The Imagery of British Churches

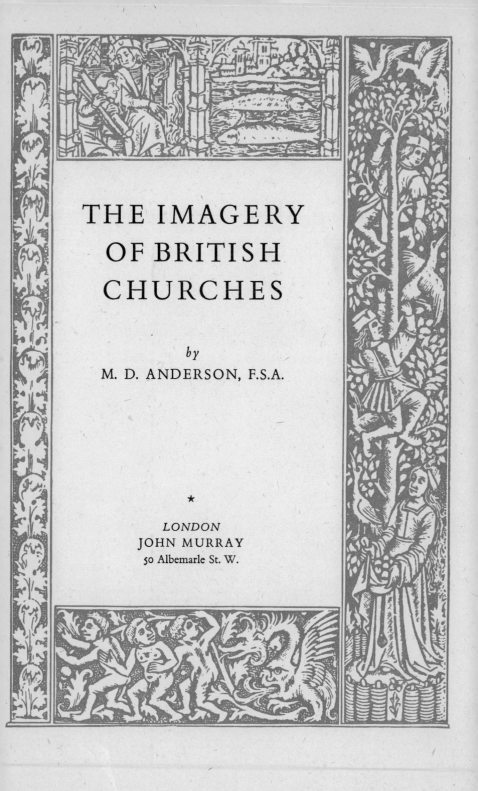

THE IMAGERY
OF BRITISH
CHURCHES

by

M. D. ANDERSON, F.S.A.

★

LONDON
JOHN MURRAY
50 Albemarle St. W.

FIRST EDITION . . . 1955

PRINTED IN GREAT BRITAIN
BY R. & R. CLARK, LTD., EDINBURGH
AND PUBLISHED BY
JOHN MURRAY (PUBLISHERS) LTD.

Contents

v

Illustrations

PLATES

Between pages xvi and 1

vii

FIGURES IN TEXT

The author's thanks are due to those whose names are in brackets after the illustrations, for their kind permission to include these in this volume.

[1] *From a photograph by the author.*
[2] *By kind permission of the Courtauld Institute.*
[3] *By kind permission of National Buildings Record.*
[4] *By kind permission of W. M. Keesey, Esq.*

Acknowledgments

In the first place my thanks are due to my husband, Trenchard Cox, who has patiently endured twenty years of cross-country motoring in search of remote churches and given unfailing encouragement, criticism and practical help during the writing of this book.

To Professor Francis Wormald I am greatly indebted for the kindness with which he has often solved my problems and rescued me from controversial quagmires in which I should otherwise assuredly have foundered.

I am grateful to Mr. W. M. Keesey for all the trouble he has taken to interpret elegantly my vague wishes as to drawings. I also thank Mr. F. H. Crossley, Mr. S. A. Jeavons, Mr. A. F. Kersting, Mr. D. Le Grice, Dr. Christopher Woodforde and Dr. G. Zarnecki for allowing me to reproduce their photographs ; also the Dean and Chapter of York for allowing me to reproduce the photograph of the York window ; also both Dr. A. R. Green and the Hampshire Field Club for allowing me to reproduce the photograph on PLATE 13*a*, and the authorities of the British Museum, Bodleian Library, the John Rylands Library and Trinity College, Cambridge, for allowing me to reproduce the subjects of the figures in text. The staffs of the National Buildings Record and the Courtauld Institute have given me much help in collecting the other illustrations, and I also thank Mr. W. G. Belsher for the skilled guidance which has made my own photographs worthy of inclusion.

Introduction

'IT is beautiful, but queer! What does it all mean ?' Exclamations such as these often express the baffled admiration with which many modern sightseers view the wall-paintings, sculpture and stained glass of medieval churches. They have heard that such imagery was designed as a picture book for the instruction of an illiterate congregation, but fail to see how some of the remaining subjects could have served such a purpose ! Undamaged Gospel illustrations are easily identifiable, and the figures of some saints have attributes which can be memorised with little effort, but much remains about which they are uncertain as to whether it should be regarded as recondite symbolism or meaningless decoration. Few sightseers realise the wide range of subjects represented by medieval artists, or that some of the most familiar themes may contain elements indicating various aspects of medieval thought, nor, even if they did realise it, could they find explanations of these elements without having recourse to specialised works, not always easy of access. Thus, all too often, they pass on with a purely aesthetic appraisal and so miss the significance which these battered, faded images show to the eyes of those who love and understand them.

How deeply we can realise the significance of medieval symbolism depends largely upon our religious convictions; the image which evokes in one mind the intense response of personal mysticism will only stir another to the impersonal interest of interpreting ancient imagery. The mystics need no guide-book, nor, if they did so, could I aspire to write one for them. Their world is timeless and the centuries which separate them from the mystics of the Middle Ages make relatively little division between their minds. It is the general public who need help in order to understand the meaning of the medieval imagery which they admire but cannot interpret. The basic beliefs of Christianity are also unaffected by time, and where these are clearly expressed in undamaged medieval imagery they need no further explanation. Here, again, it is on the humbler level of ordinary human approach that most people need help. The details of medieval iconography are the alphabet of what is literally a system of 'picture-writing', and even a little knowledge of how they became part of the accepted conventions of Christian imagery, or were used to convey a particular lesson to those who could not read, adds greatly to the interest with which we study medieval churches and also to our understanding of the psychology of the period.

It is therefore the popular understanding of medieval imagery, rather than its doctrinal or aesthetic aspects, that forms the theme of this book which aims at helping its readers to look at the structure and decoration of medieval churches through the eyes of people like themselves who lived when these churches were being built; to become in imagination those for whom the picture books of the ecclesiastical artists were designed. The gulf which we must bridge in order to achieve such understanding is wide, and, since honest recognition of obstacles is the best preparation for surmounting them, let us face our difficulties squarely.

Many people to-day are prevented from understanding the minds of the medieval church builders, not only by changes in religious education, but by an abyss of mere forgetfulness. The very term 'Gothic' architecture, imported from Italy in the 17th century to describe a style which, having had no rival in its own time had needed no name, is characteristic of the way in which the educated Englishman of the Renaissance relegated his national heritage of architecture to the limbo of despised barbarism. By the time that the sterility of later British classical architecture had led men to hope that Britain, like Italy, might find in the study of her own past the seeds of a brilliant future, all true understanding of the amazing craftsmanship which makes the structure of a Gothic cathedral almost as perfect as that of a skeleton leaf had been forgotten. The amateurs of the 18th century ecstaticised over the 'deliciously horrid' character of ruined abbeys and aped the medieval wealth of ornament without achieving the medieval sense of a harmonious whole.

If such complete ignorance of an architectural tradition had been brought about by little more than two centuries of neglect, it is not surprising that the far more complex science of medieval symbolism was forgotten. Indifference hardly needed the help it received from fanaticism to obliterate all understanding of the medieval 'picture book' from the minds of ordinary parishioners. They would probably have looked with incurious eyes at the windows, sculpture and paintings of their churches, even had these retained their pristine splendour of imagery, but this was not to be. Hardly a church in Britain, however small and remote, but shows traces of that iconoclastic lust which drove men to hack and smash and burn the adornments which had been the proud creation of their forefathers. When we stand in Kersey church (Suffolk), to take one example at random, the hard white light streams through windows which were once bejewelled with medieval glass and reveals a few battered fragments of carved stone laid on the sills; all that is left of sculptured reredos, and shrine and niche, hammered into dusty rubble. A carved cornice below the roof of the north aisle has been so battered that its imagery can no longer be deciphered, although the only figures which remain, a corpse in its coffin and a man in bed, suggest nothing more 'superstitious' than the Seven Works of Mercy. In few churches have I felt more keenly aware of the methodical savagery of the iconoclasts than at Kersey; they were not content to knock the heads off a few images of saints and smash the lower parts of the windows, I could almost hear them panting up the steep stone steps to the churchyard carrying ladders, that they might hammer out those cornices, foot by foot. At Blythburgh and Mildenhall, also in Suffolk, they tried to shoot down the great angels from the roofs with arrows and buckshot, because they could not reach them in any other way. William Dowsing, who supervised the campaign of destruction in Suffolk during 1643, claimed in his diary that he had destroyed nearly 7000 superstitious pictures in 150 churches, most of them being probably in stained glass.[1]

After the age of iconoclasm came that of neglect, and the churches were only saved from total ruin by the enthusiastic 19th-century restorers who, however, swept away many treasures which had survived the Reformation. To preserve the dramatic unities, this tragedy shall also be staged at Kersey where, in 1888, 'elaborate carved oak work in the north aisle, representing scenes from the Life of Our Lord', the pews, and a three-decker pulpit were all cleared away.[2] Early records of wall-paintings found beneath whitewash only too often end with the statement that they were destroyed. Even where medieval windows were not smashed, the glass gradually lost its original design, for the leaden binders which hold it together (and in early windows each different tone required a separate piece of glass) have to be renewed every hundred years or so. Until recently few glaziers were capable of handling old glass and fewer still understood the themes represented, so that each releading created worse confusion. When the windows of St. Michael, Spurriergate at York were recently restored, thirteen panels of the magnificent Jesse window were found divided between two windows, while the glass for five more panels was scattered throughout almost every window in the church.[3] When we remember, therefore, that for four centuries at least the imagery of our churches has been exposed to every kind of obliterative process, we shall realise how incomplete it is and how many gaps our imaginations must complete. Empty niches must be filled by the memory of statues seen elsewhere, and shadowy wall-paintings be made to glow afresh as we build up a mental image of their original design. Sometimes manuscript illuminations, or the undamaged imagery of foreign churches, guide our guesses at the subjects missing from the damaged series of carvings, or paintings, in British churches, and show us wider implications of meaning. But it is always well to remember that such imaginative reconstruction involves grave risks of error !

The vocabulary of symbolism is somewhat confusing, so it may be wise to state here the sense in which I shall use its principal terms:

A Symbol expresses an abstract idea: *e.g.* the Pelican in her piety is the symbol of Man's redemption through the Atonement of Christ.

An Emblem is used as an alternative to direct portrayal of a person, thus the Agnus Dei is the emblem of Christ, the Lamb of God.

An Attribute identifies the image of a sacred person but has no individual significance. Thus a swan or a pig enable us to identify the figures of St. Hugh of Lincoln or St. Anthony of Egypt when represented with them, but do not embody an allusion to these saints when they occur alone.

Unfortunately for clarity, there are occasions when these meanings overlap. Attribute and symbol merge when a saint is identified by an implement of his martyrdom (such as the gridiron of St. Lawrence) and does not hold the palm which is the generalised symbol of martyrdom. In late medieval art the heraldic use of some attributes, such as the keys of St. Peter, achieved an independent recognition approximating to that of an emblem.

Medieval artists did not always restrict their use of symbols to a single meaning; lions are generally symbols of good, associated with the Incarnation and Resurrection (see page 174), but they can also represent the Evil One seizing a soul in his talons. During the past fifty years scholars have established the meaning of many subjects previously obscure, but to compare these interpretations with those of older writers (who were far better qualified to guess aright than the average tourist of to-day) is to realise some of the risks we run in trying to answer our own questions. To give one example: a misericord in Lincoln Cathedral which represents the well-known medieval theme of Tristram and Iseult meeting under the tree from which the head of King Mark is shown peering was interpreted as symbolising the respect paid to the head of St. Hugh, preserved as a precious relic in the cathedral.[4] Many subjects still defy interpretation, or suggest a bewildering variety of possible interpretations. Does the composite creature on a misericord at Exeter, which has the head of a crowned man and the body of a saddled horse, allude to the story of Aristotle inveigled by a revengeful courtesan into serving as her palfrey, or is it a literal illustration of one of the locusts described in the Book of Revelation? To assume certainty is to court disillusion, but to weigh possible alternatives is to achieve a richer understanding.

Having considered some of our difficulties, let us now plan our approach. If we wish to study the churches through the eyes of a medieval person we must first decide to what sort of person those eyes shall have belonged. We had better ignore the social extremes (for neither the greatest, nor the most abjectly poor, of any land is usually typical) and also the extremes of education. The over-subtle schoolmen will not help us (for is not our modern word 'dunce' derived from those obstructive sophists, the followers of Duns Scotus ?), nor will the medieval equivalents of those whom to-day even ten years of compulsory schooling cannot teach to read or write.

Since, even if we disregard extremes, we cannot see the whole picture through one pair of eyes, let us attempt a synthesis of three points of view: those of the parson who served an ordinary parish church, the craftsman who built or adorned it, and the parishioner who generally paid for the work. I will first try to show the ways in which such men were likely to have affected church-building and the design of religious imagery. Then we must consider the choice and arrangement of subjects according to principles evolved by scholarly theologians, which were probably followed in smaller churches more as a matter of custom than because those who wrought the imagery could have explained them. It is from the imagery of the cathedrals and abbeys that we can best reconstruct the majestic design of the 'Picture Book of the Churches' although, when we understand its general structure, we can often see how this influenced the simpler imagery of parish churches. Finally, I will describe the individual subjects included in a normal cycle of illustrations to this Picture Book, in order to show the reasons which dictated the inclusion of many extra-Biblical details which have become so familiar that we rarely question their origin. Where the sources of such details are to be found in contemporary writings many medieval parsons, and some of the better educated laity, would have recognised their origin, but most of them would have been as unaware as the average church-goer of to-day that the Christian Church often borrowed its religious iconography from the art of earlier civilisations.

Most of the important source-books of the imagery of medieval churches were written in Latin, but free translations of some works calculated to edify the laity were written in the vernacular. Where such English texts are easily available I shall quote from them in preference to the Latin originals, not only for easier reading but because I hope that it will give my readers a more vivid impression of the manner in which medieval people in England interpreted the Scriptural events and religious allegories which we see depicted in the churches. It would be foolhardy to claim that, because one text contains passages which apparently explain the iconography of a particular work of art it must have inspired the artist who wrought this, and I certainly make no such claim when I associate a literary and an artistic expression of the same theme. All I hope to do is to present a generalised picture of the kind of sources from which such iconographical features were derived and to encourage my readers to seek, both in books and churches, a fuller understanding of the medieval mind, and of the thoughts which led men to create some of the finest treasures of our artistic inheritance.

I. DOOM PAINTING. ST. THOMAS' CHURCH, SALISBURY (*pages* 134-5)

2. SAXON GRAVE COVER.   WIRKSWORTH (*pages* 117, 121, 145)

3. THE JUDGMENT OF SOLOMON. WESTMINSTER ABBEY *(page 100)* ECCLESIA, MOSES AND SYNAGOGUE. SOUTHROP *(pages 75, 95)*

4. 'THE HARROWING OF HELL.' QUENINGTON (*page* 125)
THE BAPTISM OF CHRIST. CASTLE FROME (*pages* 18, 81, 111)

5. ABRAHAM AND ISAAC. WORCESTER CATHEDRAL (*pages* 20, 93)
 SAMSON AND THE GATES OF GAZA. RIPON CATHEDRAL (*pages* 22, 97)

6. CREATION OF THE BIRDS AND FISHES. YORK MINSTER (*page* 87)
THE SOWER. CANTERBURY CATHEDRAL (*page* 114)

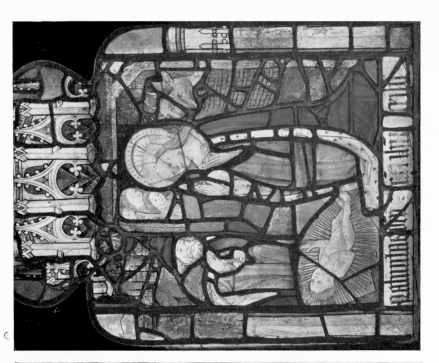

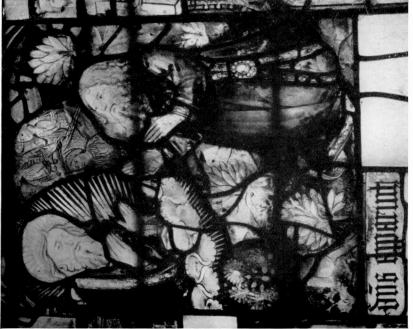

7. THE NATIVITY. MALVERN PRIORY (*page* 106)
GOD SPEAKING TO ABRAHAM. MALVERN PRIORY (*pages* 81, 92)

8. FOUR DOCTORS OF THE LATIN CHURCH. TRULL (*pages* 8, 160)
SS. JOHN, LAWRENCE AND EDWARD THE CONFESSOR. HAREWOOD (*pages* 144, 158,

9. THE RAISING OF LAZARUS AND THE THREE MARIES AT THE SEPULCHRE.
LENTON (*pages* 113, 125)

10. SEVEN SACRAMENT WINDOW.   DODDISCOMBSLEIGH (*pages 55-57*)

MASS		ORDINATION
MATRIMONY	PENANCE	BAPTISM
CONFIRMATION		EXTREME UNCTION

II. ALL SAINTS' CHURCH, NORTH STREET, YORK (*page* 165)

FEEDING THE HUNGRY   GIVING DRINK TO THE THIRSTY   TAKING IN THE HOMELESS
CLOTHING THE NAKED   VISITING THE SICK   VISITING THOSE IN PRISON

12. EMBLEMS OF THE PASSION CARVED ON BENCH-ENDS *(page* 59*)*

THE SACRED WOUNDS.   NORTH CADBURY, SOMERSET

THE ASCENSION

THE INCREDULITY OF ST. THOMAS } LAUNCELLS, CORNWALL

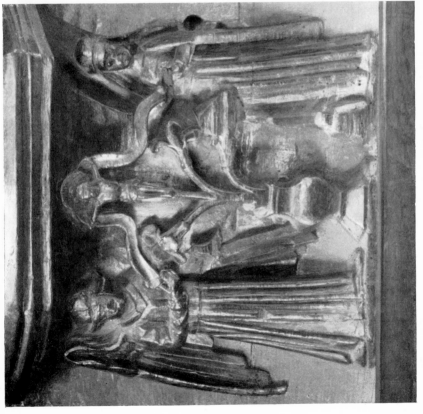

13. ST. JOHN'S HEAD. AMPORT (*page* 155)

THE ANNUNCIATION WITH LILY CRUCIFIX. TONG (*page* 103)

14. APPEARANCE OF CHRIST TO HIS MOTHER, TRANSFIGURATION, AND APPEARANCE
TO THREE MARIES AT THE SEPULCHRE. FAIRFORD (*page* 126)

15. SCENES FROM THE LIFE OF THE VIRGIN. ELFORD *(page* 143*)*

ST. JOSEPH'S ROD   PRESENTATION OF THE VIRGIN MARY   BETROTHAL OF
BURGEONS   IN THE TEMPLE   THE VIRGIN MARY

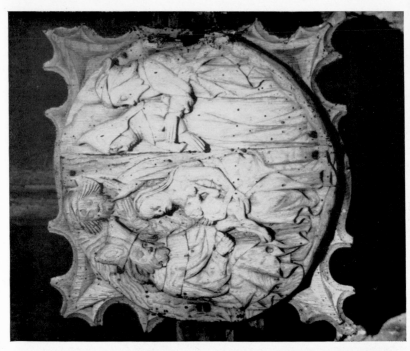

16. THE CIRCUMCISION. SALLE, NORFOLK *(page* 107*)*
CORONATION OF THE VIRGIN. LINCOLN CATHEDRAL *(page* 146*)*

17. THE APOCALYPSE BOSSES. NORWICH CATHEDRAL CLOISTER (*page* 132)

18. VIRGIN WITH THE ROSEBUSH. WILLOUGHBY ON THE WOLDS (*page* 98)
THE INCARNATION. ROSS–ON–WYE (*page* 103)

19. THE HOLY TRINITY.   WILLOUGHBY ON THE WOLDS (*page* 82)
THE SLEEPING JESSE.   ABERGAVENNY (*page* 98)

20. THE MASS OF ST. GREGORY.   STOKE CHARITY, HAMPSHIRE (*page* 58)

TRACERY OF THE ROOD-SCREEN AT LLANRWST, DENBIGHSHIRE (*page* 118)

| THE CROSS AND CROWN OF THORNS | AGNUS DEI | EMBLEMS OF THE PASSION | SACRED MONOGRA |

21. MARTYRDOM OF ST. THOMAS OF CANTERBURY. ELHAM *(page* 161*)*
ST. MARGARET. SHERBORNE ABBEY *(page* 156*)*

THE BUILDING OF
THE ARK

THE EMBARKATION OF NOAH
AND THE RETURN OF THE DOVE

NOAH PLANTING
THE VINE

DRUNKENNESS OF NOAH

TOWER OF BABEL

ABRAHAM GREETING THE AN

ABRAHAM SERVING THE ANGELS

FALL OF SODOM AND GOMORRAH

LOT'S WIFE

22. SALISBURY CATHEDRAL CHAPTER HOUSE (*pages* 87-95)

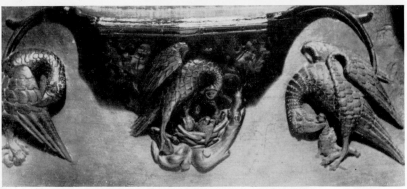

23. WOODWOSE AND LION. HOLY TRINITY CHURCH, COVENTRY *(page 182)*
THE PELICAN IN HER PIETY. LINCOLN CATHEDRAL *(page 176)*
THE CLOSED DOOR. NORWICH CATHEDRAL *(page 149)*

24. THE KNEELING CAMEL. MISERICORD AT BOSTON, LINCS (*page* 179)
THE WORST ELEPHANT! POPPY-HEAD AT SOUTH LOPHAM, SUFFOLK (*page* 178)
HART EATING WITH THE SERPENT. MISERICORD IN ELY CATHEDRAL (*page* 176)
THE TIGRESS DECEIVED. BENCH-END AT LAKENHEATH, SUFFOLK (*page* 177)

PART I

Angles of Approach

B

THE PARSON'S APPROACH

THE educational system of medieval Britain lies outside my scope but it is essential that we should remember the dominant influence which it gave to the clergy in all fields of thought. When St. Augustine brought Christianity to south-eastern England he established a school almost as soon as a church, for Christianity had hitherto spread through countries where Latin was the official language in which the services of the Church were naturally held, but the Anglo-Saxons had had little contact with Roman Europe and the missionaries had to teach their converts some Latin before these could follow the services of their new faith. The tradition by which schools were set up in connexion with important churches persisted, and in the 12th century the Lateran Council ordained that every cathedral was to maintain a master who should teach the clerks of the church and poor scholars freely.[1] By using the term 'grammar school' we perpetuate the tradition of their original function, which was to teach Latin grammar.[2]

In smaller towns and villages, where no grammar school was available, the parson, or a chantry priest, often taught the local boys in the chamber above the church porch, or in some chapel. Traces of this past use can be seen in several churches : on the wall of the vestry at North Cadbury (Somerset) the alphabet is painted in black letters ; at Long Melford (Suffolk) the multiplication table is painted on the east wall of the Lady Chapel, while the choir stalls at Blythburgh (Suffolk) have holes for ink-wells in their desks which tell of previous service in a chapel where school was taught. The value of such chantry schools naturally varied with the intellectual capacity of the chaplain, who probably aimed at little more than teaching the boys to understand the forms of worship which followed directly upon the A B C in their primer, and perhaps the psalms which they might have to sing in church. This little learning was often literally 'knocked into them' ! We might ascribe to the British working man's taste for grim slap-stick humour the carvings on misericords at

Boston, Norwich and Sherborne which show the master hard at work with the birch, did we not remember that a student graduating as Master of Grammar at Cambridge was handed a birch and a 'palmer' (specially designed for striking boys on the palm) as the symbols of his new office, and had forthwith to prove his powers of wielding them upon a boy who received a groat for his pains.[3]

When we speak of a 'clerical collar' we do not mean the symbolical napery which distinguishes professional workers from manual labourers, and the two meanings of the word 'clerical' derive from medieval usage when they were synonymous. Most grammar-school pupils would then have intended to take some degree of Holy Orders, although their later career might be that of a lawyer, teacher or states-man. Medieval education was thus chiefly concerned with the teaching of Latin as a preparation for ecclesiastical service in some form, and so entirely dominated by the Church that, in 1410, the Chief Justice ruled that the education of children was 'a spiritual matter' beyond the cognizance of the King's Bench.[4] Provisions for teaching were specified in so many chantry foundations, particularly those where large numbers of chaplains were organised into a 'college', that this word acquired its present, primarily educational, connotation.

There is no record of the exact curriculum of an important school in England earlier than the 16th century, and we know even less about the smaller ones. Broadly speaking, the advanced curriculum was divided into two parts, corresponding to the grouping of the Seven Liberal Arts, personifications of which are carved upon many French cathedrals. So far as I know, they only appear in England upon the 17th-century pulpit at Newport (Isle of Wight).

(1) *The Trivium*, or threefold way of learning, comprised Grammar, Dialectic (the study of logical argument) and Rhetoric. These would have been studied at a grammar school while, for those who found this literally too 'trivial', there was

(2) *The Quadrivium* comprising Music, Arithmetic, Geometry and Astronomy, together with the more advanced studies of philosophy and theology, which lay within the province of the Universities.

For the average parishioner, whose outlook I am trying to recon-struct, there were no provisions for adult education, outside the Universities, except such as came to him in the course of listening to sermons in the vernacular. The important part played by the medieval preachers in the development of our language, literature and social consciousness has been made the object of well-deserved study,[5] and the influence of this growing emphasis on vernacular preaching in the 14th and 15th centuries can be noted in the date of most medieval pulpits and the development of parish churches with large naves and permanent seating.

The preachers sought to hold the attention of their congregations with varied and vivid *exempla* drawn from many sources other than the Scriptures, such as classical history and travellers' tales in which the fauna of strange lands was described on the authority of ancient writers. Many grotesque creatures carved in our churches were probably derived from such sermon stories. It seems likely that the preachers would have used the imagery of the churches in which they spoke to point their lessons but such references are very rarely preserved in surviving sermon collections. On the other hand, the 15th-century dialogue between *Dives* (a prosperous but ignorant lay-man) *and Pauper* (who expresses the teaching of the Church) has much to say about ecclesiastical imagery. Commenting upon the second Commandment *Pauper* explains that such imagery does not contravene this but stirs men's hearts to devotion, 'for ofte a man is more stirred by sight than by hearing or reading' and he interprets such familiar symbols as the lily attribute of the Virgin, the keys of St. Peter or the sword of St. Paul. While some of *Pauper's* precepts might have guided *Dives* to use images as aids to devotion without falling into the sin of idolatry, others show an ingenious rationalisation of forgotten artistic conventions derived from early art which proves that, even in the Middle Ages, explanations of iconography did not always eliminate error.

Thus, at any stage of life the parishioner might learn new meanings associated with the imagery of his church, and this form of medieval education should be of special interest to us to-day for, by one of the surprising somersaults of history, the progress of science now causes a large proportion of the population to rely upon picture-papers, the cinema and television, rather than on reading to provide mental stimulus. The dignified, if sometimes obscure, iconography of medieval churches thus challenges our modern educational system with the serious question of what forms of picture-teaching we offer to our semi-literate citizens as an alternative to comic strip cartoons !

Of the many encyclopaedic works by medieval scholars which provided inspiration to successive generations of artists I have space to mention only one, my choice being guided by two reasons. The general design of the *Speculum Majus* of Vincent of Beauvais (*c.* 1190–1260) is characteristic of the structure of thought underlying much medieval imagery, for each of its sections deals with one of the facets by which human existence reflects the Divine Power. The 'Mirrors' of Nature, Science, Morals and History thus epitomise the exalted outlook of the medieval teachers who proclaimed that each object which man's senses can perceive should lead his thoughts to the contemplation of heavenly things.[6] This approach to knowledge dominated medieval teaching ; correct information about the geography of the world, or its recent history, was considered relatively unimportant compared with spiritual instruction, even if this were based upon the most grotesque misstatements of fact. Antiquity was considered as the best proof of authority, and it was the 'first word' rather than 'the last word' on any subject which the medieval scholar was proud to quote. Thus the strangest perversions of truth contained in classical writings were handed on unchallenged.

My second reason for choosing the *Speculum Majus* is that it is referred to in the only instance I know in which a medieval artist has included in his work an explicit acknowledgment of the literary source of his theme, the wall-paintings of Eton College Chapel.[7]

Under the medieval system of education many fine brains acquired added subtlety of analysis and expression, but for the average man we should perhaps accept Dr. Coulton's verdict that 'medieval education did a great deal for many centuries to divorce men from their mother tongue and thereby from a good deal of common sense'.[8] Powers of scholarly disputation were over-developed, while the basis of knowledge upon which these could be exercised was restricted by excessive reverence for ancient authorities, as opposed to personal observation. Both these characteristics influenced iconography, for the first encouraged elaborations of exalted symbolism, while the second favoured an unquestioning repetition of errors originating in classical literature, or in misinterpretations of outworn symbols.

In the title of this chapter I have used the word 'parson' with a precision of meaning often obscured by modern colloquial usage. The parson (*persona*) was the incumbent of the greater tithe, and might be an individual rector or a corporate body to which the benefice had been appropriated. In the latter case the cure of souls was delegated to a vicar, who was under canonical obligation of residence. All clergy charged with the cure of souls were technically *curati*, but in England the term 'curate' was more particularly applied to the salaried 'parish priests' who assisted, or deputised for, the rectors, or vicars, and from whose ranks the chantry chaplains were mostly recruited.

As curates had little influence on church building we will concentrate upon the parsons, in the fullest sense of that word, for a rector's importance as a link uniting a village church with the nation-wide ramifications of royal, or ecclesiastical, organisation might be greater than his personal influence. The servants of the King were often paid by preferment to ecclesiastical benefices, for, provided that no man held more than one benefice involving cure of souls, pluralism was accepted as a normal practice.[9] The rector of a village church might thus be a scholar whose prestige in the world of learning was supported by the tithes of a parish left to the care of a poorly paid vicar or a high official whose contacts at Court could secure the advice of royal craftsmen for some important rebuilding of the church. As the royal Master Masons travelled about to supervise the 'King's Works' in many parts of his realm, they sometimes gave intermittent direction to the buildings of important corporate bodies, or influential individuals.[10] Surviving contracts for parish churches show that masons and carpenters were often ordered to copy work existing in other places, with such improvements in scale or splendour as their skill, or their employer's purse, allowed, and thus one parish church designed by a distinguished master mason might inspire the local builders of a whole district.[11]

The relation between the parish churches and the monasteries was more important because it was more widespread. About 63 per cent of the churches in the county of York and 50 per cent of those in Lincolnshire were owned by monasteries at the Dissolution,[12] although the national average was lower. The effect which this monastic ownership had upon the architecture and imagery of parish churches is hard to estimate except from an economic point of view when it was generally a deterrent. Religious communities tended to regard their appropriated livings merely as sources of revenue and neither favoured, nor supported, their schemes for architectural embellishment. For one recorded case in which a chancel was rebuilt by a corporate proprietor, as at Adderbury (Oxon) or Thirsk (Yorks), there are dozens of complaints, from bishops or parishioners, that churches had fallen into ruin because the monastery had drawn all the available money away from the parish. It is noteworthy that in Cheshire, where two-thirds of the livings were owned by religious houses, some of the finest churches are to be found in the remaining parishes. Nantwich was itself collegiate, but the parishes of Bunbury, Malpas, Barthomley and Gawsworth made good use of their independence.[13]

In any case the responsibility of the *persona*, whether an individual or a corporation, was limited to the upkeep of the chancel, while the parishioners maintained the nave, and the effects of this divided burden can be seen in many churches, as at Blakeney (Norfolk) or Yatton (Somerset), where a small early chancel, patched and altered at many periods, contrasts with a large Perpendicular nave wholly rebuilt in the boom years of the wool trade. One reason why the chancel arch is so often the oldest part of a church is that it was preserved to close off the chancel while the nave was being rebuilt or, much more rarely, vice versa.

The aesthetic influence of the monasteries upon the parish churches which they owned, or which stood in near-by villages, was probably very great, for, in the 12th century particularly, the development of local styles of architecture and sculpture centred chiefly on the great religious houses.[14] When the parishioners had raised the money for a new font, or richly carved door, or a new series of windows or wall-paintings were to be designed, it seems natural that they should have sought the help of the fine craftsmen who were regularly employed in the workshops of a monastery, or had been drawn thither temporarily by some extensive building operation. The point which can rarely be decided is whether ownership, or contiguity, was the deciding factor in such influence. The remarkable 12th-century wall-paintings at Clayton and Hardham in Sussex almost certainly reflect the influence of the great Cluniac house of Lewes to which both livings belonged at that period, but paintings of the same school (now lost) were found at Westmeston which had no connexion with the Priory of Lewes other than its vicinity.[15] The wooden roof bosses at Queen Camel (Somerset) include several subjects apparently copied from the miniatures of a Bestiary to which the carver must have had repeated access,[16] unless he was given drawings made from them. The bosses may have been made in the workshops of Cleeve Abbey, to which the church belonged, but the churches of Sampford Brett and Wootton Courtenay, also in Somerset, have bosses apparently made by the same carvers, and these churches did not belong to the Cistercians at Cleeve.

The unusual beauty of the pulpit at Trull (Somerset) (PLATE 8) may be connected with the fact that the church belonged to the Priory at Taunton, but Southrop (Glos), where the font (PLATE 3) (together with its fellow at Stanton Fitzwarren) must surely have been produced in the workshops of some great monastery, was owned by the Knights Hospitallers of Quenington, who were not prominent in the development of the arts. These few conflicting instances must suffice to indicate a complex problem which should be considered by those interested in the history of old churches, when they find ornament of unusually high quality and erudite design.

A few individual rectors, such as William Longthorne of Fen Stanton (Hunts) and Richard Pottesgrave of Heckington (Lincs), rebuilt the chancels of their churches and lie in the founders' tombs, but such cases are rare. An unusual brass at Fovant (Wilts) records that 'Sir George Rede' was rector when the tower was rebuilt in 1495, and shows him kneeling, in his ordinary habit and holding a large rosary, before the scene of the Annunciation, but does not define his rôle in the building operations. As a general rule, I think, we may assume that the average parson would have been more concerned with the significance of the imagery than with the style of the structure, a matter which was decided between the craftsmen and those who financed their operations.

How far can we estimate the nature of a parson's directions? The *Rationale Divinorum Officiorum* of William Durandus (c. 1220–1296) [17] illustrates the lengths to which medieval scholars would go in devising symbolical meanings for every feature of a church (see page 36), but, although this work was greatly respected in the Middle Ages, many of its spiritual rationalisations of architectural features would probably have been as unfamiliar to the average village parson as they are to us. The outlook of an enlightened ecclesiastic on the decoration of churches is also expressed in the preface to a 13th-century treatise on this subject, known as *Pictor in Carmine* and probably written by an Englishman.[18] He expresses grief that the sanctuary of God should be full of foolish pictures and misshapen monstrosities, but considering that it would be difficult to dispense altogether with meaningless paintings in churches, he suggests that the parishioners 'should enjoy at least that class of picture which, as being the books of the laity, can suggest divine things to the unlearned and stir up the learned to the love of the Scriptures'. *Pictor in Carmine* is predominantly concerned with *what* should be shown, not *how* it should be shown. It was the era of the educator and the artist-craftsman, not yet that of the art critic.

Although we shall never know the exact part played by the individual rector in designing the imagery of his church, we shall not misrepresent the general lines on which medieval iconography developed if we imagine priest and craftsman in conclave over designs for new windows or wall-paintings; similar work recently done in the neighbourhood would be discussed, a miniature, or a symbolical diagram, in some book owned by the priest might be displayed, or his recollection of a fine manuscript seen elsewhere be described or roughly sketched. If the design were originated by the craftsman, then the priest might urge that more emphasis be placed upon some feature symbolising an important lesson, or forbid the repetition of an ancient symbol which was now frowned upon as likely to suggest heretical beliefs. To-day our minds are so conditioned by life in a literate world that only a sustained effort of imagination can make us realise the responsibility which rested upon those who directed the adornment of a church in the Middle Ages. When few could read, even if they could afford to own a book, the imagery of their parish church

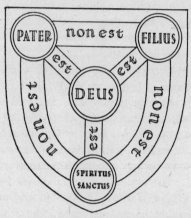

FIG. 1. ARMS OF THE HOLY TRINITY

offered the only version of the Scriptures which was always available to the laity. It was therefore desirable that the images should express the theological, as well as the historical, aspect of their theme. Scholars designed diagrams expressing matters of doctrine, and symbols which represented the abstract ideas implicit in some Gospel subjects. Sometimes they were successful. It would be difficult to imagine a more concise and effective statement of the triune individuality of the Holy Trinity than the heraldic device (Fig. 1) which appears in many churches, as for instance in the south-east window of Newark (Notts). While the designer has not here entirely dispensed with words, the illiterate person to whom the device had once been explained would have had no more difficulty in recognising its meaning than *we* have when we see carvings of it from which the painted letters have worn away. Most of the moral allegories found in wall-paintings are in effect pictorial sermons.

The task of the symbolist was more difficult when a detail in some historical scene was devised to express a point of religious teaching, for ignorant men were liable to interpret such symbols literally and thus fall into heresy. In his posthumous book, *Of the History of Holy Images, for their true Use against Abuses* (1593), Molanus, a learned and orthodox professor of Louvain, argued that few images were really an occasion of error to simple folk, as claimed by the heretics, although admitting that they seem such. 'For in certain places, in the story of the Annunciation and the Lord's Incarnation, there is painted a little human body among rays diffused by the Holy Ghost descending to the most blessed Virgin's womb ; which picture might seem to offer an occasion, not only of perilous, but even of heretical, error.'[19] St. Antonino (1389–1459), Archbishop of Florence, condemned, not only this treatment of the Annunciation, which we find in several British churches (see page 103 and PLATE 18), but also the artists who showed 'the Trinity as one person with three heads, which is a monster in nature' (see page 82) nor are they praiseworthy when they paint apocryphal things, as the midwives at the Virgin Birth, or the Virgin Mary at her Assumption leaving her girdle to the Apostle Thomas (see pages 106 and 145).

Many pre-Reformation sermons deplore the danger of idolatry created by ignorant superstitions among the common people. On the other hand, John Mirk, Canon of Lillieshall, whose *Festial* and manual on *The Duties of a Parish Priest* [20] are helpful illustrations of a 15th-century point of view, stated boldly that thousands of people could not imagine in their hearts how Christ hung upon the Rood unless they learned it from images and paintings. He considered that, if people were well taught, they would not be misled by the Evangelistic symbols into thinking that SS. Matthew, Mark, Luke and John 'wern suche bestys and not men', yet the records suggest that even in this very modest hope he may sometimes have been disappointed. Contemporaneous writers denounce priests who, so far from teaching people to avoid vulgar errors, were apt to originate them. Giraldus Cambrensis tells of a preacher who described the Canaanite woman in the Gospel as being half-dog, half-human, because he thought the text called her 'a canine woman'.[21] Under such guidance it is not surprising that misunderstandings of obscure symbols gave rise to picturesque legends. Both wise and silly priests thus played a part in creating the iconography of our churches, the first by helping to evolve symbols expressive of Christian beliefs, the second by allowing popular imagination to interpret such symbols according to its own fashion. While the Church tried to remedy such abuses it also taught that ignorance did not hinder the work of salvation. In the wall-paintings of Eton College Chapel and Winchester Cathedral we see illustrations of the Blessed Virgin's intervention to justify the ignorant priest who could only say one Mass, that of Our Lady, and who was therefore suspended by his Bishop, and many other legends of a like nature were current.[22]

Archbishop Peckham's Constitutions (1281) directed all clergy to expound in the vulgar tongue 'all fourteen articles of the Faith with regard to the Holy Trinity and Christ's humanity, the ten Commandments, the two Evangelical Precepts . . . the Seven Works of Mercy, the Seven Deadly Sins, the Seven Virtues and the Seven Sacraments',[23] but medieval sermons covered a much wider range of subjects, particularly after the advent of the preaching friars.

Many of these friars were men of intellectual distinction who could have expressed the most abstruse subtleties of medieval theology in flawless Latin, but who turned these powers to the education of the unlearned by preaching in a style at once forceful and familiar. Parallels are plentiful between the *exempla* of the preachers and the subjects of the craftsmen, but it would be rash to over-stress their connexion. The preachers' descriptions of the Hounds of God protecting the sheep from the wolves, or the geese from the fox (*i.e.* Christian souls from the devil), or of Christ as the great huntsman loving to hunt for souls, obviously did not inspire all the carvings of hunting scenes, or of foxes carrying off poultry which we see on capitals, and misericords, but even if we assume no more than that both preacher and craftsman were using the experience of their own lives to enrich their service to Holy Church, the parallels show that neither would have found such imagery incongruous in a church.

The preaching friars denounced clerical abuses as well as social, and castigated the tyrannical over-lord no more acidly than the wealthy ecclesiastic who neglected his spiritual duties, or the parish priest who did not instruct his flock. Naturally the victims of these rankling shafts were quick to retaliate when the growing wealth of the Mendicant Orders led to corruption among their members. A craftsman's wry recollection of an extortionate friar, expressed in one of many carvings of a cowled fox preaching to a flock of geese in order to lure one within range of his teeth, would not have been unwelcome to the beneficed clergy whose privileges had been attacked. While resentful ecclesiastics might have suggested this subject at any time after the coming of the friars in the 13th century, it is not until the 15th century, when the justice of the satire was apparent, that it becomes common. It is amusing to speculate whether some friar inspired the counter-attack carved upon a strikingly fine bench-end in the church of Brent Knoll (Somerset) which shows the fox in the garb of a mitred abbot, preaching to birds and beasts, and which is locally supposed to refer to the frustrated efforts of the Abbot of Glastonbury to recover this benefice which he had previously exchanged for several others ! [24]

Two somewhat contradictory lines of thought with regard to the building and adornment of churches are expressed in medieval sermons. It was praiseworthy to make 'fair paintings and images' in order to help simple folk to worship, but it was reprehensible to 'clothe timber and stone' with adornments while neglecting 'the naked necessity of the poor'.[25] We must not generalise, for the manner in which priests inspired, directed or discouraged their parishioners to rebuild or adorn churches must always have depended upon the temperament and convictions of the individual, but it is clear that enlightened ecclesiastics did not regard all such offerings as dictated by pure piety. In *Dives and Pauper* the teacher comments that 'I dread me that men do it more for pomp and pride of this world, to have a name and worship thereby in the country, or for envy that one town hath against another, not for devotion but for the worship and the name that they see them have by array and ornaments in Holy Church'.

CHAPTER 2

THE CRAFTSMAN'S APPROACH

WHILE the different types of medieval Churchmen speak to us with a confusing multiplication of voices the craftsmen confront us with an equally perplexing silence, for what can we know of men who only appear in the fabric rolls of some great building as 'John of X . . .' paid so many shillings or pence for his work ? Before the introduction of hereditary surnames men were often distinguished by their places of origin, and the fabric rolls of the Cistercian Abbey of Vale Royal (Ches) and of the Castles of Beaumaris (Anglesey) and Caernarvon, dating from the late 13th century or early 14th, show us that many masons then came from the stone-quarrying districts.[1] This probably applied still more to the Norman period when houses were mostly built of wood and plaster and the sudden demand for masons created by the immense number of churches then being built could only have been met by recruits from the quarries. Such men would have risen by their natural skill in handling stone, rather than by theoretical education, and most of them would have been illiterate.

The crafts connected with church building were probably hereditary in many families ; masons, carpenters and glaziers followed in their father's trades, particularly in the later Middle Ages. At Ely the monastery employed one family of hereditary goldsmiths for 200 years.[2] It has been suggested that masons' marks tend to grow more complicated in the later periods because they were sometimes passed on from father to son, with slight differences, like coats of arms.[3] In the Norman period most marks contain only two or three lines, while those of the Perpendicular masons may have as many as eleven. Apprenticeship among masons was confined chiefly to master masons perhaps because the nomadic existence of the ordinary journeyman mason would have made it impossible for him to feed and house an apprentice. The Master Mason of a Lodge attached to a cathedral was often required by his contract to train an apprentice, but the relatively high wages which such apprentices received suggest that they were already skilled masons qualifying, by further instruction, for the designing and supervision of building operations. An interesting case, which may indicate a wider preparation, is that of Thomas, son of Hugh le Peyntour of Durham, who was apprenticed to a barber in 1386 but whose apprenticeship was later sold to Thomas Canoun, marbler, probably a member of the famous family of carvers from Corfe.[4] Since a barber-surgeon was paid for services connected with the making of the bronze effigy of Richard, Earl of Warwick, in the Beauchamp Chapel at Warwick, which shows an unusually scientific observation of the veins on temples and hands,[5] it is permissible to wonder whether the painter's son, wishing to be a sculptor, chose to make a special study of anatomy, or to learn the art of making death masks, before beginning his training under an 'imager', or whether he was simply a foolish boy who could not decide on a trade.

Our present concern is less with the master masons who influenced the development of architectural styles than with the craftsmen who carved, or painted, religious imagery. Broadly speaking, there were three phases in the evolution of professional status among such craftsmen. In the 12th century even stone carvers skilled in the technique of their craft needed the guidance of artists working in more precious, and tractable, media, for the design of any figure-work. During the 13th century the mason emerges as an independent artist ; religious themes were, no doubt, still selected by clerical patrons but the carvers were capable of expressing such themes naturally in the idiom of their own material. The final phase, in the 14th and 15th centuries, is characterised by an increasing amount of shop-work. Effigies, or complete tombs, alabaster retables and other fine carvings, as well as stained glass, were made to order in centres where fine material and skilled men were available and the 'imagers', or glaziers, who directed this trade became important merchants and employers of labour. Unfortunately this development brought about a much greater measure of mechanical repetition, particularly among the alabasterers whose products were exported to all parts of Europe.

Craftsmen who had had little education outside their technical training must have been dependent upon instructions, or models, provided by literate employers for any subject outside a strictly limited repertory. All they were likely to originate, so far as iconography was concerned, was an occasional variation due to misunderstanding ! How were designs presented to them ? We know that as a preparation towards the rebuilding of Canterbury Cathedral after the fire of 1174, William of Sens 'delivered molds for shaping the stones to the sculptors who were assembled and diligently prepared other things of the same kind'.[6] These 'molds' were probably wooden patterns from which the profiles of mouldings could be copied, but were the 'other things' drawings of carved work made on plastered boards, or actual models of capitals, etc.? Before the discovery of paper, preliminary designs for carvings or stained glass were often drawn upon plastered boards, and survived their immediate usefulness no longer than the next demand for the board. For the outlines of simple tracery a sanded floor might suffice, and the bold scratches on the Chapter House doors at Wells are thought to have served as the setting-out lines of the great inverted arches in that cathedral.

The controversy as to whether monks built their own churches has proved that masons' work was done by them only in times of financial stringency, as when the monks of Gloucester vaulted their nave in 1242. It is, however, true that Benedictine and Cluniac monks illuminated manuscripts (although the Cistercians condemned such occupation) and that exceptionally talented monks did fine goldsmith's work, carved crucifixes, and were occasionally concerned with the design of stained-glass windows. If we assume that the early masons required models for any work more ambitious than geometric patterns, and that this direction was often given by monastic craftsmen whose natural medium of expression was in paint or precious metal, we should expect this interrelation of media to be apparent in the carvings, and so it often is.

Early Norman is soldiers' architecture. Bold and simple in design and massive in construction, it could be built by quarry-trained men under the direction of a few skilled masons, for the proportion of carved work to plain walling is small, and the ordinary enrichments of the mouldings, billet, chevron or roll would have been easily repeated. The artistic tradition of Scandinavian wood-carving, lingering among the British carvers, may have suggested the 'beak-head' mouldings, which occur earlier and more often in England than in France.[7] Some of the primitive Norman tympana, on which figure sculpture has been most unsuccessfully attempted, such as Little Paxton (Hunts), Danby Wiske (Yorks) or Wordwell (Suffolk),[8] make it clear how greatly the masons needed help when something beyond abstract decoration was required of them. It was probably the painter who directed their first attempts at figure sculpture. Not only the plain surfaces, but also the capitals and tympana of Norman churches were decorated with painted designs, and on detached capitals preserved in Hereford Cathedral, and in the triforium of Westminster Abbey

(PLATE 3), we can study figure subjects treated in such flat planes that the carver may only have enhanced the effect of a painted design by cutting away the background and marking the folds of drapery by incised lines. Even such a comparatively sophisticated work of art as the Prior's Door of Ely Cathedral suggests some such co-operation between carver and painter, for in the curiously distorted arms of the angels, leaning forward to support the mandorla round the Christ in Majesty, the carver has clearly misunderstood a foreshortened drawing. Whenever we see early carvings executed in flat planes, with the modelling expressed in incised lines, we may cautiously conjecture that the carver has followed the design which another man had painted.

At the next stage of professional development the carver probably worked from a design painted or drawn upon parchment, either as a miniature in an illuminated manuscript, or a rougher sketch on a piece of parchment; such sketches perhaps formed a pattern book in the possession of the master mason. Sometimes we can see that a carver has reproduced the contour lines of a pen drawing, without realising that the three-dimensional nature of his own medium made them superfluous. Thus on some figures upon the late 12th-century font at Coleshill (Warcs) we see the lines of shading by which the original draughtsman had indicated the modelling of the thigh copied as meaningless incisions by the carver, contradicting, rather than emphasising, the curve of the stone. In some cases the carver's model was apparently a drawing belonging to an earlier period. The demi-angel carved on a 12th-century tympanum at Halford (Warcs) seems to follow an Anglo-Saxon drawing of at least a century earlier, and some Norman reliefs at Barton-le-Street (Yorks) also look like copies of drawings of the Winchester School.[9] The practice continued in the later Middle Ages when the 15th-century wooden bosses of Queen Camel (Somerset) seem to have been based on a late 12th- or early 13th-century Bestiary. These later copyings can rarely be detected and probably only occurred when the carver was asked to depict unusual themes. The bosses in the Norwich cloister which represent subjects from the Apocalypse (PLATE 17) were almost certainly based upon the miniatures of an illuminated manuscript (*see* page 132). I do not suggest that the great Apocalypse belonging to Trinity College, Cambridge,[10] was connected with the Norwich bosses, but the miniature showing 'The Second Trumpet' (Fig. 7) contains all the elements which are present in the carving, and I think that we shall better appreciate the virtuosity of a medieval carver if we attempt to visualise a design for a roof boss which shall include all these momentous elements before turning to the photograph which illustrates his masterly solution of the problem.

The emergence of the medieval figure sculptor from a copyist to a creative master can best be studied upon early tombs. The prototype of the magnificent memorial effigies preserved in many parish churches is perhaps to be seen in the crude figures incised upon the wooden coffin of St. Cuthbert in Durham Cathedral. From wooden coffins such graffiti spread to stone grave slabs, but the designer's conception remained purely two-dimensional. He drew a standing figure upon the last page of life's record and cared not whether this was to be placed upright or horizontally. The canopy above the head, a supporting corbel beneath the feet, and the parallel folds of the drapery all belong to a vertical conception of form.

The series of memorials to 13th-century Abbots of Peterborough, in that cathedral, show a gradual increase in the carver's sense of modelling, but it was not until the second half of the 13th century that carvers began to express a recumbent figure in terms of their own medium, and the extent of their success in this matter is a criterion of date in these early monuments. The crossed legs picturesquely, but erroneously, associated with the Crusaders, may have been introduced with this aim in view.

Some of the carvings we have been considering seem to imply the active co-operation of a painter to direct the carver's chisel, but as the masons advanced in technical skill the mere sight of designs executed in other media was enough to guide them.[11] From the workers in metal they borrowed the design like plaited wire which surrounds the font at Castle Frome (PLATE 4) and the moulding of linked medallions round the famous 12th-century door of Kilpeck (Herefs), or the font at Stottesdon (Salop). A drawing of such ornament, which did not indicate its setting, might be mistaken for some rich necklace of gold and enamel. The miniature arcades, each arch framing a single figure, which the goldsmiths had used for their reliquary chests (inspired perhaps by classical sarcophagi) were copied by humbler workers in lead or stone, on fonts (Hereford Cathedral or Dorchester, Oxon) or for the heads of doorways at Pampisford (Cambs) or Syston (Lincs). On the Norman tympanum of the Virgin and Child, so inappropriately placed beneath the dazzle of the west window at Fownhope (Herefs), the draperies of the Virgin's robes are outlined by fine parallel groovings like those with which the early workers in gold or ivory often indicated such detail.

In some cases foreign characteristics give additional evidence that the carvers copied works in other media. The Saxon angel at Breedon-on-the-Hill (Leics) raises his hand to greet or bless, with the gesture of the Eastern Church (see page 84). The eastern legend of St. Anthony and St. Paul breaking bread in the desert appears on the late 7th-century Ruthwell Cross, where other figure compositions suggest affinities with Syrian paintings[12] and on the carved stone at Nigg (Aberdeen) which also suggests an eastern prototype.[13] The vine scrolls of Mediterranean decorative art find their counterparts on some Anglo-Saxon cross-shafts, and many Norman carvings of confronted animals evidently reproduce the designs of silks brought from the east to deck the sanctuaries of important churches. A few precious scraps of such silks survive in the library of Canterbury Cathedral, preserved by their use as seal-bags.

On stained glass and wall-paintings the dominant influence was that of the artists who illuminated manuscripts. In the 12th century particularly the wall-paintings are sometimes so closely allied in style with the miniatures of contemporary manuscripts as to suggest that the same artists were concerned with their design.[14] The general popularity, in the 13th century, of round medallions containing figure subjects, linked together by foliate designs, is reflected in all forms of ecclesiastical craftsmanship. The small round drawings of the Guthlac Roll in the British Museum, and the design of grouped medallions in a 13th-century manuscript in the library of Eton College, could so aptly have been translated into stained glass, or roundels of enamel, that they may even have been drawn for this purpose. Similar designs were painted upon the cathedral vaults of Canterbury, Rochester, Norwich, Ely and Salisbury, as well as on the walls of Brook (Kent) and Romsey Abbey. The last-named example is of special interest because of its similarity with the carved tympanum at Higham Ferrers (Northants). Both the figure subjects within the roundels, and the foliate star which occupies the space between them, have the same stylistic character.[15] The tympanum of Croyland Abbey (Lincs) on which roundels containing scenes from the life of St. Guthlac are combined into a large quatrefoil may also be associated with this group, which shows that in the 13th, as in the 12th, century the character of designs was not determined by the medium in which they were to be executed.

Some late 14th-century misericords in Worcester Cathedral which represent rare Old Testament subjects (see pages 93 and 95) are of particular interest because they were carved from designs closely akin to the 12th-century paintings formerly existing at Peterborough and

Worcester. The design of the misericord shown in PLATE 5 appears with unmistakable similarity in a Psalter in the Royal Library at Brussels (No. 9961) among miniatures which are accepted as records of the typological paintings which once surrounded the choir of Peterborough Cathedral.[16] This design, and those of two other misericords, occur on the 12th-century enamelled 'Warwick' and 'Balfour' ciboria (now on loan to the Victoria and Albert Museum) accompanied by inscriptions derived from a set of Latin verses which originally explained the paintings in the Chapter House at Worcester.[17] These paintings probably survived until the Chapter House was partly rebuilt in 1400, about twenty years after the making of the new choir stalls.

Not only did the carvers copy religious subjects, where their desire for guidance was natural, but also grotesque subjects. It has recently been established that a capital in the crypt at Canterbury Cathedral, showing an animal playing on a flute, corresponds closely with a miniature in a 12th-century manuscript from the scriptorium of Canterbury, and this also includes a lightly clothed man, gathering grapes into a basket, that we see carved upon a capital at Castor (Northants).[18] The definite identification of the source of a carving is a very rare prize, and even when we can say with certainty what has been copied we can hardly ever tell how it came to be copied. I know of only one case in which all the wished-for evidence seems to have been miraculously preserved : the late 15th-century paintings upon the stalls of Carlisle Cathedral. Some of the best of these illustrate the life of St. Cuthbert and it has been established that they are closely connected with a 12th-century manuscript of Bede's *Life of St. Cuthbert*, now in the British Museum but formerly belonging to the monastic library of Durham.[19] Out of 17 panels at Carlisle 13 correspond so closely to the miniatures of the manuscript that these could well have served as original designs, and the remaining 4 panels were perhaps based on miniatures which are now missing. The painter did not make a slavish copy, the backgrounds are different, the colours vary and sometimes a figure is shown in a different pose, but the general grouping is identical and proves that the painter must have been able to make outline sketches from the manuscript, or have had such sketches provided for him. The intermediary who made this possible was probably Richard Bell who was Bishop of Carlisle, 1478–95, when the paintings were being made, and who had previously been Prior of Durham. The catalogue of the Durham Library, made in 1416, mentions that the *Life of St. Cuthbert* had been in the possession of Richard le Scrope, Archbishop of York, and it is possible that its loan had been requested in order that the glazier making the St. Cuthbert window in the south choir aisle of York Minster could derive his subject-matter from such a venerable source. Unfortunately he felt competent to produce his own designs and only one panel, that of St. Cuthbert's horse pulling out the thatch of the house to reveal the food miraculously concealed there, shows any similarity with the miniatures of the manuscript.

For the later medieval periods the glaziers provide us with the best evidence of how designs were conveyed.[20] Until the mid-15th century cartoons for windows were drawn upon plastered boards which were supported on trestles. These 'tables' served both as model and work-bench, for the craftsman cut and leaded his material upon the blank end of the board. Since their bulk made difficult the storage of many 'tables', the same designs were constantly repeated, slight alterations in their details increasing the range of their subject-matter. The identification of most saints depended only upon an attribute, so that, by varying the attributes, one cartoon could easily do service for all saints within a given group, identified by their clothing as apostles, Popes, bishops or deacons. This repetition was particularly easy when all the windows of a cathedral clerestory had to be filled, for then the subjects would be far above the eye-level of carping criticism. In the clerestory of the western choir of York Minster a five-light window showing a central pope flanked by a king and an ecclesiastic on each side is repeated six times with slight variations, and at Malvern the same cartoon served for both Edward the Confessor and William the Conqueror. The late medieval practice of filling each light of a window with a single figure made their balance most important, and many glaziers achieved symmetry by the lazy process of reversing the cartoon for use in the corresponding light. Thus, in a window in North Cerney (Glos), we can see three female saints worked from one cartoon. In one case this has been reversed and in the other two a change of attribute, or the introduction of the Child Virgin beside St. Anne, was all that was needed. A single cartoon of a shield-bearing angel could serve to fill the tracery lights of many windows and when the family of a donor were shown kneeling behind him, the same child could be repeated in descending scale as often as was required.

The introduction of paper, or parchment, to replace the boards increased this repetition, for it was easier to store such 'scrolls' over long periods of time. The wills of medieval master glaziers record bequests of 'scrowles' as well as of tools to their heirs or partners. In St. Michael-le-Belfrey, York, there is a St. Christopher in a window probably put up after the rebuilding of the church in 1528–36 which is identical in design with one in All Saints, North Street, supposed to be the work of John Chamber the younger, who died in 1451. The scroll bearing this design had therefore been handed on from one master glazier to another, and used, as need arose, over a period of eighty years at least. Had more churches retained their ancient glass we should probably have seen other windows taken from this cartoon in districts served by the glaziers of York. At Bolton Percy (Yorks) the saints represented in the east window include a bishop taken from the cartoon used for the figures of St. John of Beverley and St. William of York in the Parker window, and an archbishop repeating the figure of St. Paulinus in the Wolveden window in York Minster.

Even groups and subject pictures were sometimes composed from cartoons already drawn for a different purpose. Miraculous cures at the shrine of a saint often had a similarity of which the glaziers were quick to take advantage, and in the St. William window at York two cartoons have been repeated without change while two others have been varied by a mutual interchange of the blind and the crippled coming to the shrines. It is thus obvious that very little clerical supervision would have been necessary in the glazing of a later church, even if cartoons for the subjects chosen were not already in stock. An important master glazier would probably have had some list of the attributes of the outstanding saints in his workshop, so that the cartoons could be correctly adapted, and the co-operation of an ecclesiastical adviser would only have been necessary when rare subjects were required.

The same process of repetition characterises the later shop-work of the carvers, particularly those who made alabaster panels. Sometimes these repeated their designs *ad infinitum*: fifty-six 'Heads of St. John the Baptist' (see page 155) were sent out in a single consignment, but the unusual imagery of such panels, as 'St. Boniface overthrowing the Tree of Thor ' (in the Victoria and Albert Museum), suggest that a cleric may have designed them.

The invention of paper, followed by that of printing, made possible the wide distribution of single woodcuts, and of illustrated books which were not too precious to be used directly as models. The designs of the block-book *Biblia Pauperum* (Fig. 4) appear in glass and carving in many churches, and the glaziers of Malvern made such frequent use of the woodcuts of the *Speculum Humanae Salvationis* that these have been used as the basis for restoring shattered panels in these windows.[21]   Not only figure subjects but abstract ornaments were copied by the carvers. Almost all the carved ornament on the de la Warr chantry at Boxgrove (Sussex) was copied from the borders of French Books of Hours (of which one is reproduced on the title-page of this book), and some of the same designs were copied by the carvers of the misericords in Bristol Cathedral.

The medieval craftsman was evidently no more averse to working from other men's designs than his descendants, even when he did not understand them. While the finer craftsmen gained independence both as regards economic status and technique of expression, they remained subject to the informed direction of ecclesiastical employers in their renderings of sacred themes, or responded to the vivid, but often misleading, stimulus of popular imagination. The carver's share in originating such popular innovations was no more important than that of any other parishioner and it is in terms of the parishioner's outlook that we must consider them.

CHAPTER 3

THE PARISHIONER'S APPROACH

THE approach of both parson and craftsman was largely determined by their professions, but that of the parishioner was,
literally, nation-wide, since, when there was only one Church,
every citizen was a parishioner. I must therefore make my own
limitations and discuss only three aspects of the parishioner's relation
to his parish church:

(1) His share in general parochial efforts to raise money for repairs
or rebuilding.

(2) The material provisions which he made for the future well-
being of his soul.

(3) The effect of popular imagination upon iconography.

First let us try to picture the activities, involving all inhabitants,
of a village or small town, when any important work on the parish
church was in progress. The records of such operations rarely survived but a lucky chance preserved the financial records of the rebuilding of Bodmin church in 1469–72. Crumbling away, but still legible,
these were discovered in an old chest in the parvise of the church
porch and published in the *Camden Miscellany* for 1875. The Priory
of St. Petrock, which owned the living, apparently contributed nothing
to the rebuilding, for this did not include the chancel. The provision
of funds was largely organised through the forty gilds in Bodmin, of
which five were craft gilds while the others had been founded for
religious or social purposes. Out of the £196: 7: 4 raised during the
first years of the work, the gilds contributed £86: 11: 5 from their
own funds and a further £24: 13s. raised through the craft gilds by a
levy of 1d. or ½d. per man. Voluntary contributions from the
parishioners, bequests and the sale of old materials from the church
made up the balance. The records of these sales show us that complete
windows were sold to other parishes, and some glass in the north
aisle of St. Kew (Cornwall) is traditionally supposed to have come
from Bodmin at this time. Glancing through the receipts one gets a
moving impression of the little community pooling all its resources to

glorify God through the beauty of their new church. Every inhabitant seems to have given according to his means and those who could not give money gave their free labour. Many gave both labour and gifts of produce to be sold: here a lamb and there a goose, and further on we read that Cicely Serle gave her 'crokke' (or cauldron) which was sold for 20d. The vicar gave his whole year's salary and the 'parish people' who lived outside the town also contributed. There is a list of 460 inhabitants who made voluntary contributions, but there seems to have been some compulsion, for several men are listed as having had some household effect seized because they failed to pay, and small fines upon those who did not do their promised day's work in the quarry are also recorded. Some of the principal contributors are still commemorated in the church. The windows given by Thomas Lucombe and Bartholomew Trote have been lost, but the Lucombe arms are carved upon the roof bosses and Trote's merchant's mark appears on the bench-ends. Since there is no reason to think that Bodmin was unusual in any way except in the preservation of its records, we may take the picture which these present as typical of the efforts by which the small medieval communities created churches whose unstinted splendour puts to shame the dingy mediocrity of many built at the apogee of England's industrial wealth.

The accounts of Bodmin represent a special effort, but where the building operations were on a smaller scale the necessary funds were sometimes obtained from sources not mentioned in these accounts. Fines for misdeeds were applied to church improvements although I know of no medieval instance which has left so clear a record as the 18th-century font at Tollesbury (Essex), which is clumsily inscribed:

> Good people all I pray take care
> That in ye church ye doe not sware
> As this man did,[1]

and the records for 1718 tell how John Norman came drunk to church and paid £5 (spent on a new font) to avoid being prosecuted for this offence. A more important source of income was the 'mortuary' or 'corpse-present' which, from a voluntary offering, became practically compulsory. Even if the priest did not break the laws of the Church by exacting payment for the Sacraments, and such offences are frequently denounced, his deathbed influence was well-nigh irresistible.[2] Those who could not make a written will, and the majority of citizens were in this case, had to make their testamentary dispositions verbally before a priest, and one can imagine how vividly the terrors of Hell, as they were painted upon the walls of most churches, could be recalled to the minds of the dying in order to secure an important bequest.

Where a gift to the church took the form of a window, pulpit or painted screen, an inscription often recorded the names of the donors and exhorted the beholder to pray for their souls. With the same intention of serving as a pictorial Bede Roll the figures of kings and nobles who had been important benefactors were represented in the windows of great churches, such as Malvern or Tewkesbury. The appeal 'Ora pro nobis' can still be read on the worn scrolls of memorial brasses, inlaid upon the stone floor of the church, or in the lower panels of windows where it is often accompanied by a small figure of the kneeling donor, who is sometimes shown holding his gift in his hands. The invocation may be addressed to a particular saint: SCT EDMUND ORA P NOBIS in crowned letters of stone is inlaid on the flint walling of his church at Southwold (Suffolk), or an appeal for the prayers of the passer-by may be reinforced by a grim reminder that they too will soon be in like need of intercession.

In all pious foundations of the Middle Ages there was an implicit agreement, sometimes specified in the bequest, that Masses should be offered, and special prayers said, for the deliverance from Purgatory of the souls of the founder and his family. Modest endowments provided for the saying of Masses upon the anniversary of death, or some other chosen day, either for a period of years or in perpetuity, while wealthier testators founded perpetual chantries whose chaplains were primarily concerned with the saying of such Masses. Important benefactors to religious communities shared vicariously in the prayers and good works of their members, and sometimes letters of confraternity accorded them the privilege of being admitted to the Order upon their death-beds, so that they should die in the habit of a monk, or nun. A man thus admitted was known as *monachus frater ad sucurrendum*.[3] The Franciscans zealously promoted this practice and it is the Franciscan habit which covers the mail shirt and coif of a layman upon an effigy at Conington (Hunts).[4] Such effigies are very rare; the great of the land generally preferred to be represented upon their tombs in all their worldly finery even if they had died in the rough robe of a monk.

It is in the 13th century that we first hear of chantries being endowed so that soul-masses should be said in perpetuity for the soul of the founder.[5] Edward I gave the Abbey of Westminster the revenues of twenty-two manors to endow services of intercession for his beloved queen, Eleanor of Castile, and Masses were also endowed at the places where her body rested on its last journey and which were subsequently marked by the famous Eleanor Crosses. In the 14th and 15th centuries these chantries multiplied so rapidly that there was hardly a church that had not one at least, while in many cases there were several, so that the plan and general structure of parish churches were changed by the building of additional chapels. At Newark-on-Trent, for example, there were fifteen chantries in the parish church whose chaplains had free control over their particular altars and endowments but who were bound to assist and obey the rector in matters concerning the parish services in the choir. This obligation, which applied generally to chantry chaplains, explains why so many parish churches have fine choir stalls with carved misericords. Suitable seating for all the chantry priests had to be provided in the choir, and when these were sufficiently numerous to be organised into a College its establishment was often celebrated by the making of new stalls.

Some chantry foundations included almshouses, or hospitals, whose occupants were to pray daily at the tomb of their founder, and who wore a long hooded robe embroidered with his badge, or arms. Such figures are often included among the 'weepers' upon tomb-chests and they generally hold rosaries which are disproportionately large. The reason for this is to be found in the many medieval wills which specify that 'Our Lady's Psalter', or the Rosary, shall be recited to ensure the dead person's rest.[6] An unusual reminder of the prayers to be said in connexion with such foundations occurs on two brasses in the church at Morley (Derbs). One of these shows John Stathum (d. 1454) and his wife kneeling before St. Christopher and records his endowment of an annual dole of bread. The second brass specifies the prayers to be said for the souls of three generations of his family.[7]

The terrible Black Death of 1349 and the lesser outbreaks in succeeding years led to a rapid increase in the number of chantries, for the imminence of death brooded upon men's minds. We can feel some of the despair in the minds of parishioners who had seen almost all their neighbours die of the plague, and half the benefices in the country left without priests, when we try to decipher the inscription scratched upon the wall of the church at Ashwell (Herts). The abbreviated Latin graffito may be rendered:

1350. Wretched, savage and violent, a wicked populace survives to witness and in the end of the second [pestilence ?] with a violent wind Maurus thunders in the world. 1361.

The meaning of the last line is explained by a verse in Harding's

Chronicles which follows an account of the plague:

> In the same yere was on St Maurys Day
> The great wind and earthquake mervelous.[8]

In the 15th century this preoccupation with death also found expression in the ghastly cadavers carved beneath some tombs, as, for instance, those of Bishop Fleming at Lincoln and Bishop Beckington at Wells. At Feniton (Devon) we see the cadaver on the top of the tomb-chest, and this morbid cult for realism reaches its apogee at Tewkesbury where the 16th-century Wakeman cenotaph shows the dead body being devoured by a snake, frog, mouse and snail.

The founding of a private chantry was only possible to the wealthy, but the poor were just as much afraid, and so the 14th century also saw the foundation of many gilds by which men and women bound themselves together to support chantries for the spiritual welfare of all members, past and present.[9] These religious gilds were distinct from the craft gilds which existed primarily to control the economic organisation of a trade, but both types maintained lights before the altars of their patron saints in their parish church and endowed Masses for the souls of their members. Much of our knowledge about their early history comes from the returns which their officers made in 1389, when the government of Richard II, apparently suffering from the common delusion that financial disruption can be cured by *questionnaires*, demanded information about all gilds. Only 507 returns have survived and their distribution is erratic: 164 from Norfolk, and only 1 from Staffordshire, 51 from Kings Lynn and only 1 from Canterbury, but the reasons for their foundation given by some gilds are relevant to our present study. In 1114 the Gild of Holy Sepulchre was founded in Cambridge for the special purpose of building, in honour of God and of the Holy Sepulchre, the Round Church which still stands. The canonisation of a British saint sometimes led to the foundation of a gild. Two years before the death of Henry II a Gild of St. Thomas à Becket was founded at Wymondham (Norfolk) and dedications to him occur in about a dozen of the surviving returns. A Gild of All Souls, founded in London in 1379, found the chapel of the charnel house in St. Paul's Cemetery in a ruinous condition, 'its windows broken and its altars so foul that none of the chaplains of chantries there could sing for the souls of their founders', and they repaired it. Another return is movingly simple: 'The poor men of the parish of St. Austin (Norwich) founded this gild for the help and amendment of their poor parish church'. Sometimes the creation of a work of art gave rise to a gild. At Spalding, in 1358, John de Rughton painted a beautiful image in honour of St. John and, with the help of others, maintained a light before it, and later provided a chaplain. The Gild of the Invention of the Holy Cross at Grantham was formed in connexion with the Rood carved by Roger de Wolsthorp in 1347.

Only about 36 gilds specified in 1389 that they had contributed in any way to their parish church, but we have seen from the Bodmin accounts how important a part they sometimes played in the building or adorning of churches. Visible evidence of this is rare, but some painted screen panels in St. Matthew's Church, Ipswich, include what is probably a portrait group of the gild which gave the screen. The men kneel in front, the foremost bearing a heavy purse, which may indicate that he was Master, or Treasurer, and the women members form another group behind. Among the saints painted upon the other panels is one holding the hammer attribute of St. Eloy. It is tempting to guess that the painter meant to represent the windlass of St. Erasmus, for records show that there was a Gild of St. Erasmus connected with this church, but it must not be more than a guess !

The east window of Holy Trinity Goodramgate, at York, which shows God the Father, holding the body of the dead Christ, in the central light, flanked by SS. Christopher and George, certainly refers to gild membership. John Walker, who gave this window in 1470, also made bequests to the city gilds of Corpus Christi and of the 'Holy Martyrs Christopher and George'.[10] Until the air raids of 1942 there were four representations of Corpus Christi in the windows of York churches, and the figures of the two patron saints occurred so often as to constitute almost a trade mark of the York glaziers.[11]

The gilds of Corpus Christi form a distinct group. In about 1264 Pope Urban IV directed that the Feast of Corpus Christi should be celebrated, and indulgences were granted to those taking part in the elaborate processions of the Holy Sacrament which marked this festival. The feast was not generally observed in England until the 14th century and the Corpus Christi gilds were formed to organise the processions. Their members included many who belonged to other gilds and the craft gilds also co-operated by producing mobile 'pageants'. The texts of the surviving play cycles, such as the Chester, or York, Plays, or the *Ludus Coventriae* whose original location is uncertain, give us a clear idea of what these pageants were like. At York the Corpus Christi gild had a Creed play of their own which they performed every tenth year, and in the 14th century a special gild was formed to produce a Paternoster play.[12]

The mention of these plays brings us to my last theme. Both in the *exempla* of medieval preachers and in the texts of the play cycles, we find the same robust, vivid handling of solemn themes. Local names and turns of speech, which call up the atmosphere of the English countryside, mingle with the words of the Bible, and characters only chronicled anonymously in the Gospels are allotted roles of racy comedy or macabre horror. The theatrical 'business' accompanying such interpolated scenes impressed itself upon the minds of the artists and was sometimes reproduced by them when they were called upon to express the same themes in the imagery of local churches. So the popular element gained acceptance in the minds of the parishioners as it was bandied to and fro from theatrical producer to artist-craftsman. Some instances of this theatrical influence I have noted in a former book,[13] and others will be mentioned in connexion with the subjects it affected, so we can pass on to consider another manner in which popular imagination affected religious imagery.

Every period has its own artistic conventions which appear so natural to contemporary eyes that their symbolism passes for reality, but, just as the outrageous artistic innovation of to-day becomes the academic platitude of to-morrow, so the generally accepted symbol will in the course of years become mysterious once more. Since there was no written record of the symbolism of early Christian art, the features not retained in common use lost their original meaning for the people, who therefore invented new legends to explain them. Thus a new saint, or a new episode in the life of an old one, was added to the iconography of Christian churches.

An interesting, if somewhat grotesque, example of this process is to be found in the legend of St. Uncumber (also known as St. Wilgefortis) whose statue in Henry VII's Chapel at Westminster shows her as a woman with long hair and a full beard, holding a book and a Tau cross. On the screen of Worstead (Norfolk) she is shown as a bearded and crowned woman on a cross. Her legend tells that she was a princess of Portugal who prayed that some disfigurement might save her from being forced to marry. She immediately grew a beard and her father, maddened by this unnatural obstacle to his plans, crucified her. So ran the tale by which medieval folk tried to explain the robed Christ on such early Roods as that at Langford (Oxon) where although the head, which perhaps wore a crown, has gone, the long straight robe reaching to the feet and wrists and girdled with a sash, might well suggest a woman. Thus ignorance created a new saint who was credited with the power to rid women of their unwanted husbands!

In the same way the early Christian convention of showing the less important figures on a smaller scale added to the story of St. Nicholas of Bari the picturesque episode of the three children miraculously resurrected from the tub in which their bodies had been cut up and salted. Originally this saint had been honoured for the great numbers of converts whom he had baptised and three small figures standing in a tub-shaped font at his feet became his attribute which was later so strangely interpreted ! [14] The symbol of an eye, placed beside St. Lucy by early painters, as an identifying reference to her name Lucia (light) gave rise to the later legend of how the saint plucked out her own eyes and handed them to the suitor who sought to make her break her vows of virginity by praising their beauty.[15]

Thus in a confusion of faith and fear, mysticism and muddle, some of them serving in genuine piety, others actuated by social ambition or uneasy conscience, medieval men and women approached their parish church, and it is time that we also turned to the buildings themselves to examine what meanings underlie their structure and decoration.

PART II
Structure and Plan

CHAPTER I

THE SIGNIFICANCE OF PLAN

THE stylistic developments of church architecture do not concern us here, but I think it is relevant to my theme to consider how far the ground plans of British churches were dictated by the demands of ritual, by symbolism, or by architectural expediency.[1]

The origin of the basilican type of early church is obscure and need not be considered in detail. One theory derives it from the public halls used by the Romans for justice or commerce and another from the inner hall of a Roman house. We know that some Roman villas in Britain were owned by Christians, for symbols of the Faith have been found at both Chedworth (Glos) and Frampton (Dorset), but these do not seem to have included any specially designed places of worship. Foundations generally accepted as those of a Romano-British church were uncovered at Silchester (Hants) in 1892 and these resemble the plans of the first churches in North Africa. Thus, while the apse is at the west end, and the aisles have western transeptal projections, like the original basilica of St. Peter's at Rome, the narthex extends the whole width of the façade, following eastern models, and the projecting parts of the aisles are closer to the *Diaconicon* and *Prothesis* of the eastern churches than to Roman transepts, for the ritual distinction between these chambers was early abandoned in Rome. The first opened into the chancel and was used for keeping holy vessels, while the other was entered from the nave by those who brought offerings.[2]

When we come to consider medieval churches the symbolical interpretation of the cruciform plan seems so obvious that one is tempted to accept it as having been the guiding principle of the early church-builders, but if we study the earlier ground plans we shall see that considerations of stability and convenience, rather than symbolism, dominated their tentative evolution.

If we disregard the early 'bee-hive' oratories of Ireland, the most primitive churches, such as the ruined chapel at Heysham (Lancs), had only one narrow chamber, but it was soon felt that the altar should be set in a place apart and a small second chamber was built on for this purpose. This formed the aisle-less nave and square chancel which is common to many early British churches, particularly in the north. The fine Saxon tower of Barton-on-Humber (Lincs) has a small contemporary structure projecting to the west of it and the foundations of a corresponding eastern chancel have been traced, so that the ground floor of the tower formed the central one of three chambers arranged in line, but there were no lateral projections. The western tower at Bradford-on-Avon (Wilts) had large north and south porches, one of which remains, and small chapels abut upon the central towers of St. Mary-in-Castro, Dover, and Breamore (Hants), or opened from the eastern part of the nave at Britford (Wilts) or Worth (Sussex). These chapels are not, however, true transepts. In the later periods, when central towers were raised upon high arches, transepts were a structural necessity and the cruciform plan would thus have come into being even if it had not possessed such appropriate symbolical associations. Even so, it was not universally adopted and the little importance attached to its symbolism by later builders is made clear by the way in which they built on chapels until a church which had been regularly cruciform became an illogical agglomeration of parallelograms like Burford (Oxon).

The divergent opinions of people in the Middle Ages are effectively illustrated by comparing this circumstantial evidence of the masons' indifference to symbolism, with the assertions of Durandus that cruciform churches signify that we are crucified to the world, while round ones symbolise how the Church has been extended throughout the circle of the earth. 'The foundation is faith, which is conversant with unseen things : the roof charity, which covereth a multitude of sins', while the cock on the summit of church typifies the preacher who calls to repentance those who sleep in their sins through the night which is this world. 'The glass windows of a church are Holy Scriptures, which expel wind and rain, that is all things hurtful', but transmit the true sunlight of God into the hearts of the faithful. 'The door of the church is Christ, and the Apostles also are called doors. The chancel, that is the head of the church, being lower than its body, signifieth how great humility there should be in the clergy'.[3] While realising that such symbolical interpretations of church architecture are often only later spiritual rationalisations, we should also remember that the views of Durandus were probably shared, with individual variations, by many scholarly clerics of the Middle Ages and that they may also have heightened the reverence with which the educated laity regarded the structure of their churches.

Before we leave the subject of plan two features, to which the symbolists have attached mystical meanings, must be discussed. Starting from the belief that the transepts represented the transom of Christ's Cross, they related the corona of chapels which radiate from the ambulatory surrounding the main apse at Canterbury, Gloucester and Norwich to His crown, and interpreted the irregular alignment of many chancels as symbolising the weary drooping of His head upon the Cross. The first point need not be discussed at length, it is merely a case of an over-ingenious interpretation of an arrangement which was designed to provide a number of chapels and a dignified passage for processions, or for the pilgrims who came to worship at the different shrines within a great church. Had the symbolical meaning of the corona been generally accepted, even the austere Cistercians would hardly have abandoned it in favour of the square-ended chancel. Their first house in England, at Waverley (Surrey), had an aisle-less cruciform church, square-ended and with only two transeptal chapels.

The peculiarity of plan known as a 'skew', or 'weeping', chancel, of which the side walls are not in alignment with those of the nave, occurs to a varying extent in many churches. The late Mr. C. J. P. Cave made a systematic survey of 642 churches [4] and found that in 99 (that is to say in 15·4 per cent) the chancels were perceptibly crooked. Of these 56 inclined to the north and 43 to the south, so there was no agreement as to the direction of deviation, as might have been expected with any symbolical tradition, particularly as almost all medieval crucifixes show Christ's head drooping onto His right shoulder. The angles of deviation varied from $\frac{1}{2}$ to 8 degrees; the extremes being represented by St. Martin's, Exeter, which slants 8 degrees to the north, and Bosham (Sussex) which is 7 degrees to the south. More than half the churches surveyed had deviations of between 1 and 3 degrees, more easily attributable to accident than intention. The early church builders were frankly careless in setting out their foundations. It is quite common to find a church in which either nave or chancel is not a true parallelogram; at Sherington (Bucks) the chancel is 18 inches wider at the east end than at the west.[5] When the 14th- or 15th-century masons had to build on to such an irregular structure it was impossible for them to produce a correctly aligned addition since their elaborate roofs made parallel walls essential. If they prolonged one wall of the original building, the opposite side of their new work had to 'weep' in order to keep this parallel. The most usual method was to set out the new work at right angles to the chancel arch, but if this was set crooked, and at Wiggenhall St. Mary Magdalene (Norfolk) it is at a marked angle, then a 'weeping chancel' was inevitable.   .

Mr. Cave's study of weeping chancels was brought about by his interest in the orientation of churches and, since no more appropriate context for this study will occur in this book, I will here summarise his findings.   Out of the 642 churches measured only 10 were orientated due east; 405 were north of east and 227 south of east.   A similar study of Scottish churches by Dr. F. C. Eeles produced the same percentages.[6]   It has sometimes been suggested that orientation was fixed by the point of sunrise upon the festival of the patron saint of the church, but this theory does not stand up to detailed tests.   Mr. Cave preferred the common-sense explanation that the foundations were orientated to the point of sunrise at the time when they were first cut.   The preference for a northerly deviation would thus be explained by the fact that building operations generally began early in the spring when the sun is north of the Equator.   A later start would mean a different orientation.

CHAPTER 2

THE STRUCTURAL SETTING OF IMAGERY

IT would be inappropriate for me to attempt any description of the
rites and ceremonies for which special structural provisions were
made in medieval churches, beyond the briefest possible indication
of the original purpose of the remaining structures. The bibliography
on page 199 will help my readers' next step towards a more adequate
study of them. This chapter is merely intended to indicate the probable
whereabouts of interesting imagery to be noted in the course of a
walk round a medieval church, the itinerary being arranged in the
following order:

The Churchyard Cross	Lecterns
The Exterior Imagery	Chantry Chapels
Consecration Crosses	Tombs
Mass Dials	Rood-screen
The Porch Imagery	The Altar
Holy Water Stoup	Sedilia
The Font	Piscina
Benches and Stalls	Aumbry
Pulpits	Easter Sepulchre

THE CHURCHYARD CROSS.—Although few of them still stand in
their original positions, many churches contain fragments of Saxon
crosses which perhaps marked the gathering places for worship before
any church was built. The simpler examples are only decorated with
interlacing patterns but the greater crosses, such as those at Ruthwell
(Dumfries) and Bewcastle (Cumbs), include scenes from the Gospels
and the figures of saints, while subjects from Norse mythology mingle
with Christian iconography on crosses at Leeds, Halton (Lancs) and
Gosforth (Cumbs) and on many carvings in the Isle of Man. Later
medieval churchyard crosses generally have a tall, slender shaft rising
from a steeply stepped base which sometimes served as an outdoor
pulpit. The cross head often takes the form of a square panel under
a gabled roof; on one side is carved the Crucifixion and the other
often shows a figure of the Virgin and Child. Occasionally figures

are carved on the cross shaft, for instance, St. Michael and the Dragon at Drayton (Somerset).

EXTERIOR IMAGERY.—Before entering the church it is well to walk round the exterior at a little distance from it, for interesting statues sometimes remain in the niches on late medieval towers, too inaccessible to have been deliberately damaged. On the west face of the tower at Beaminster (Dorset) there is a Rood Group with the Resurrection and Ascension carved on reliefs above it. The patron saint of the church may be represented by a single statue on the tower, or be accompanied by others, as at St. Austell (Cornwall). More rarely, such images appear over the east window. Coats of arms or merchants' marks carved on the tower sometimes recall its founders.

CONSECRATION CROSSES.—Incised crosses, sometimes framed in a circle, appear on the outer walls of some churches, marking the spots anointed by the bishop during the consecration of the building. The usual number of places so anointed was 24, 12 inside and 12 outside the building, but often the crosses were only painted on the wall and have weathered away, or been covered over. Painted crosses survive on interior walls in some places, as at Overbury (Glos), while at Edington (Wilts) they seem to have been inlaid with brass. The 11 consecration crosses on the exterior of Yetminster (Dorset) may mark a 15th-century reconsecration of this church after the nave and tower had been rebuilt.

MASS DIALS.—The radiating lines of a sundial can be seen on many churches, particularly near to the south door. Although some Saxon dials, such as those at Kirkdale (Yorks) and Daglingworth (Glos), divide the day into four 'tides' of three hours each, most medieval dials show only noon and the hours of Mass and Vespers. Where other lines are shown on a dial the line representing the hour of Mass is sometimes distinguished by a cross-bar.

THE PORCH.—The imagery of the main door into the church will be discussed later (see page 65), but other features should be noted. A niche in the side wall of the porch is a feature particularly common in the Cotswolds, and, although these niches are mostly empty now, the remains of images which probably once occupied them can be seen at Coberley and Great Rissington in Gloucestershire. In most cases the figure probably represented the saint to whom the porch altar was dedicated. In some early churches, such as Bradford-on-Avon (Wilts), Bishopstone (Sussex) and Stottesdon (Salop), we can see that the door into the church is markedly to the west of the central line of the porch to allow room for the porch altar.

When the porch is a vaulted stone structure the roof bosses should be noticed, for these sometimes include unusual subjects, as, for instance, the strange form of Holy Trinity, with a large eye carved below the Three Persons, which occurs on the central boss at Thorverton (Devon).

The HOLY WATER STOUP usually occurs on the right-hand side of the main door, but many examples were broken or blocked up at the Reformation. The lower part of the bowl may be carved, at Cleobury Mortimer (Salop) it shows a human head, but such carvings rarely have any special significance.

THE FONT.—This is always near the door, just as Baptism is the Doorway to the other Sacraments. The large bowls of early fonts sometimes stood directly on the floor, and it is, therefore, interesting to note how often the base of a Norman font is later than the bowl. The varied imagery of early Norman fonts includes biblical scenes, events in the life of Christ or of the saints ; the Psychomachia (see page 164), calendars and symbolical animals. Later medieval fonts have a more restricted range of subjects : the Crucifixion or the Baptism of Christ, figures of the Virgin and Child, Holy Trinity, the Evangelists in human form or represented by their Emblems (see page 130), religious or secular heraldry, are the most usual subjects. The Seven Sacrament fonts are a group apart (see page 54). Figures of saints are sometimes carved round the shaft of the font, as an alternative to the more usual lions and woodwoses. Some fonts have angels holding scrolls, from which the inscriptions have worn away, but at St. Margaret's, Ipswich, the words SAL ET SALIVA are carved on an angel's scroll referring to the usage of placing salt in a child's mouth and anointing its nose and ears with saliva, during the baptismal service.

Symbolical explanations of the form of font bowls are sometimes put forward, but the fact that, even when the scheme of imagery demands a seven-sided font, as in the case of the Seven Sacrament fonts, this mystic number was set aside in favour of the more easily set-out octagon seems to disprove any such intention. An exception may be made for the chalice-shaped fonts of which Castle Frome (PLATE 4) is an early example.

BENCHES AND STALLS.—Before the late 13th century the nave of a parish church would always have been clear of seats, as we still see it at Grosmont (Herefs), and even later the worshippers in most churches would have stood, or knelt, upon a rush-strewn floor. Those who through age or infirmity were too weak to stand throughout the Mass 'went to the wall', where a stone bench, running along its base, or surrounding the piers of the nave, gave them rest. At Perranzabuloe (Cornwall) such a wall-bench runs all round the small ancient church, and sections of it can be seen in several churches.

The earliest wooden benches are those at Dunsfold (Surrey) dating from *c.* 1290, but in the 14th and 15th centuries carpenters must have been busy in most churches. The carved wooden bench-ends show us a wide variety of popular imagery, but rarely include motives of great iconographical interest. Figures of the Virgin and Child, or of saints, are sometimes represented, particularly fine series of such figures occurring on the benches of two Norfolk churches, Wiggenhall St. German and Wiggenhall St. Mary the Virgin. Emblems of the Passion are very often shown, as on the Cornish bench-ends at Poughill, Kilkhampton and Launcells, or the richly carved bench-back at Fressingfield (Suffolk). Vices and virtues personified in terms of racy caricature, strange animals drawn from the Bestiary (PLATES 23 and 24), heraldic devices and the merchants' marks of donors, besides an endless variety of grotesque subjects are to be found.

In many churches the bench-ends curve inwards at the top and end in richly carved finials, known as poppy-heads. The name is derived from the Latin *puppis*, a small image, and sometimes the finial does take this form, but grotesque animals or luxuriant foliage are more frequently seen (PLATE 24). Some bench-ends, particularly in the eastern counties, have figure subjects carved on projecting arm-rests, generally in the form of animals. The finials of choir stalls occasionally represent biblical scenes, as, for instance, at Tong (Salop) where the Resurrection and Ascension are so depicted.

I cannot attempt to enumerate the types of subject which are found on the misericords, those carved brackets on the under-side of the hinged seats of choir stalls. With the possible exception of scenes from the Passion I can think of no form of imagery occurring elsewhere in churches which does not occur on some misericord, and illustrations of secular literature are chiefly to be found in these carvings (PLATES 5, 13, 21, 23). For those who have the interest and the leisure to undertake the dusty, back-breaking task of turning up a long series of misericords, examining and then replacing them, the study is well worth its pains.

PULPITS.—If we except the 13th-century reading pulpit in the refectory of Beaulieu Abbey (Hants), which is now the parish church, no pulpit is earlier than the 14th century. One of the oldest may be that at Mellor (Derbs), which is cut from a solid block of wood. It is comparatively rare to find imagery on a medieval pulpit, and when this appears it often takes the form of statuettes, or paintings, of the Four Doctors of the Latin Church, as at Trull (Somerset) (PLATE 8). The figures carved on the stone pulpit at Frampton-on-Frome (Dorset) are very unusual in that they represent preaching friars, perhaps the two great Franciscans, SS. Bonaventura and Peter of Alcantara.

LECTERNS.—The most popular form for the great lecterns of wood or brass is that of an eagle, the bird which alone can gaze undazzled at the sun (see page 179). Examples remain in more than fifty churches. Much more rarely we find lecterns in the form of a pelican, the symbol of Christ's sacrifice, as, for instance, in Norwich Cathedral and at Middleton (Hants) and Stanton Fitzwarren (Wilts). Beautifully carved stone desks, probably made for some great abbeys, are now in the Worcestershire churches of Norton and Crowle.

CHANTRY CHAPELS.—If we could see an important medieval church in its original condition we should immediately notice the much greater extent to which it was divided into separate chapels, each screened off by tracery of wood or stone. The aisles might be entirely occupied by such chapels, for it was often to provide space for chantries that an aisle was added on. There is no 'normal position' for a chantry chapel and their erratic arrangement has given to British churches a fascinating variety of ground plan. In a cathedral, or abbey church, chantry chapels often took the form of cages enclosed with exquisite stone tracery, and framed in the arches surrounding the High Altar. Sometimes small figures of saints stand in niches on this tracery, as on Prince Arthur's chantry in Worcester Cathedral, and the bosses, and other detail carvings, of the interior of such chapels are often worthy of study.

One of the most magnificent chantry chapels in England, the Beauchamp Chapel in St. Mary's Church at Warwick, has preserved the greater part of its imagery, glass painting and statuary, all combining in a coherent iconographical scheme, but this is very unusual. The most common form for a chantry chapel was an aisle added to the nave, or, more often, to the chancel. The detail carvings of the aisles added as chantry chapels to the Devon churches of Tiverton and Cullompton are almost biographies in stone of the rich clothiers who built them, so many trophies of their trade are included. In many of the chapels which open from the chancel, or the transepts, of parish churches we now see only the tombs of the great family which probably founded a chantry in them, but at Stoke Charity (Hants) the beautiful carving of the Mass of St. Gregory (PLATE 20) was probably the reredos of the chantry altar.

43

TOMB CHESTS.—The splendid monumental effigies which lie on tombs in parish churches throughout the country are the finest examples of medieval sculpture which have been spared to us, but their historic and stylistic interest lies outside my theme. The late medieval tomb chests often have small figures arranged in niches all round them. Some of these represent 'weepers', fashionably dressed men and women or cowled bedesmen, but other tombs have preserved series of saints' figures which are hard to equal elsewhere (PLATE 8). Sometimes scenes from the Gospel, particularly the Annunciation, are included, as on the tomb at Ross-on-Wye (PLATE 18), or figures of the Virgin and Child or the Holy Trinity (PLATES 18 and 19). The magnificence of an effigy should never make us ignore the details of its tomb chest.

THE ROOD-SCREEN.—The importance of the chancel arch in the iconographical scheme of the church, and of the Doom painting above it, must be discussed elsewhere (see pages 68 and 134). I need only say here that, when the lower panels of a rood-screen are painted, these should be carefully studied. It is here that we are most likely to find national, or local, saints represented: King Henry VI at Barton Turf and Gateley in Norfolk and Eye (Suffolk); St. William of Norwich, shown being crucified by the Jews on the screen at Worstead (Norfolk); and Sir John Schorne, the 13th-century healer of gout and ague, who 'conjured the devil into a boot' at Gateley and Suffield in Norfolk. At Southwold (Suffolk) the screen panels show the Nine Orders of Angels in elaborate costumes, and at Bradninch (Devon) the twelve Sibyls.

Except in a few churches, mostly in Wales or the west country, the rood-screens have lost the lofts which once gave access to the great Crucifix which was decked with rich clothes for festivals or sadly veiled for Lent. They may also have accommodated the instrumental music. Only the rood-loft stairs remain, narrowly contrived in the thickness of the wall, and now leading to a suicidal drop into empty space. The richly carved fronts of these lofts may once have boasted a wealth of imagery, for that at Llananno (Radnor) is closely set with small niches for images (now restored), and at Strensham (Worcs) a rood-loft with 15th-century painted panels is still used as a western gallery. It shows the figures of Christ and the twelve apostles as well as bishops, kings and other saints. Most of the surviving lofts, however, are decorated only with exquisitely carved trails of foliage, predominantly vines.

THE ROOD.—Even when a solid screen did not entirely shut off the nave from the choir, as in monastic churches, the division between the two was more marked in the Middle Ages, and the great Rood above the chancel arch, or framed within its head, dominated the view of the congregation in the nave. The Saxon word 'rod' originally meant only the timber baulk of the Cross, but came to include the whole group together with the figures of the Virgin Mary and St. John. All Roods were condemned to destruction in 1547, and only a few fragments remain from the images which must have represented the apogee of medieval wood-carving. At South Cerney (Glos) the head and one foot of a small 12th-century Rood figure were found walled up beneath a consecration cross, and the sensitive rendering of the weary anguish on Christ's face leaves no doubt that this was the work of a master. At Cartmel Fell (Lancs) a rough wooden figure from a Rood remains, the arms broken and the legs charred away.

During the Marian reaction churches were ordered to replace their Rood figures, and the Crucifixion roughly painted on a wooden tympanum inside Winsham church (Somerset) may have been an attempt to do this quickly.

Although the Roods have vanished, some of their adjuncts remain. Rood beams can be seen *in situ* in several churches, but the most interesting example, carved with the rocks and skulls of Golgotha, lies in the nave at Cullompton (Devon). At Woolpit (Suffolk) a Canopy of Honour projects from the chancel arch, but in most cases the celure over the Rood was achieved by decorating the roof of the eastern bay of the nave more richly than the rest, as, for instance, at Mobberley (Ches). To prevent the dazzle from the east window obscuring the Rood, a wooden tympanum was sometimes fitted into the head of the chancel arch and the Last Judgment painted upon it. The best surviving example is at Wenhaston (Suffolk), and others may yet be discovered beneath the Royal Arms which were often painted over them.

THE ALTAR.—When we pass through the screen into the chancel we naturally turn first to the High Altar, but very little medieval imagery is to be found in connexion with it to-day. Where the stone slab of a medieval altar is exposed to view we can see the five crosses incised upon its surface, indicating the spots anointed by the bishop in the service of consecration. Their normal position, one in each corner and the fifth irregularly centralised, is probably an allusion to the Five Wounds of Christ, but examples are known which have more, or fewer, crosses. In the presbytery of St. David's Cathedral a stone altar slab shows a rectangular seal of a different stone inset above the receptacle in which holy relics were preserved.

REREDOS.—One reason why we rarely find a medieval reredos in connexion with a High Altar may be that the east window served it in this capacity, portraying in vivid imagery the lessons of Christian belief or subjects connected with the dedication of the church. The side chapels of some churches retain the tracery of magnificent reredoses. In the Lady Chapel of St. Cuthbert's at Wells the reredos must once have illustrated the earthly descent of Christ, for the outline of the figure of Jesse can be seen at its base although the carvings have been smashed. A similar reredos at Christchurch (Hants) has kept its Jesse figure and also a central relief showing the Adoration of the Magi. At Abergavenny (Mon) a large wooden figure of the sleeping Jesse (PLATE 19) is one of the grandest surviving examples of British wood sculpture, and this was probably the base of a reredos. That the Tree of Jesse was considered particularly suitable to the ornament of a reredos perhaps accounts for the fact that it was often made the subject of an east window, as in the cathedrals of Bristol, Gloucester and Wells.

Oxfordshire is particularly rich in medieval stone reredoses. At Somerton the Last Supper is carved on a long panel with each figure framed in one arch of a miniature arcade; other examples remain at Enstone, Hanwell and Bampton. To see one of the great Nottingham alabaster retables, built up of many panels illustrating the life of Christ, or of some saint, we must go to foreign museums or churches, but panels from simpler reredoses have been recovered in several places. At Drayton (Berks) there are five panels carved with scenes from the Passion and the life of the Virgin Mary, and at Elham (Kent) two scenes from the life of St. Thomas of Canterbury (PLATE 21) flank a fine carving of the martyrdom of St. Catherine.

SEDILIA.—The group of stone seats we often see on the south side of the chancel was built for the celebrant, the deacon and the sub-deacon to occupy during those parts of the Mass which were sung by the choir. In the earlier medieval examples the seats are on different levels (see Fig. 2a), the eastern seat, reserved for the celebrant, being the highest; but from the 15th century onwards the seats are generally all on the same level, perhaps because the multiplication of chantries brought more chaplains in full priest's Orders to assist at the Parish Mass. Sedilia are often richly carved with foliage, with human or grotesque heads, or with angels, but they rarely show any didactic imagery.

PISCINA.—Immediately to the east of the sedilia on Fig. 2b we see an ornamental niche containing a shallow basin from which a drain

Fig. 2. COMPOSITE VIEW OF A CHANCEL
(a) sedilia ; (b) piscina ; (c) aumbry ; (d) Easter sepulchre

carried the water used in ceremonial ablutions through the wall and on to the consecrated earth of the churchyard. Piscinae may be found in many parts of the church, marking the former positions of minor altars. From the mid-13th to the mid-14th century the piscina was made with two drains, while before, or after, this period it only has one. After the doctrine of Transubstantiation had been definitely stated it was felt unseemly that the chalice should be washed at the piscina also used for washing the priests' hands, and, with the superb medieval disregard of all proportion save utmost ability to serve, even such a modest village church as Culmington (Salop) was given a double piscina worthy of a cathedral. A further change in the 14th century introduced the custom of the celebrant drinking, at the altar, the wine and water in which the chalice had been rinsed and, thereafter, a single piscina was once more considered adequate. At Seaham (Durham) a hand raised in blessing is carved at the back of one arch of a double piscina, presumably to mark the different purpose of the two drains.

THE AUMBRY.—This cupboard in the wall, for keeping the sacred vessels, is almost always on the north side of the chancel, and in England it is merely a square recess which has generally lost its original door (Fig. 2c). This door remains at Rothersthorpe (Northants), and its snake-like iron hinges seem to defy unlawful approach. In Scotland the aumbry was used for the Reservation of the Sacrament and was called the Sacrament House. This name is inscribed on the fine example at Deskford (Banffshire), and both here and at Cullen (Banffshire) and Kintore (Aberdeens) angels are carved above the recess, holding a monstrance. At Auchindoir (Aberdeens) the whole Sacrament House is shaped like a monstrance with a lobed foot and pyramidal cover.

THE EASTER SEPULCHRE.—This is always on the north side of the chancel (see Fig. 2d). Here the crucifix from the High Altar was laid on Good Friday and 'watched' until it was restored to the Altar on Easter morning. Here also the dialogue between the angel and the three Maries at the Sepulchre was enacted by priests during the Easter services. The elaborate Sepulchres not only formed an impressive setting for this liturgical drama at Easter but also recalled its significance throughout the year. At Heckington (Lincs) the risen Christ is carved above the central recess, and at Hawton (Notts) the Ascension is shown with the Apostles gazing upwards. Christ rising from the tomb is carved above the recess on the simpler Sepulchre at Patrington (Yorks) (see Fig. 2d). In all these cases, and in several others, the bottom panels of the Sepulchre are carved with the figures of the sleeping guards. Where no special Easter Sepulchre existed an ordinary tomb recess in the correct position was used, or a wooden structure brought in and placed on a flat table tomb. Medieval wills often directed that the testator's tomb should be made to serve as an Easter Sepulchre and this intention is reflected in the painting of the Resurrection at East Bergholt (Suffolk), and in the carving of this subject at South Pool (Devon), each placed at the back of a tomb recess.

I must regretfully pass over such interesting features as squints, low-side windows and the openings from anchorites' cells, but these were purely functional and never bear any imagery. I will, therefore, end this chapter with a reminder that interesting imagery may be found in the most inconspicuous places. Roof bosses so high that they can only be seen through strong field-glasses are sometimes carved with illustrations of rare legends, or unusually rich sequences of biblical subjects. Capitals or corbels may furnish isolated examples of interesting subjects, although they are more often carved with angels, shields bearing sacred or secular heraldry, or human heads, more or less caricatured. Complete stained-glass windows imperatively command attention, but a careful watch should be kept for interesting fragments of glass as for memorial brasses, which often lie hidden beneath protecting mats. Wall-paintings, even though they have faded far beyond hasty recognition, also yield their meed of interest and aesthetic pleasure to those who will wait and watch until the design seems to emerge once more from the stains and shadows of the plastered wall.

PART III

The Picture-Book of the Churches

CHAPTER I

THE SEVEN SACRAMENTS AND DEVOTIONAL IMAGES

BEFORE discussing the general design and individual illustrations of the Picture Book of the churches, we must briefly consider a few subjects which actually represent medieval religious rites or typify the part played by certain forms of imagery in the private devotions of the people.

Since the origin of all ritual lies in the desire of the individual to enter into communion with the Divine, let us first consider the attitudes of prayer.[1] The original attitude of Christian prayer was standing with the arms raised to Heaven, but in the 3rd century Tertullian advised the faithful to abandon this pose as too reminiscent of pagan worship, and he advocated that they should either hold out their arms, as on a cross (an attitude which figures largely in the legends of Celtic saints as being maintained for phenomenal periods of penance), or with the elbows bent, like the classical *orante*. Early Celtic carvings at Llanhamllech and Llanfrynach in Brecon include figures in this posture, which also appears at Stowell (Glos), where a 12th-century wall-painting shows the Blessed Virgin interceding for mankind, and in the Baptism of Christ carved on the Norman font at Lenton (Notts). A secular example occurs on the tomb of Princess Joan, from the Franciscan Friary of Llanfaes, which is now at Beaumaris (Anglesey). In this posture of prayer the hands are held palms outwards, but when they are laid open upon the breast the pose may indicate lamentation, as in some early representations of the Virgin and St. John beneath the Cross.

The posture with hands joined was unknown alike to pagan antiquity and early Christianity; it appears first in the 8th century but did not become common until the 12th century. Dom Louis Gougaud suggests that it may have been derived from a Teutonic feudal ceremony since it was known as a juridical form of homage long before it was adopted as a devotional attitude. The kneeling vassal placed his hands, held palm to palm, between those of his over-lord who, when the oath of allegiance had been pronounced, kissed him and accepted him as his liege man.[2] This ceremony has a sinister illustration upon the 14th-century carving on the altar screen of Beverley Minster which shows Theophilus of Adana swearing fealty to the Devil, and it survives to-day in the conferring of degrees at some older universities. In the Middle Ages it probably suggested a spiritual counterpart to feudal loyalty, and this may explain why, on most medieval effigies, we see the finely tapered hands pressed palm to palm as though they awaited in confidence the accepting clasp of their Creator.

Turning from personal to corporate worship, we find two types of illustrations of the rites of the Church: the incidental and the deliberate. When medieval artists visualised Jewish religious cere-monies, they often introduced details from contemporary Christian usage. Thus, in the marriage of the Virgin and St. Joseph, they showed Mary with her hair flowing loosely from under a chaplet of flowers or jewels, like any medieval bride who was a virgin. In the background of the Presentation in the Temple one can often see figures bearing the candles of the customary Candlemas procession, but such chance allusions to medieval ceremonies are far less important than the direct illustrations carved upon the Seven Sacrament fonts which are the glory of East Anglian churches, or represented in the closely allied Seven Sacrament windows.

There are about forty Seven Sacrament fonts and, with the excep-tion of two stragglers at Farningham (Kent) and Nettlecombe (Somer-set), they are all in Norfolk or Suffolk.[3] They have octagonal bowls mounted on high shafts which are often surrounded by statuettes of the Evangelists, or saints, or by alternating lions and wood-woses (see page 182). The bowls are carved with panels of figure sculpture, each representing one of the Sacraments, while the eighth subject is often the Baptism of Christ or the Crucifixion. Carvings of the Holy Trinity, the Virgin and Child, or some saint, occur more rarely in the eighth panel. Both the position and character of these panels exposed them to damage, but many carvings can still be deciphered, sometimes with the help of emblems, representing each Sacrament, carved on the chamfer of the bowl. At Salle (Norfolk) we see angels holding the following emblems: a chrismatory, or casket for holy oils (Baptism); a mitre (Confirmation); an altar stone (Mass); a rod (Penance); a soul rising from a shroud (Extreme Unction); a chalice (Ordination). Under the panel illustrating Matrimony there is an angel with a musical instrument, but I fear that this is not intended to suggest that well-attuned marriages are made in Heaven, but simply to accompany the adoring angel which is carved beneath the Crucifixion upon the eighth panel!

Although specialists in liturgical accessories may study the less damaged panels of these fonts with keen interest, the ordinary sightseer will not be able to distinguish evidence of the early existence of rare forms from mere careless carving. I will, therefore, leave my readers to seek a detailed analysis of the subjects represented on these fonts in the articles quoted on page 200, and will only point out a few features of general interest which are clearly apparent.

BAPTISM.—The grouping almost always shows the priest behind the font, about to immerse a naked infant. Sometimes there are acolytes holding the chrismatory and the open service book. At Little Walsingham, Badingham and Nettlecombe a woman holds the white linen cloth in which the child was wrapped after it had been anointed, and in which it was buried if it died before the mother had been churched. The frequent appearance upon medieval tombs of dead babies in their Chrisom cloths, bound with diagonal bands, is a grim reminder of the rate of infant mortality. Early representations of infant baptism are rare, so the panel on the 12th-century font at Thorpe Salvin (Yorks) is worth mentioning, although this is not a Seven Sacrament font.

CONFIRMATION.—The children being presented to the bishop are always very small, sometimes infants in arms, for the Synod of Exeter in 1287 decreed that children must be confirmed before the age of three. In a window at Doddiscombsleigh (Devon) (PLATE 10) we see the bishop wearing a red out-of-door habit together with his mitre and stole, which reminds us that bishops sometimes confirmed children in the open air as they rode about their dioceses.

MASS.—Generally the carvings represent the Elevation, either of the Host or of the Chalice. At Brooke (Norfolk) an acolyte is shown holding the rope of the sanctus bell, while at Badingham (Suffolk) and Marsham (Norfolk) he holds in his hand a small sacring bell, such as was rung at the moment of the Elevation in the Low Masses of chantry chapels.[4] Candles upon the altar are only shown at Badingham (Suffolk) and Gresham, Little Walsingham and Walsoken, all in Norfolk. At Great Glemham and Woodbridge, in Suffolk, the priest is giving the sacrament to a man and woman who hold the Houseling Cloth, or long towel which was held before communicants in order to catch any particles of the Host which they might let fall.

PENANCE.—John Mirk's *Duties of a Parish Priest* confirms the evidence of these fonts that, in the 15th century, the confessor still sat openly on a chair in the nave, or on the special shriving pew shown at Denston and Woodbridge in Suffolk, while the penitent knelt before him.[5] At Marsham confession is being heard in a little gabled structure with a bell, but this may be merely a symbolic church. At Gresham (Norfolk) and Nettlecombe (Somerset) the penance of scourging is indicated and several other fonts emphasise the spiritual significance of penance by showing a demon trying to grasp the penitent but being repelled by an angel.

EXTREME UNCTION.—This rite usually consisted of anointing the dying person with holy oil on eyes, ears, nose, mouth and feet, but the Use of York also directed that they should be anointed over the heart, and this is shown on the font at Woodbridge. At Gresham a dish upon the bed presumably contains the wisps of wool with which the priest wiped the places anointed and which were subsequently burned, or buried in the churchyard. The windows at Doddiscombsleigh (Devon) (PLATE 10) and Crudwell (Wilts) show the Communion of the sick, rather than Extreme Unction ; the priest holds a paten in his hand and behind him stands an acolyte holding the candle prescribed in the rubric.

ORDINATION.—The laying on of hands is usually shown, and informed observation of the vestments is necessary to decide to what degree of Holy Orders the ordinand is being admitted. At Gresham a clerk in the background bears a thurible, the only reference to the use of incense on these fonts. At Nettlecombe a barber is shaving a tonsure on the head of a seated candidate while another kneels before the bishop.

MATRIMONY.—As the joining of hands always took place at the church door, we sometimes see the building indicated in the background. On the font at Brooke (Norfolk) the women standing behind the bride hold something which may be meant for the 'care cloth' which was held over the heads of the bridal pair (if neither of them had been married before), from the Sanctus of the Eucharist to the conclusion of the Nuptial Benediction. When a marriage legitimised previously born children, according to civil law, these too sometimes knelt under the care cloth.[6]

The Sacraments were obviously appropriate subjects for a font, and they also appear on the carved bench-ends of the Suffolk churches of Tannington and Wilby, but the few surviving Seven Sacrament windows express more clearly the deeper meaning of this imagery. In these windows small panels illustrating the Sacraments surround a figure of Christ and are connected to His Holy Wounds by crimson lines.[7] The intended lesson is manifest: even as the heart drives life-giving blood through all members of the body, so Christ crucified gives life to all members of the mystical body of the Church by means of the Holy Sacraments. Many fonts show the Crucifixion upon their eighth panel which suggests that their original design was the same as that of the windows, but once the carvers came to consider the Baptism of Christ as being equally appropriate, the subject of the eighth panel soon became a matter of personal choice.

The Seven Sacrament windows remaining in England [8] are contemporary with the fonts, and the theory that their inspiration came from the Netherlands is supported by the fact that East Anglia, where almost all such fonts are found, was particularly affected by Flemish influence owing to the commercial relations of the wool traders. The design may have been based on a devotional woodcut, or one of the carved wooden reredoses which were exported in large numbers from Antwerp.

No complete example of a Seven Sacrament window survives, but we can get a clear impression of what they were like by comparing the two best preserved examples. At Crudwell (Wilts) we still have the medieval Christ, crowned with Thorns and displaying His wounds, but two of the Sacraments are lost and the others damaged. At Doddiscombsleigh (Devon) the Christ is modern, but the panels of the Sacraments are medieval and the angles at which the crimson lines on these are drawn show that they were originally connected with the Five Wounds. A third window, closely related to the others, is at Melbury Bubb (Dorset). Here only the upper part of the figure of Christ remains and one Sacrament, but it is interesting to see how the red line ends on the hand which the bishop raises in blessing, while his other hand rests upon the head of the ordinand. In the south and west of England the central figure of Christ is shown displaying His Wounds and wearing the Crown of Thorns, while in the north He is shown upon the Cross.

The figure of Christ showing His wounds, known as the 'Christ of Pity', occurs frequently, either alone or in representations of the vision vouchsafed to St. Gregory while celebrating Mass. These images were probably based upon the commemorative picture which the Pope is said to have placed in Santa Croce in Gerusalemme at Rome and which showed a half-length figure of the dead Christ standing upright in a sepulchre at the foot of the Cross.[9] The legend of the Mass of St. Gregory is not mentioned in the *Golden Legend*, nor do the Bollandists accept it, but it was frequently represented in the

15th century, because thousands of years of pardon were claimed for those who, being in a state of grace, said certain prayers before an image representing it. This indulgence, said to have been originally granted by St. Gregory, was increased to astronomical proportions by later Popes, and pilgrims to Rome probably carried back to all parts of Europe images of this subject, which gradually became more elaborate, developing from the single figure of Christ into the full panoply of the Papal Mass. Out of 21 English devotional woodcuts of the 15th century, listed by Mr. Campbell Dodgson,[10] 12 represent the Christ of Pity (Fig. 3). Such pictures were copied in many media in parish churches; at Roxton (Beds) the Christ of Pity is painted on the rood-screen, and at Diddington (Hunts) there is a fine example in stained glass, while carvings of the Mass of St. Gregory occur on Bishop Oldham's Chantry in Exeter Cathedral, the Kirkham Chantry at Paignton (Devon) and in that lonely little church of the lovely name, Stoke Charity, in Hampshire (PLATE 20). The last-named carving was found built into the walls and wonderfully undamaged; the shining pallor of the stone gives an unearthly beauty to the figure of Christ which dwarfs (by majesty even more than by mere size) that of the Pope, kneeling before the altar with the Host in his hand. At Paignton we see a later convention, in which the large half-length Christ had evidently given place to a small, full-length figure striding forward upon the altar and probably causing the Blood from His wounded side to spurt into the chalice, as we see it carved on an English alabaster retable now at Montreal (Yonne).[11] This figure has been broken away at Paignton, but even if intact it would have been less prominent than the figures of the kneeling Pope and the two cardinals standing behind him. These last present a curious problem. Could the designer of a monument which is distinguished by the scholarly arrangement of its imagery have been so ignorant of Papal ceremonial as to show these cardinals assisting at Mass in their outdoor habit and, still more improbably, wearing their hats after the Consecration?[12] A more plausible answer is suggested by a devotional woodcut preserved in the Bodleian Library, Oxford, which shows the Mass of St. Gregory happening in the background of two groups of figures : representatives of the Church, under the banner of St. Peter, and the wielders of secular power led by an Emperor.[13]

The Christ of Pity was a favourite subject on tombs, chantry chapels and memorial brasses, for it was believed that the soul of the departed would profit by the indulgence if the specified prayers were said by the tomb. An interesting example occurs on the brass of

Robert Legh (1506) at Macclesfield (Ches). Beside the figure of the dead man is a scroll inscribed : *A dampnacoe ppetua libera nos dne*, and beneath the Mass of St. Gregory is written: '*The pdon for saying of v pater nost' & v aues and a cred is xxvi thousand yeres and xxvi dayes of pardon*'. Brasses on which are engraved similar promises of indulgences may be seen at Hellesdon (Norfolk) and Hurstmonceux (Sussex).[14]

On some devotional woodcuts the Christ of Pity is represented within a border composed of the Instruments of the Passion (Fig. 3), while others show these Instruments alone, displayed heraldically, and with the promise that 'Whosoever devoutly beholdeth these arms of Christ hath 6,765 years pardon'. The glass and carvings of many churches still illustrate these emblems, blazoned separately or in conjunction upon shields held by angels. Special honours were paid to the Instruments of the Passion from the 13th century onwards, but it is in connexion with the private devotions of the medieval parishioner that they chiefly concern us here.

While exalted minds found in such emblems a focus of mystical contemplation, the humbler folk associated each emblem with some form of human weakness from which they craved deliverance. Roughly written verses in the vernacular, accompanied by drawings of the Emblems of the Passion, were probably widely distributed, and from the surviving copies we can learn something of the devotional meditations of the ordinary parishioner. It is perhaps relevant to mention that *The Lay Folks Mass Book*, an English transcript, *c.* 1400, of a lost original probably in 12th-century French,[15] shows that the people were expected during Mass to occupy themselves with private devotions rather than to attempt to follow the prayers said by the celebrant. The imagery of the nave may thus have influenced the form of their prayers by recalling those associated in these poems with the Emblems of the Passion.

Beside the thirty pieces of silver . . .

> The pens also that Judas told
> Wherefore Jesus Christ was sold
> Lorde shield me from treason and covetys
> Therein to sin nowise

Beside the lantern which gave light . . .

> When Christ was taken in the night
> Lorde kepe me from the night of sin
> That I ne'er be taken therein.

Spitting Jew   Cock   Vernicle   High Priest   Pilate

Striking Hand

Lantern

Pestles & Mortar for Myrrh

Pillar & Scourges

Rods

Ladder

Pelican

Seamless Robe

Hammer Pincers

Sword & Staff

30 Pieces of Silver

Dice

Hand plucking Hair   Boxes of Spices   Ewer   The Chalice   Nails

FIG. 3. 'CHRIST OF PITY' DEVOTIONAL WOODCUT

> Swords and staves that they bare
> Jesus Christ therewith to fear,
> From fiendes Lord keep thou me
> Of them afeared that I not be.

The vessel of vinegar and gall is associated with a prayer not to be poisoned by sin; the sponge on a reed for . . .

> All that I have drunk in gluttony
> Forgive me Lorde e'er that I die.[16]

The heads of the spitting Jews suggest a prayer that all who have offended the supplicant may be forgiven and the final drawing of the Sepulchre is accompanied by a prayer to be cleansed of all sin before death and to rise without fear of damnation.

The most elaborate series of carvings of these emblems is that on the vaulting bosses (early 16th century) in the choir of Winchester Cathedral,[17] and others have already been mentioned. The wood-cut reproduced in Fig. 3 could have served as a model for many such series and the nature of their iconography can be seen in PLATE 12. The long-shafted cross with its floating banner, which is the usual attribute of Christ in His post-Resurrection appearances, is here the emblem of His person, and the feet disappearing into a cloud and leaving their prints on the rock beneath is a common convention for the Ascension (see page 127). The hand touching the wounded Heart probably here illustrates the Incredulity of St. Thomas, but it may also allude to the special devotions of the Sacred Wounds which we must now consider.

During the first millennium of Christianity, piety was not particularly concerned with the wounds of Christ, and none of the many prayers in honour of the Five Wounds preserved in Books of Hours is older than the 13th century.[18] The early Fathers of the Church had taught the symbolical significance of the wounded Side, as the Door of Grace from which issued the sacraments of Baptism and the Eucharist, but it was probably the Stigmatisation of St. Francis in 1224 which gave the greatest impetus to the cult of the Five Wounds. Angels often figure in scenes of the Crucifixion, swooping down to hold chalices to catch the Holy Blood; in a window at Bowness-on-Windermere (Westmorland) they are shown beneath each of the Five Wounds.[19] Later medieval artists evolved a blazon of the Five Wounds, the Hands and Feet being arranged round the wounded Heart as on the bench-end at North Cadbury (Somerset) (PLATE 12). The words from Isaiah xii. 3, 'Ye shall draw waters of joy out of the

Saviour's fountains', which were used in the Office of the Sacred Heart, caused the Wounds to be referred to as 'Fountains' or 'Wells' in the 15th century,[20] and the windows of Froyle (Hants) and Sidmouth (Devon) include shields showing five almond-shaped cuts dropping blood, each surmounted by a golden crown and with the inscriptions: 'Wel of Wisdom, Wel of Mercy, Wel of Everlasting Lyf, Wel of Grace, Wel of Gudly Comfort'. This blazon of the Five Wounds was particularly popular in England, and when the Dissidents rose against Henry VIII in the Pilgrimage of Grace they placed it upon their banners. The Well of Everlasting Life was the Sacred Heart upon which the devotions originally paid to all Five Wounds tended later to become concentrated. In the Brudenell Chapel, in Deene Church (Northants), there is a reredos of carved and gilded stone in honour of the Sacred Heart, which bears the date 1635. The Sacred Heart is carved in the central panel, covered with drops of Blood and with flames rising from it, while the side panels show ears of corn drooping over a paten, on which lie the Holy Wafers, and a vine with grapes hanging immediately above a chalice. This may have come from the private chapel of the first Earl of Cardigan, a devout Roman Catholic, although the date may imply Laudianism.

British artists do not seem to have favoured those strange illustrations of mystical iconography, the Fountain of Life and the Christ of the Winepress, by which those on the Continent expressed the later cults of the Sacred Blood and the only example, in a British church, of which I know is the Flemish early 16th-century glass in Marston Bigot (Somerset). This shows the Cross raised in a circular basin, round the exterior of which are carved the heads of the Evangelistic symbols. The Blood from the Five Wounds of Christ flows into this fountain and thence, through the mouths of these heads, into a rectangular basin below. In the background is an altar with a chalice upon it, and the Host, shown in a glory of light.[21]

So far I have written only of devotions common to all parishioners, but to end this chapter I will mention one record of planned, private meditation, which is unique in British churches. At Bishop's Cannings (Wilts) there is a curious desk, or pew, which has been variously described as confessional, the seat for a shrine-watcher and a monastic 'carol'. On the panels of the back is painted a large hand, with a scroll on the wrist inscribed: *Meditare debes quod* . . . which introduces the subjects of suggested meditation upon the miserable condition of man upon earth and the inevitability of death and condemnation, each inscribed upon a scroll corresponding to one of the five fingers.[22]

While the mystery surrounding its origin prevents us from considering it as typical of the meditations of a devout medieval parishioner, it may point our way to a better realisation of that discipline of spiritual abnegation by which many of them approached the contemplation of divine truths.

CHAPTER 2

THE SIGNIFICANCE OF POSITION

IN matters of construction we can assume that the master mason had the final word, while in the arrangement of space for particular forms of worship he was subordinate to his ecclesiastical employers. The scholarly symbolist had no part in this planning, although he might evolve mystical explanations of forms created for practical reasons, but his influence often dominated the design and disposition of imagery. In the ecclesiastical schools of the Middle Ages iconography became a complex science, to whose laws even the placing of subjects had to conform, each motive in a decorative scheme thus adding its particular significance to complete the whole. It was a science of which the elementary rules could have been expounded by an intelligent parish priest, or a travelling friar, to the moderately educated parishioners while its recondite developments were probably as mysterious to the majority of laymen in the Middle Ages as they are to their modern descendants.

By the 7th century, Greek ecclesiastical writers had attached symbolical meanings to the architecture of a church as a whole, as well as to its several parts, and the tradition thus created altered little with succeeding centuries. The French archaeologist Didron found an ancient Manual for the guidance of Painters still being used on Mount Athos which not only specified the subjects to be chosen from Old and New Testaments to epitomise the Divine scheme of Salvation, and the inscriptions which should accompany each figure, but also described the position appropriate to each subject on the walls and cupolas of a Greek church.[1] This Manual is now considered to be by an early 18th-century writer, Dionysiat of Fuma, whose main source-book was written by an anonymous painter *c.* 1566 [2] and may have incorporated earlier texts. The evolutionary traditionalism which created most medieval art thus continued to function in this timeless sanctuary.

The plan of western churches required a different scheme of iconographical arrangement, and unfortunately we lack a western 'Manual for Painters' to codify our traditions. All we can do here is to study the painted decorations of a few early churches, and the stained glass of some later ones, which still show some over-all plan of dogmatic decoration, and thus try to make out what rules once governed the placing of imagery in a British church. As the British have never been a consistently logical race, we need not expect to find one generally accepted scheme but, if we know at least some of the factors which may have been considered, we shall understand more fully the significance of what remains.

All the resources of medieval art were used to stress moral contrasts; Sin and Redemption, Good and Evil were portrayed in the most dramatic opposition of beauty and ugliness, and the contrast between the blessed state of those within the fold of Holy Church and the hideous doom awaiting all others meets us, literally, at the doors of our early churches. While later doors have generally lost what little figure sculpture they originally possessed, most Norman tympana survive unscathed, perhaps because their symbolism puzzled the iconoclasts as much as it does unspecialised tourists of to-day ! It is rare to find a tympanum completely battered out as at Brimpsfield (Glos). The subject index of Mr. C. E. Keyser's *Norman Tympana and Lintels* immediately makes it clear that the words of Durandus, 'The door of the church is Christ, according to the saying in the Gospel "I am the door" ', are largely borne out by the carvings. Out of 197 examples listed, 126 allude to Christ in one way or another. The more proficient sculptors represented Our Lord in Majesty surrounded by the symbols of the Evangelists, as at Rochester Cathedral, Elkstone (Glos) or Pedmore (Worcs), or else in a vesica borne aloft by angels as at Ely Cathedral, Water Stratford (Bucks) or Rowlestone (Herefs). He is shown in the Virgin's arms at Fownhope (Herefs) and Inglesham (Wilts) and harrowing Hell at Beckford (Worcs), Quenington (Glos) and Shobdon (Herefs). Humbler craftsmanship could represent the Agnus Dei (32 examples) or the Tree of Life (28 examples), whilst the merest tyro could produce some sort of cross (39 examples). Many of these carvings still make clear their message that, as it is only through the door that we can enter the church, so only through the atonement of Christ's Passion can men come to salvation, but sometimes the symbols appear strangely incongruous. Thus the Tree of Life between confronted monsters is an image which suggests the abstract designs of eastern textiles rather than any didactic intention, yet the fine example at Dinton (Bucks) bears an explanatory inscription which may be rendered thus:

If any should despair of obtaining reward for his deserts let him attend to the doctrines here preached and keep them in mind.

(*Praemia pro meritis si quis desperet habenda audiat hic praecepta sibi quae sint retinenda.*) [3]

The carving thus proclaims that the Church is the source of spiritual sustenance for the souls of all who enter her gates.

I have written first of the Norman tympana because their evidence is numerically more impressive, but the association of figures of Christ with the entrance to a church was expressed by Anglo-Saxon sculptors with a dignity surpassing that of the noblest Norman tympanum in Britain. Above the western door at Headbourne Worthy (Hants) can be seen the outline of a great Rood group carved on the surface of the outer wall.[4] The figures have been hacked down until all their modelling is lost, but even in this pitiful state they show a majesty of conception which must place them among the lost masterpieces of art, and our imaginations can recapture something of the awe with which early worshippers must have passed into this church through the narrow archway cut at the very foot of the Cross. The famous Saxon angels above the chancel arch at Bradford-on-Avon (Wilts) probably flanked a Rood, or some other representation of Christ, with the same intention of showing that only through His mediation could man enter into the spiritual life. The concentration of ornament upon the arch mouldings of entrance doors and chancel arches, which we notice in most Norman churches, may not have been exclusively due to the influence of this symbolical tradition but it should not be forgotten when we pause to admire the barbaric richness of their ornament.

The further statement of Durandus, 'the Apostles also are doors', is not borne out by the iconography of Norman tympana. With the possible exception of the figures within an arcade above the doors of Syston (Lincs) and Pampisford (Cambs), the Apostles certainly do not appear in groups, and even if we rashly identify as Apostles all figures not clearly meant for other saints, they still would be outnumbered by the figures of St. Michael, or St. George, whose conflicts with dragons symbolise the eternal conflict between Good and Evil. How far the threshold of the church was considered as the physical frontier line of such supernatural warfare it is as impossible to say as it is to answer the frequent question as to the meaning of the gargoyles along the eaves of churches. In the latter case my own belief is that, if their makers had any intention beyond that of adorning a waterspout, it was to enhance the contrast between the demon-haunted world outside the protection of the Church and the spiritual security within. A similar suggestion of deadly peril escaped may have been expressed by the 12th-century closing rings of church doors (often erroneously called Sanctuary Rings) which show a human figure emerging from the jaws of a monster, as at Norwich, St. Gregory, and Gloucester, St. Nicholas.

The symbolical significance of church doors seems to have lost ground with later church builders in Britain. A plain arch, decorated only by fine mouldings, and sometimes surmounted by a niche for the statue of the Virgin and Child, or of the patron saint, was considered enough for most parish churches, while the western façades of Wells Cathedral and the abbey church of Croyland were entirely covered with a screen of figure-work in which the door was merely a necessary interruption.

The iconographical arrangement of the figure sculpture on the façade of Wells merits careful study.[5] The lowest tier of figures, the foundation upon which rests this great *Te Deum* of sculptured praise, represents the prophets who foretold the coming of Christ. In other niches stand statues of those who testified to His presence upon earth; the saints and confessors, many of them Anglo-Saxon kings and queens, nobles, bishops and abbesses. In quatrefoils within the spandrels of arcades we see angels, and scenes from the Scriptures, while the upper part of the façade illustrates the Second Coming of Christ. Above the Resurrection of the Dead stand the Nine Orders of Angels, the Apostles, and, in the topmost gable, the figure of Christ as the supreme Judge. Instead of the Norman conception of the Church as an austere fortress of refuge against the powers of evil, the west front of Wells offers us a magnificent frontispiece to that Picture Book of the Church which is the main subject of our study.

Medieval symbolism was all-embracing and the scholarly disposition of subjects could make the humblest village church portray the entire Universe of space and the ultimate limits of Time. Its roof, and particularly that of the chancel, represented the sky and therefore the glories of Heaven were painted upon it, so long as the plain surfaces of early barrel vaults allowed this to be done effectively.[6] The 12th-century paintings at Kempley (Glos) are now in poor condition; their tints have faded to a reddish darkness flecked with white patches from which the plaster has crumbled, but by patient staring we can make out details of the Apocalyptic Vision, the Four Beasts, the Cherubim and Seraphim and the golden Candlesticks. The Christ in Majesty which was originally in the crown of the vault has largely perished.

Paintings of the signs of the Zodiac on the soffit of a chancel arch, as at Copford (Essex), or the Labours of the Months carved upon the voussoirs of Norman doors, like those which are now reset in the interior of the tower at Calverton (Notts), emphasised the symbolism of this archway as a division of Time and also the lifelong labour to which man was doomed at the Fall.

Since the nave was the domain of the laity, its windows and wall-paintings fitly illustrated the earthly lives of Christ and His saints, or moral allegories intended to instruct the parishioners. The chancel symbolised the spiritual life, or else Heaven as it would appear at the Last Day, and on the wall above the chancel arch (PLATE 1), or on a tympanum framed within it, was depicted the Last Judgment which should decide whether the soul might pass into eternal life. Most of these painted Dooms are now half-obliterated, but even if we can see no more than the horns and tail of a demon to the north of the chancel arch, we should remember that the whole once presented to the fearful congregation a vivid impression of the dread Judgment which should decide their fate, and added an urgency of significance to the great crucifix framed in the head of the chancel arch.

The ubiquity of Doom paintings in this position probably accounts for the rarity of the subject in stained glass. The great Doom Window at the west end of Fairford church is a notable exception and its placing, as well as the style of the glazier's art, may have been influenced by Continental traditions. These taught that the west end was the appropriate place for scenes of death and Judgment, not only because of the obvious association between the final hours of the world and the setting place of the sun, but by a false etymological link between 'Occident' and the verb *occidere* (to kill).[7] The same association of the west end with Hell and Death appears at Chaldon (Surrey) and Clayton (Sussex) where the 12th-century wall-paintings are of outstanding, and somewhat mysterious, interest.

At the west end of the north wall at Clayton is the figure of an angel about to sound the Last Trump and the subjects of the Resurrection of the Dead and the Weighing of the Souls have also been identified. Beyond this a procession of the Blessed advances towards the Heavenly Jerusalem (shown as a hexagonal walled enclosure) and the great figure of Christ, enthroned in a mandorla above the narrow chancel arch. The iconography of the south wall has proved a fertile subject for learned disagreements, which should warn the amateur against hasty interpretations! Trouble starts as soon as our eyes, travelling westwards along this south wall, have passed a great Cross, upheld by four angels, on the left hand of Christ. The next figure is of an angel with arms exaggeratedly crossed over its breast, one hand holding a banner of the Cross, the other making some gesture towards a group of figures, several of whom wear crowns. The Guide to the church invites visitors to see in this strange pose the angel's rejection of those who, in their lifetime, ignored the Cross, but other writers have explained it as an eastern gesture of intercession [8] or one of greeting, as in the case of the Angel of the Annunciation at Hardham (Sussex). Leaving the future fate of the group of figures thus uncertain, we come to the next mystery: the legs and body of a quadruped and the lower part of its rider. Human hands emerge from a blank space, caused by damage, just beneath its forelegs, and appear to beg for mercy. Beyond these are figures crowded together, and then another angel. Is it the Beast of Revelation with the False Prophet, one of the Four Horsemen, or Death with an ox, and do the imploring hands belong to a lost soul in the Bottomless Pit, or to a prostrate victim? I would claim no certainty beyond the fact that this unknown Rider belongs to the forces of Evil, for he clutches the hair of a figure in the first group and appears to drag it westwards, away from Christ and nearer to the huddled crowd who seem to stand in the shadow of Death.

Part of a Doom painting, which includes a weighing of the souls, remains on the north wall at Stowell (Glos), and this unusual position may indicate that the Norman painters had in mind an over-all scheme akin to that of Clayton. At Stowell a parallel between the ultimate Judgment of God and man's ephemeral justice is perhaps indicated by a slight sketch of two men taking part in an 'ordeal by battle' which is painted beneath the Doom.

What we know of the original placing of the subjects in the windows of Canterbury Cathedral suggests a wholly different scheme, based upon the dedications of altars in various parts of the cathedral. The windows of the choir of 'Christchurch' were appropriately filled with figures of Christ's earthly ancestors (now in the south transept or in the west window) except for the five eastern windows which illustrated scenes of His earthly life or those of Moses and St. John the Baptist, the first and last prophets of His Coming. The crypt below the Corona, which originally served as a Lady Chapel, has recently recovered some of the glass which there expressed the glorification of the Blessed Virgin, and nine windows illustrating the posthumous miracles of St. Thomas of Canterbury are still in the Chapel (now Trinity Chapel) where stood his golden shrine until it was destroyed in 1538. Medallions representing scenes from the lives of SS. Alphege and Dunstan, now in the triforium of the north choir aisle, are thought to have come from windows near the altar tombs of these canonised archbishops.[9]

The north choir aisle seems to have been considered the most suitable place for windows of a directly educational purpose. At Canterbury there were originally twelve Theological windows illustrating the relation between Old and New Testaments (see page 75), and Thomas Habington tells us that, in the early 17th century, the windows of the north choir aisle at Malvern represented 'the Pater Noster, Ave Maria, the Creede, the Commandments, the Masse, the Sacraments issuing from the wounds of Our Saviour ; my memory fainteth. But to conclude all in one, there is the whole Christian doctrine and the fower doctors of the Latin Church.'[10] Unfortunately only scraps of this glass survive to support Habington's description.

The south clerestory windows at Malvern originally contained panels illustrating the lives of Old Testament patriarchs, some of which are now in the south choir aisle (PLATE 7). This placing marked a break with the tradition that subjects connected with the Old Law were shown on the sunless north, as in the rose windows of the transepts at Canterbury, where Moses with the Synagogue, the four Cardinal Virtues and the major prophets are still represented on the north side, although only a modern conjectural reconstruction in the south rose shows us Christ, the Church and the four Evangelists. A later, and humbler, example occurs on the stalls in the nave at Astley (Warcs) which are clearly now reversed as their return seats face west. What were originally the south stalls have the haloed figures of apostles painted on the panelled backs of the seats, while the corresponding figures on the north represent the prophets, wearing caps or turbans.[11] At Fairford the windows of the nave clerestory oppose the enemies of the Church, on the north, to the saints in the southern windows.

This mention of Fairford brings me to my last and finest example, for the early 16th-century windows of this magnificent parish church show us one of the most complete schemes of didactic decoration surviving in Britain,[12] although the wall-paintings have mostly faded and the carved Rood group which originally faced the nave has been destroyed.

Beginning at the north-west corner, the windows of the north aisle represent the twelve prophets who foretold the coming of Christ, each holding a scroll on which is indicated the relevant verse (see page 188). The window immediately before we enter the Lady

Chapel represents four of the Old Testament subjects which were associated with the Nativity. The Temptation of Eve, who brought sin into the world, while the Virgin brought forth Man's Redemption; Moses and the Bush which burned but was not consumed, a type of the Virgin Birth; Gideon's Fleece on which alone the dew fell, typifying the Incarnation of Christ; and the Queen of Sheba bringing gifts to Solomon as the Magi were to lay their offerings before the Child at Bethlehem. The windows of the Lady Chapel illustrate the birth of the Virgin and the infancy of Christ, the historical sequence being interrupted by the Assumption of the Virgin in the window behind the altar. Across all the upper lights of the great east window is shown the Crucifixion but below the transom each light represents one of preceding scenes of the Passion, from the Entry into Jerusalem to the Bearing of the Cross. The south window of the chancel represents the Entombment. Above the altar in the south chapel, the window (PLATE 14) shows us the Transfiguration and post-Resurrection scenes including the rare apocryphal subject of Christ appearing to His mother in the house of St. John (see page 126). The windows of the south aisle contain the Apostles, each bearing upon a scroll the appropriate phrase from the Creed (see page 152), and the Doctors of the Latin Church (see page 160). The south clerestory windows have figures of saints, kings, an emperor, cardinals and a pope, each with an attendant angel and representing the defenders of the Church, while on the north side the character of such oppressors as Annas, Judas, Caiaphas, Herod and Herod Antipas is made clear by the flaming background to each figure and the demon beside it. The three windows in the west wall are the climax to the whole scheme. In the centre we see the Last Judgment, a design of impressive simplicity and glowing colour whose dignity is not lessened by the macabre humour which represents the damned as undergoing tortures akin to the processes of manufacturing glass. The flanking windows illustrate the Old Testament types: the Judgment of Solomon, and David and the Amalekite.

Here we can see how the medieval imagination, by its universal scope and the deep sincerity underlying its curious idiom, could express all the fundamental teaching of the Church within the narrow limits of windows or walls. It would be rash to assume that such ambitious schemes were generally understood and that only lack of means prevented their more frequent expression. In many medieval parishes the priest could probably not have interpreted fully such a scheme as that of the Fairford windows, let alone designed it, and the

71

congregation would have understood it even less. Yet, even a partial understanding of the religious ideas thus associated with different parts of the church must have helped the ignorant parishioner to grope his way towards true worship, while, to the better educated members of the congregation, the religious significance of each subject would have gained intensity of meaning from being included within so majestic a conception of the whole.

CHAPTER 3

THE CHOICE OF SUBJECTS

HAVING achieved some idea of the principles which governed the placing of imagery in a medieval church we must next consider why certain Scriptural subjects recur frequently whilst others, which appear to have equal claims, are hardly ever seen. Why was Jonah a favourite figure while Joshua is almost unknown ? Why was Noah's Ark preferred to the Passage of the Red Sea ? Why also, when a certain story had been chosen, did the artist almost always illustrate the same incident from it until extreme familiarity has made us accept as normal what is really both surprising and significant ?

Since the practical usefulness of iconography depends upon general recognition of its symbols, both the selection and representation of these naturally tend to become traditional. Some of the Old Testament subjects which are most often represented even in the depleted imagery of British churches, and which must have been familiar to all medieval church-goers, are to be found in the earliest examples of Christian art, the paintings in the Catacombs of Rome,[1] and the close parallel between these subjects and certain early prayers in which God was besought to deliver His servant as He delivered 'Isaac from sacrifice . . . Daniel from the den of lions . . . or the Children of Israel from the fiery furnace . . .', with other examples drawn from the Old Testament, suggest that the artists were directly inspired by these prayers. It is interesting to note that several monuments of Early Christian art in Ireland and Scotland show the same range of subjects as the Roman Catacombs. On an 8th-century cross base at Seir Kieran (Offaly) the Fall of Man, the Children of Israel, the sacrifice of Isaac and Jonah emerging from the whale are all carved while Daniel and the Lions occurs singly on several sculptured stones in each country. Most of the High Crosses of Ireland which show such subjects were carved during the period of the Viking wars, when the lives of Christians were as precarious as in pagan Rome and their fearful supplications may have been expressed in the same form, for the '*Ordo Commendationis Animae*', which influenced the imagery of the Catacombs, was known in the Celtic Church.[2]

Early Christian artists also used subjects from both the Old and New Testaments to express the spiritual benefits of the Sacraments. Thus Noah in the Ark, Moses bringing forth water from the rock and the healing of the paralytic by the Pool of Bethesda were sometimes combined in a decorative scheme with a direct illustration of a baptism. The Miracle of the Loaves and Fishes (shown in highly conventionalised form on some Irish crosses) and the changing of water into wine at the Marriage in Cana were similarly associated with the Eucharist.

These traditional subjects were severely formalised; not only were subsidiary details suppressed but the moment of time depicted was always that which saw the witness of divine deliverance. Noah reaches up his hands to welcome back the dove (Fig. 6 and PLATE 22), and the raised arm of Abraham is poised over the kneeling figure of Isaac at the very moment when its fall was halted by the voice of God, just as these subjects were to be represented by countless artists throughout the Middle Ages.

The establishment of the Peace of the Church in the 4th century brought important changes to religious art. Henceforth the artists who adorned great churches were free to evolve long series of Biblical illustrations, such as the mosaics in the nave of Sta Maria Maggiore at Rome, but where a more restricted choice of subjects was necessary they concentrated upon those subjects which most clearly expressed the significance of the great Church festivals. The differences of opinion in the early Churches as to which events should be celebrated as festivals need not concern us here; it is enough for our present purpose if we remember that, during the Middle Ages, the events commemorated by the main Feasts of the Church, and which were therefore exemplified by imagery were: the Birth of the Blessed Virgin, the Presentation of the Virgin in the Temple (late), the Annunciation, Nativity, Epiphany, Presentation in the Temple, Transfiguration (late), Entry into Jerusalem, Crucifixion, Resurrection, Ascension, Pentecost, Assumption of the Virgin and Exaltation of the Cross.

Although the whole range of the Bible was theoretically available to the artists who adorned our churches, their choice of subjects was actually limited to those themes which were particularly associated with Church festivals or to which Christian teachers had given a mystical interpretation. Origen admitted the impossibility of believing literally in parts of the Scriptures, but explained that: 'Forasmuch as man consisteth of body, soul and spirit, so in the same way doth the

Scripture'.[3] The simple man might be edified by the 'flesh' of literal meaning, but the moral and mystical interpretations were reserved for those of deeper understanding. He ridiculed those who believed literally that God clothed Adam and Eve in aprons of skins, and taught that these garments symbolised the mortality which came upon them after the Fall.

The Doctors of the Latin Church gave support to such allegorical interpretations; St. Augustine tells of his joyous relief at hearing St. Ambrose teach 'that "the letter killeth but the Spirit giveth life" whilst he drew aside the mystic veil laying open spiritually what, according to the letter, seemed to teach something unsound',[4] and this scene is represented in the paintings at the back of the choir stalls in Carlisle Cathedral. This 'mystic veil' covering the inner truth of the Old Testament was associated with that of the Temple which was rent at the moment of Christ's death, when the Old Order gave place to the New. Where the symbolical figures of Church and Synagogue are included in scenes of the Crucifixion, or are associated with Moses, the Law-giver of the Old Order, as on the font at Southrop (Glos) (PLATE 3), the Church is shown as a stately woman, crowned and holding a book, while Synagogue, blindfolded and holding a broken spear, lets fall the crown from off her drooping head. The finest English examples of such figures flank the Chapter House door in Rochester Cathedral. This multiple interpretation of the Scriptural subjects should always be borne in mind when studying medieval iconography, for it lends a dignity of implied meaning even to the least eloquent artistic expression.

The selection of certain Old Testament subjects as prefiguring types of events in the Gospels was a most important factor of choice in the Middle Ages. This 'typological' teaching drew its authority from the words of Our Lord : 'O fools, and slow of heart to believe all that the prophets have spoken ! Ought not Christ to have suffered these things, and to enter into his glory ? And beginning at Moses and all the prophets, he expounded unto them in all the scriptures the things concerning himself' (St. Luke xxiv. 25-7). A more precise parallel is recorded by St. Matthew (xii. 40) : 'For as Jonas was three days and three nights in the whale's belly, so shall the Son of man be three days and three nights in the heart of the earth'. The swallowing of Jonah by the whale, and his miraculous deliverance, thus became accepted symbols of the Resurrection and an affirmation that the Passion of Christ had been ordained in its least detail from the beginning of time.

This didactic scheme of imagery was introduced into Britain very early. Bede tells us that Benedict Biscop brought back from Rome in 685, to adorn his church at Jarrow, 'Paintings showing the agreement of the Old and New Testaments, most cunningly ordered; for example, a picture of Isaac carrying the wood on which he was to be slain was joined (in the next space answerable above) to one of the Lord carrying the cross on which He likewise was to suffer. He also set together the Son of Man lifted up on the cross with the serpent lifted by Moses in the wilderness.'[5]

It was in England that this iconographical tradition found its fullest expression in church decoration. Twelve 'Theological Windows' are recorded in Canterbury Cathedral, of which enough remains to fill two windows in the north choir aisle.[6] Fragments of what may have been a similar series of 13th-century windows remain in Lincoln Cathedral.[7] A full series of typological paintings is known to have existed in the choir of Peterborough Cathedral [8] and another in the Chapter House at Worcester. Medieval scholars developed the science of typology until each important event in the Gospel story was associated with a varying number of 'types' taken not only from the Old Testament, but also from secular history, old Jewish legends and the curious lore of the Bestiary. Two books which summarised these parallels were among the most important source books of medieval art: the *Biblia Pauperum*, of which the earliest manuscripts date from *c.* 1300,[9] included only Biblical parallels, while the slightly later *Speculum Humanae Salvationis* [10] drew also upon secular sources.

When the invention of paper made possible the printing of block-books, with a brief text explaining the relations between the various pictures on each page (all cut on the same wooden block), these two works were among the earliest to be so reproduced. A list of the subjects given in a 15th-century block-book, *Biblia Pauperum*, is given in Appendix I, while the arrangement of pictures and text are shown by Fig. 4. In the *Biblia Pauperum* the New Testament anti-type is always the central subject, flanked by two Old Testament types, while above and below it appear half-length figures of prophets who sometimes hold scrolls inscribed with an indication of their relevant quotation. The remaining spaces on the block are filled by much abbreviated texts explaining the relation between type and anti-type. The block-books of the *Speculum Humanae Salvationis* have their associated subjects spread out over the double-page spread of the book. These block-books, which were largely of German or Netherlandish origin, were widely distributed, and direct copies of their woodcuts, made by crafts-

FIG. 4. A PAGE FROM THE *BIBLIA PAUPERUM* BLOCK-BOOK

men working in various media, can be seen in several churches. Four misericords in Ripon Minster are copied from the *Biblia Pauperum* and comparison of the carving reproduced in PLATE 5 with the woodcut in Fig. 4 will show how close the carver kept to his model.[11] The windows of the church at Tattershall (Lincs) were originally filled with glass reproducing such designs, and some panels are still there, while others have been moved to St. Martin's Church, Stamford. At Stamford we can see the Deposition, Entombment and Resurrection, together with Moses striking the rock, Samson with the gates of Gaza, and David and Goliath. These books were also used by the designers of the windows of King's College Chapel, Cambridge, and of Henry VII's Chapel, Westminster, and many adaptations of them appear in the windows of Malvern. The miniatures of earlier manuscript versions may have been copied but are more difficult to identify.

Although British churches offer no equivalent to the sublime statues on the south portal of Chartres, where Abraham, Melchizedek, Moses, Samuel and David appear, to quote the simile of M. Émile Mâle, as columns in a symbolical avenue of approach to Christ,[12] it is in this sense that we should consider the statues of these patriarchs on the façade of Wells Cathedral, or in the windows of Canterbury, Malvern or Fairford. Each was associated with a particular aspect of Christ's life. Adam, because he was the only other man to enter this world free from sin; Abel by his accepted sacrifice and as the first shepherd; Melchizedek, High Priest and King, who offered bread and wine to Abraham, was the type of Christ instituting the Eucharist. Joseph, sold by his brothers and welcomed in Egypt, prefigured the Betrayal of Christ by the Jews and the acceptance of Christianity by the Gentiles. These few examples must suffice to illustrate the sort of association which may have led clerical patrons to set up whole windows illustrating the lives of these Old Testament figures, as at Malvern, but its influence is rarely apparent in the smaller churches.

To end this chapter I will describe two surviving examples of the way in which this typological teaching was expressed in church decoration. The carvings on the great south door of Malmesbury Abbey (Wilts) are now badly weather worn, but in 1925 Dr. M. R. James identified the medallions carved on the inner order of the arch as representing the Creation of Man with the Temptation and Fall, the Expulsion and, perhaps, the death of Cain.[13] The next order showed Noah's Ark, the sacrifice of Isaac, the Burning Bush, Moses striking the rock and receiving the Tables of the Law; Samson fighting the lion, bearing away the gates of Gaza, and pulling down the columns of the roof; David in combat with the lion and again with Goliath. On the outside order of the arch were carved New Testament anti-types such as the Annunciation, Nativity, Adoration of the Magi, Baptism of Christ, Entry into Jerusalem, Last Supper, Crucifixion, Resurrection, Ascension and Pentecost. The relation between Old and New Testament scenes is not regularly observed; some Gospel anti-types have three types, others have none. Thus the Fall of Man (through the fruit of a tree), the sacrifice of Isaac and Samson pulling down the columns, were all regarded as types of the Crucifixion.

The windows of the north choir aisle of Canterbury Cathedral show us the remains of a more exact typological arrangement, dating from about 1200. Of the 174 medallions which were originally grouped in 12 windows, only 33 panels now remain and only 18 of these are in their original position. Fortunately a manuscript roll has been preserved in the Cathedral Library which gives all the titles which appeared in these windows, together with Latin verses explaining the relations between associated subjects. The large script of this roll suggests that it may have been hung up in the cathedral for the guidance of those who found the teaching of the windows hard to understand.[14] To-day it tantalises us with the knowledge of how much has been lost, but also helps us to imagine the remaining medallions in their proper context.

The iconographical grouping of the subjects which are still *in situ* is shown in Fig. 5. The central subjects from the New Testament are each flanked by Old Testament types, starting at the top with the Journey of the Magi, between Balaam prophesying 'There shall come a star', and Isaiah, 'Kings shall come to the brightness of thy rising'. The Presentation in Temple has lost its second type and the gap is filled by the panel of The Sower (PLATE 6) brought from another window. The east window of the Corona at Canterbury is slightly later in date and its sequence of pictures is confined to the Passion and Resurrection. Around the medallion of the Crucifixion (much restored) are grouped four types: Moses striking the rock (Exodus xvii), the sacrifice of Isaac, the marking of the lintels with the blood of the lamb at the first Passover (Exodus xii) and the spies bearing the grapes (Numbers xiii).

Few people are able to memorise all the associated types enumerated by *Pictor in Carmine*, for this work, possibly compiled by a 13th-century English Cistercian, associates 508 types with the 138 anti-types from the New Testament.[15] Even the much simpler series provided by the *Biblia Pauperum* may be beyond the scope of our memories, but we shall see the imagery of our churches in truer perspective if we remember that it was intended primarily to teach the people the meaning of the great Church festivals, and to strengthen their faith in the divine pre-ordination of the events so celebrated by prophetic parallels chiefly drawn from the Old Testament. The craftsmen may have understood very little of the theological science underlying the choice of subjects, and not every priest would have been able to explain it to his parishioners, but the main lines of medieval iconography were nevertheless determined by a noble tradition.

CHAPTER 4

GENERAL CONVENTIONS OF RELIGIOUS IMAGERY

W E must now turn from the general scheme of the Picture Book of the Churches to study the way in which individual subjects are represented. The ease with which we recognise important themes from the New Testament tends to make us accept as 'Gospel truth' details which in truth no Gospel mentions, and some knowledge of the sources from which these were derived adds greatly to the interest with which we study them. A single detail may express the fulfilment of a prophecy, the vision of a mystic or the teaching of a great scholar, while another may have been introduced through the 'business' of a mystery play or the similes of a preacher. Medieval teachers enriched the iconography of our churches by writing many 'devout imaginations and likenesses, stirring simple folk to the love of God and the desire of heavenly things',[1] and though some of their imaginings may seem to us crude and indifferent to historic truth, their interpretation of the Scriptures has a vivid intimacy not always found in works of accurate scholarship. Their light was a smoky fire compared to the glare of our present scientific knowledge, but they saw pictures of unearthly beauty within its glowing heart.

Before considering the illustrations individually let us note some conventions which are common to all imagery.

God the Father is rarely shown in human form in early churches, where the symbol of His intervention on earth is the Hand of God reaching down from Heaven to create, or protect, as we see it above the head of Christ on the famous Saxon Rood of Romsey Abbey, or on the Castle Frome font (PLATE 4). It is thus that the Divine Architect is also represented in the Creation panels of the east window of York Minster (PLATE 6), but the late medieval artists more often based their representation of the Creator upon the vision of the 'Ancient of Days' described in Daniel vii, and depicted Him as an old man with flowing beard and hair. A window at Malvern (PLATE 7) shows God speaking to Abraham, leaning out of Heaven, which opens in a glory of fire upon a blue sky crowded with the heads and wings of angels. I have chosen this illustration because it shows so well the combination of homeliness and soaring imagination which characterises medieval art. In the later medieval work God the Father sometimes wears an early form of the papal tiara, with the three crowns mounted on a steeple-shaped cap. A striking example of such a head is carved upon an arm-rest of the stalls of Lincoln Cathedral, but it must remain one of the problems of the medieval mind whether a carver would have chosen, or been allowed, to represent so lofty a theme in such a lowly place.[2]

The imagery of British churches is not old enough to illustrate the conflicting traditions of the Early Church as to the physical appearance of Christ.[3] It is possible that the Hellenistic type of young, beardless Christ is carved on the Bewcastle Cross and on a fragment of a cross-shaft from Rothbury (Northumberland), now in the Blackgate Museum, Newcastle-on-Tyne, but the weathered stone denies us certainty.[4] The Norman painters of the 12th century, when they showed a great figure of Christ in the apse, or dominating the vault of the chancel, drew His eyes unnaturally wide open, with staring pupils to convey His all-perceiving vision.

The usual manner of presenting the Holy Trinity is that carved upon the tomb at Willoughby-on-the-Wolds (Notts) (PLATE 19), or on the beautiful alabaster carving at Kinlet (Salop). God the Father is shown crowned and enthroned, holding the Crucifix between His knees, while the Holy Dove hovers above. On the Suffolk fonts at Snape and Orford the Holy Dove is omitted. On the rare occasions when all Three Persons are represented anthropomorphically, as in windows showing the Coronation of the Virgin at Holy Trinity, Goodramgate, York, East Brent (Somerset) or Doddiscombsleigh (Devon), they all bear the traditional physiognomy of Christ, including the cruciform nimbus. At Doddiscombsleigh the Three Persons are shown with golden faces, a bizarre and unsuccessful attempt to express in yellow stain the radiance of the Divine Presence.

This representation of the Holy Trinity by three identical figures was denounced by theologians as tending to tri-theism, and some artists attempted to avoid such heretical suggestions by showing the Holy Trinity as partly threefold in form and partly united. On a misericord at Cartmel (Lancs) and on a bench-end at Lansallos (Cornwall) there are carvings of a triple face beneath a single crown. These triune forms appeared in the 14th century but were too grotesque to win approval.[5]

The halo of light round the heads of sacred persons, which is one of the most familiar features of Christian art, has a long history of evolution. Radiating lines of light surrounding the head have been accepted as a symbol of supernatural power in many religions, and it was as a symbol of power rather than sanctity that it was first used by Christian artists. Thus both Christ and His apostles were shown nimbed in scenes of the Last Judgment before the halo was applied to them in historical scenes.[6] While the halo round the head was a personal attribute, the mandorla, or almond-shaped glory surrounding the whole figure, was associated with certain manifestations of divine power.[7] In British churches it is used chiefly in connexion with the Transfiguration (PLATE 14), Ascension, or Second Coming, of Christ, or the Assumption of the Blessed Virgin. The mandorla is often supported by flying angels.

The AGNUS DEI, or Lamb of God, has remained the most familiar of all emblems of Christ. It can be identified from all other lambs, naturalistic or symbolical, by the cross-shafted banner which it holds in an uplifted foot (PLATE 20). As we have seen, this banner, or *vexillum*, is sometimes used separately as an emblem of the risen Saviour.

THE FISH.—This early Christian emblem of Christ, sometimes also used for a Christian soul, was derived from the initial letters of 'Jesus Christ, Son of God, Saviour' which form the Greek word for a fish. It is rarely seen in British churches, but a late vaulting boss at St. Just-in-Roseland (Cornwall) has three fishes painted upon it with the word ΙΧΘΥΣ above them.[8]

SACRED MONOGRAMS occur frequently in ecclesiastical art. The oldest and most famous is the Chi-Rho which the Emperor Constantine placed upon the shields of his soldiers after he had seen it in a vision as a sign of future victory. This appears in its original form ⚹ (based on the two first Greek letters of the name of Christ) on several primitive memorial stones in Galway and on a cross at St. Just-in-Penwith (Cornwall).[9] On later examples the X gave way to a horizontal transom crossing the shaft of the P. From the 12th century onwards a monogram taken from the three first Greek letters of 'Jesus' IHC was used and in western Europe was often written IHS and taken as the initials of *Jesus Hominum Salvator* (PLATE 20).

The clothes in which Christ and His disciples are always represented mark the period at which His physical appearance became traditionally accepted, for the long mantle draped round the body and over the shoulders was the usual garb for teachers, or other persons

of dignity, in the 4th century.[10]   The bare feet which distinguish
Christ and the Apostles from other figures in a group may have
originated in a copyist's misunderstanding of sandals, but so simple an
explanation did not satisfy the medieval mind.   In *Dives and Pauper*
we read: 'Commonly all the apostles ben paynted barefote in token
of innocence and of penance.   Natheless they wente not always fully
barefote, but sometyme with galoches, a sole byneth and a fastenynge
above the fote. . . . Also the apostles . . . ben paynted with manteles
in token of the vertue and poverte whych they hadde.   For, as sayth
Seynt Gregory, "all these worldly goodes ben noughte ellys but a
clothynge to the bodye and a mantele is but a loose clothynge, not
faste to the bodye but loose and lyghtly maybe done awaye.   For
they were . . . alway redye to forsake all for Crystus sake." '

Fantasy rather than tradition governs the costumes in which Old
Testament figures, or the Jewish dignitaries in Gospel scenes, were
clothed by medieval artists.   At Malvern Abraham and Noah wear an
upper garment open at the sides like a dalmatic and fastened with
jewelled clasps (PLATE 7).   Their hats are of strange forms, with
pointed bi-lobed, or draped crowns (see Fig. 3), and sometimes with
high brims turned up and adorned with jewels.   Jewish priests are
sometimes vested as bishops (PLATE 15).   Where military accoutrements are shown, on warrior saints, the murderers of St. Thomas of
Canterbury (PLATE 21) or the soldiers of Pilate's guard, these are
contemporary with the work of art, or slightly outmoded.

In many illustrations of Scriptural scenes the speaker is distinguished
by having one hand raised, often with the two first fingers extended.
This is the old Roman gesture betokening speech, and it gave rise to
the bishop's gesture of benediction with the two first fingers raised
and the others held down by the thumb.   The equivalent Greek gesture,
in which the fourth finger is bent over to meet the thumb and three
fingers are held erect, is shown by the Saxon carved angel in the tower
of Breedon-on-the-Hill (Leics).

In the following sections the subjects are arranged in their Biblical
order, as being most familiar to my readers, and I will assume their
knowledge of the Biblical account of each event.   The textual references will enable them to refresh their memories should they need to
do so.   It is the allegorical, or extra-Biblical, elements in these subjects
which need explanation.   When quoting literary counterparts to this
or that detail, I claim no decisive identification of its source.   Even
among the writings which have survived, the same themes of contemplation, the same legendary enrichments of detail occur in several

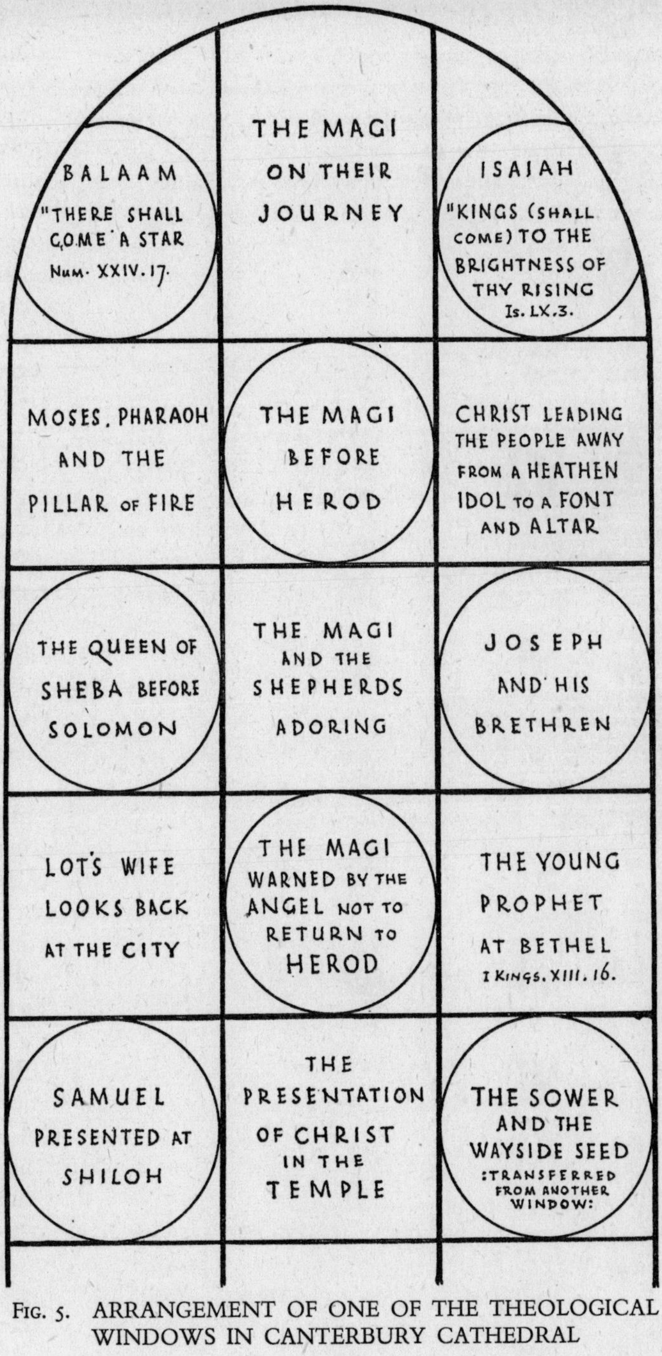

BALAAM "THERE SHALL COME A STAR Num. XXIV. 17.	THE MAGI ON THEIR JOURNEY	ISAIAH "KINGS (SHALL COME) TO THE BRIGHTNESS OF THY RISING Is. LX. 3.
MOSES, PHARAOH AND THE PILLAR OF FIRE	THE MAGI BEFORE HEROD	CHRIST LEADING THE PEOPLE AWAY FROM A HEATHEN IDOL TO A FONT AND ALTAR
THE QUEEN OF SHEBA BEFORE SOLOMON	THE MAGI AND THE SHEPHERDS ADORING	JOSEPH AND HIS BRETHREN
LOT'S WIFE LOOKS BACK AT THE CITY	THE MAGI WARNED BY THE ANGEL NOT TO RETURN TO HEROD	THE YOUNG PROPHET AT BETHEL I KINGS. XIII. 16.
SAMUEL PRESENTED AT SHILOH	THE PRESENTATION OF CHRIST IN THE TEMPLE	THE SOWER AND THE WAYSIDE SEED :TRANSFERRED FROM ANOTHER WINDOW:

FIG. 5. ARRANGEMENT OF ONE OF THE THEOLOGICAL WINDOWS IN CANTERBURY CATHEDRAL

books, and other alternative sources must have been lost. I only aim at giving in the aggregate a sketch of the sort of literary influences affecting the craftsmen who decorated British churches, and to explain some of the strange elements they represented in the actual words which might have been known to a medieval parishioner, even if the vernacular text is somewhat later than the work of art.

CHAPTER 5

OLD TESTAMENT SUBJECTS

FULL series of Old Testament pictures were evolved at an early date, and during the Middle Ages glaziers working for the major churches devoted whole windows to the lives of such patriarchs as Noah, Abraham, Jacob, Joseph and Moses. Some scattered panels from these windows are sometimes found, and a rich sequence of Old Testament subjects occurs in the 13th-century carvings round the interior of the Chapter House at Salisbury, but in this chapter I will concentrate chiefly upon those subjects which were apparently considered as complete in themselves.

THE CREATION.—Although the six Days of Creation had been illustrated in manuscripts as early as the 7th century,[1] no full representation of them survives in a British church which is earlier than the 15th century. An unusual series of carvings, perhaps brought from some church, are set on the exterior of Stapleford Hall (Leics). By far the finest illustration of the Hexameron is the east window of York Minster, c. 1410, in which the keynote of the whole design is struck by the figure of God the Father, at the head of the window, holding a book inscribed with the words *Ego sum alpha et omega*. The first and the last things being as one in His vision of the Universe, the upper panels of the window, which show the Creation, find an appropriate counterpart in the Apocalypse represented in the lower part of the window. The imaginative power of these panels can be but poorly represented by a single detail (PLATE 6), although in this the rhythmic movement of the birds and fishes seems to speak their worship of their Maker as eloquently as the kneeling adoration of the angel above them. In some panels the Hand of God is shown with a cruciform nimbus to recall the Son's participation in the Creation: 'All things were made by him; and without him was not any thing made that was made' (St. John i. 3). This idea is sometimes expressed by showing the Creator in the traditional likeness of Christ.

In a *Te Deum* window of the south transept of York Minster the Creator holds an orb in one hand and a large pair of dividers, or compasses, in the other.[2] This motive, which also occurs in the glass at Malvern and on a boss in the nave of Norwich Cathedral, refers to the description of the Lord God in Isaiah xl. 12 : 'Who hath measured the waters in the hollow of his hand, and meted out heaven with the span . . . and weighed the mountains in scales, and the hills in a balance ?' Some Anglo-Saxon manuscripts show the Creator holding both scales and compasses, but in church imagery the Architect of the Universe wields the instrument used by medieval masons and of which an actual example is preserved in York Minster.

On the 12th-century Tournai marble font at East Meon (Hants) we see God creating Adam, who stands rigidly before Him, and in the east window of York Minster Adam seems to be let down from Heaven, but generally this subject is much rarer than the Creation of Eve. A miniature in the 13th-century *Emblemata Biblia* in the Biblio-thèque Nationale, Paris, makes clear the reason for this preference. At the foot of the Cross, God the Father draws Eve from the side of the sleeping Adam, while, from the wounded side of Christ, emerges the personification of Holy Church, a naked woman, crowned and holding a chalice in which she catches the Blood of the Redeemer. Further expression of this contrast between the Old Law and the New is given by the figure of Moses on the left hand of Christ opposed to a baptismal scene on His right hand.[3]

THE TEMPTATION AND FALL OF MAN (Genesis iii).—The design of our first parents standing one on each side of the Tree, round the stem of which the Serpent is coiled, figures in art from the 3rd century onwards, and became an accepted tradition so early that it may have been adapted from a pre-Christian design such as the contest between Athene and Poseidon, standing beside the olive tree which was some-times shown encircled by Erichthonius in the form of a serpent.[4] Early carvings of the Fall, on stone crosses in Ireland and Iona, already show this traditional pattern.[5] The 12th-century wall-paintings at Hardham (Sussex) are unusual in that they show Adam and Eve on the same side of the Tree. Here Eve takes the apple from the Serpent's mouth, a detail which recurs on the woodcuts of the block-book *Speculum Humanae Salvationis*, and probably alludes to the honeyed poison of flattery by which the Serpent beguiled the woman. It may have been to express this same meaning that the Serpent was first shown with a woman's head, but Vincent of Beauvais accepted the existence of great snakes with the faces of virgins, and Petrus Comestor explains that the Devil so disguised himself because 'like things applaud like'. As the dialogue between Eve and the Serpent developed in the later mystery plays, the popularity of the human-headed serpent increased, and there is a tendency for the Tree to become a thick bush in which the body of an actor could have been hidden while his tail was prominently displayed below.[6]

Medieval artists often anticipate the consequences of the Fall and show our first parents already veiling their nakedness with their hands, or with large leaves, before the forbidden fruit has been tasted. 'Adam's apple' is such a generally accepted symbol of the Fall that we are apt to forget that Genesis does not specify what fruit was borne by the Tree of Knowledge. The apple was not generally accepted by early Christians; the orange and cherry found some supporters and the Eastern Church reasoned that, since fig leaves are mentioned, the Tree was some kind of fig.[7] I can think of no work of art in a British church which definitely shows Eve taking a fig, but the belief must once have been current in Britain for the *Dialogue of Solomon and Saturn* speaks of Adam tasting 'the forbidden fig-tree's fruit'.[8]

THE EXPULSION.—Although in Genesis iii the angel with the flaming sword is posted at the gates of Eden only after Adam and Eve have been driven thence by their Creator, the medieval artists consistently show an angel as the instrument of the Expulsion. On the font at East Meon we see this angel in kindlier mood, his sword laid aside and teaching Adam how to dig. The influence of the early forms of drama can be seen here, for the action takes place before the façade of a great church. The political and historical associations of the jingle:

> When Adam delved and Eve span,
> Who was then the gentleman?

have made this subject so familiar that some might find it hard to say whether or not these occupations are mentioned in the Bible, which shows how easily symbols become accepted as facts. 'In the sweat of thy face shalt thou eat bread, till thou return unto the ground' was the doom of Adam symbolised by these essential tools of medieval life. A misericord in Worcester Cathedral shows a man and woman in contemporary dress holding a spade (broken) and a distaff, and as several other misericords illustrate the Labours of the Months,[9] the carver may have wished to emphasise the way in which these fulfilled man's doom. It is in this context that we should consider the calendars on the fonts at Brookland (Kent) or Burnham Deepdale (Norfolk) as well as the 'Labours' which occur singly in windows or wall-paintings. (For chart of these Labours of the Months see Appendix 2.)

CAIN AND ABEL.—Although the acceptable sacrifice of Abel typified that of Christ, it is rarely shown in the surviving imagery. It is carved in the Chapter House at Salisbury, and on the tomb of Henry Fitzroy (1536) at Framlingham (Suffolk). Where both brothers are shown sacrificing, the acceptance or refusal of their offering is indicated by the smoke rising from the altar. The designer of the Creation window at St. Neot (Cornwall) seems to have been inspired by 'the great bush of smoke' which is described in the contemporary Cornish Creation Play as being blown downwards from Cain's irreverent sacrifice of cow-dung and thorns.[10]

The murder of Abel (Genesis iv), which typified the Crucifixion, often has one detail which deserves special note. In almost all British examples Cain uses a jaw-bone to strike down his brother, and this weapon is mentioned in vernacular texts from the 9th century onwards, except when Cain is said to have bitten his brother to death. The tradition appears to have originated in these islands, for the jaw-bone is indicated on 10th-century Irish crosses, whereas Byzantine artists make Cain use a stone. Perhaps it originated in a confusion between the word *cinbán* (a jaw-bone) and the title *Cain-bana* (Cain, bane of his brother) used in *Solomon and Saturn*.[11]

Where the scene of God rebuking Cain is shown (as in a 12th-century wall-painting at Kingsdown near Sevenoaks and also in the Salisbury Chapter House), a tiny figure is shown rising from the earth behind Cain to express the text 'Thy brother's blood crieth unto me from the ground' (Genesis iv. 10). The symbolism of this motive may be explained in the words of the 14th-century mystic, Walter Hilton: 'Right as the blood of Abel cried to God from the earth, right so Christ's blood crieth to the Father, asking forgiveness of sins to all those that with faith and love will open their mouths to receive it'.[12]

The mysterious exclamation of Lamech: 'I have slain a man to my wounding, and a young man to my hurt' (Genesis iv. 23), was explained by an old Jewish legend which may have become familiar to the artists through the *Historia Scholastica* of Petrus Comestor. When Lamech grew old and blind he took his young son Tubalcain with him to direct his footsteps and the aim of his bow. Seeing movement in the bushes, the lad told Lamech to shoot, but when the fugitive Cain fell mortally wounded, Lamech, in horror at his own act, slew Tubalcain. This scene is shown in one of the quatrefoils on the façade of Wells Cathedral, on a boss in the nave of Norwich Cathedral and in the Creation window at St. Neot.[13]

NOAH (Genesis vi–ix).—The prayer from the service of Baptism:
'Almighty and everlasting God who of thy great mercy didst save
Noah and his family in the Ark from perishing by water . . . figuring
thereby Thy Holy Baptism' recalls the symbolism which made Noah

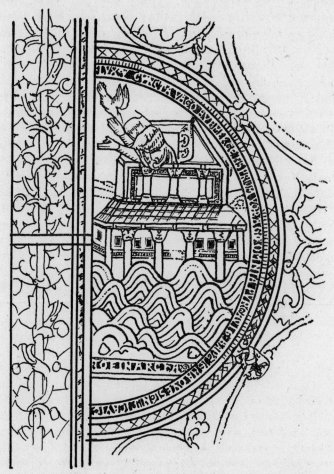

FIG. 6.   NOAH IN THE ARK.   CANTERBURY CATHEDRAL

in the Ark a favourite subject with early Christian and medieval artists.
It also symbolised the Church, guided by Christ amid the troubled
waters of the world.

A complete lack of realism generally characterised this subject.
In the Catacombs the painters showed the Ark as a square box with an

upraised lid, the *arca*, or shrine, which was the symbol of deliverance, and in the Theological windows of Canterbury Cathedral (Fig. 6) the Ark is still more shrine than ship. Most other British illustrations of Noah's Ark show a ship of sorts, albeit of most doubtful sea-worthiness ! On the façade of Wells Cathedral its upper structure is roughly pyramidal, probably because Gregory the Great taught that the Ark was broad enough at the base to hold all beasts and reptiles, and then narrowed by successive stages to accommodate first the birds, and, above them, man. It thus symbolised the Church in which the many are carnally minded, the few spiritual, and only Christ is without sin.[14] The carver of a boss in the transepts of Norwich Cathedral shows beasts, birds and men divided on three arcaded decks, but, not understanding the symbolism of this arrangement, he has put the birds on top. At Salisbury (PLATE 22) there are only two decks, but birds and beasts are clearly separated. Confusion as to the meaning of the word 'tristega', sometimes used for such a three-storeyed structure, may have caused the carver of a misericord in Ely Cathedral to give his Ark three battlemented towers. One supporter of this misericord shows the dove with the olive branch and on the other is carved a raven feeding upon carrion. In the 14th-century poem *Cursor Mundi* we read:

> Noe opened his window high,
> A raven let he forth to fly.
> He flew up and down and sought alwhere
> A stead to sit upon somewhere.
> Upon the water soon he found
> A drowned beast that lay floating,
> Of that flesh he was so fain
> To ship came he not again.[15]

Some panels from a complete Noah window at Malvern, now reset in the south choir aisle, show some rare episodes in the story. Noah kneels to receive the commandments of God in one panel, for which the glazier has used the same cartoon as for the Covenant made with Abraham (PLATE 7). The building of the Ark (which is most beautifully carved in a quatrefoil on the west front at Wells) has been lost in the Malvern glass, but the rare subject of the animals entering the Ark is there, the entry of Noah's family into the Ark, the return of the dove and Noah's thank-offering. Three more panels are devoted to Noah planting the vine, and his drunkenness, a subject which occurs more often than might have been expected because it was held to prefigure the stripping and mocking of Christ. It occurs at Salisbury (PLATE 22), on the Fitzroy tomb at Framlingham and in glass at York Minster and St. Michael, Spurriergate, York.

ABRAHAM.—Three incidents in the life of Abraham were treated as having more than historical significance; his meeting with Melchizedek and the offering of bread and wine by that Royal High Priest (Genesis xiv. 18) which occurs in the east window of York Minster; the visit of the three angels announcing the birth of Isaac (Genesis xviii) and the sacrifice of Isaac (Genesis xxii). In later medieval 'typology' the visit of the three men (who are generally shown as winged angels) was a type of either the Annunciation or the Transfiguration,[16] while some commentaries upon the Old Testament explained that they represented the Holy Trinity. One carving at Salisbury shows Abraham kneeling before the angels and the next shows them at table in the house of Abraham, who serves his guests with a towel over his hands (PLATE 22). This detail probably alludes to the fact that Abraham's service was regarded as a type of Christ washing the feet of His disciples, and these two subjects were associated in the Canterbury windows.

Three misericords in Worcester Cathedral which show the circumcision of Isaac, Abraham leading Isaac to the mountain in Moriah and his arrested sacrifice belong to the group of typological subjects already mentioned as being taken from 12th-century designs (see page 19). Such iconographical features as the marked diagonal crossing of the faggots on Isaac's shoulders (PLATE 5), to stress the parallel with Christ bearing His Cross, and the fact that Isaac kneels upon a draped altar, emphasise the typological aspect of these subjects. The Hand of God emerging from a tree to seize Abraham's sword (probably the carver misunderstood the conventional rendering of a cloud) also belongs to the early traditions of iconography. Later artists generally substituted an angel.[17]

LOT AND HIS DAUGHTERS (Genesis xix).—The fall of Sodom and Gomorrah is dramatically portrayed at Salisbury by toy towers and gateways tilted at all angles (PLATE 22). In the next spandrel of the arcade we see Lot and his daughters advancing towards the hills of refuge, whilst behind them stands a human-headed 'pillar of salt'. The fate of Lot's wife was not only a direct warning against disobedience, but foreshadowed the angel's warning to the Magi that they should not return to Herod.

JACOB.—The loss of Esau's birthright was associated with the rejection of the Jews, while Jacob typified the Gentiles who were established in the Christian Church. This subject, carved at Salisbury, is there followed by Rebecca sending Jacob to Laban, a type of the Flight into Egypt. The next carving, Jacob wrestling with the Angel, has one interesting detail which recalls earlier iconography. The angel touches Jacob's thigh with a wand, like that with which Christ is shown performing miracles in the Catacomb paintings. Two angels poised on a diagonal line here indicate Jacob's Ladder (Genesis xxviii), but this rare subject is more effectively shown on a stall-end in Chester Cathedral. What appears to be a Jacob's Ladder on the west front of Bath Abbey, with the descending angels shown head downwards, is more probably an illustration of the dream which inspired Bishop Oliver King to rebuild the church in 1499.[18]

JOSEPH (Genesis xxxvii-xliii).—Although Joseph was considered as prefiguring Christ, and six episodes from his life were connected with events of the Passion in the *Biblia Pauperum*, such episodes are rarely found singly. Full series of illustrations were developed early and were further enriched in the Middle Ages by apocryphal details, some of which appear in our richest surviving series, the carvings at Salisbury. After Joseph's dream, and the vengeance of his brothers, the carver diverges from the Bible by showing Joseph sold, not to the company of Ishmaelites, but to a single man who rides off with the lad on pillion behind him. Who is this man? He also appears in Queen Mary's Psalter, and the Anglo-Norman verses which accompany those exquisite drawings of Old Testament scenes tell us that he is Seneschal to the King of Egypt. This manuscript is a generation later than the carvings but both may have been based upon the same metrical French paraphrase of the Bible, although none now extant gives the explanations adopted in the Psalter.[19]

In both the Psalter and the carvings the Seneschal sells Joseph direct to Pharaoh, whose own wife, not that of Potiphar, plays the temptress, and both show the dreams of Joseph's two fellow-prisoners being fulfilled in one illustration. The Baker hangs upon a tree while the Butler kneels before Pharaoh, offering him a cup. Neither series illustrates the actual dreams, but a fragment of glass in the north choir aisle at Malvern evidently belonged to a panel showing the baker asleep, with the birds eating Pharaoh's bakemeats from the basket upon his head.

In a carving of 'Joseph supervising the threshing of Pharaoh's corn' at Salisbury a man is throwing straw into the river and this action, also shown in Queen Mary's Psalter, may be explained in the words of the *Cursor Mundi*.

> The chaff of corn as I you say
> In a water he cast away,
> Into a flume atte ran there,
> To Jacob's house the wind it bare. . . .

In defiance of geography the Nile carried it to Palestine where Jacob saw it:

> Childer, he said, ye list and lete
> I saw chaff on the water flete.
> Withern it comes I can not rede
> But down it fleets full good speed. . . .

He advised them

> Agayne the flume to follow the chaff
> Corn there shall we find to have.[20]

The remaining carvings at Salisbury which show the brethren buying corn; the hiding and discovery of the cup in Benjamin's sack, and Jacob's journey into Egypt, call for no comment.

MOSES.—It was in his capacity as Law-giver that Moses typified Christ; receiving the Tables of the Old Law from God, as Christ brought down the New Law from Heaven. He is mostly shown as a single figure holding the Tables of Stone as on the font at Southrop (Glos) (PLATE 3). Although Christ Himself compared His Crucifixion to Moses lifting up the serpent in the wilderness (St. John iii. 14), this subject (Numbers xxi. 7-9) is now surprisingly rare in British churches. One of the typological misericords in Worcester Cathedral shows the Brazen Serpent upon a column in the centre, while the fiery serpents are coiled upon the supporters. The medallion on the 16th-century manorial pew at Holcombe Rogus (Devon) was probably copied from an early printed Bible.

The destruction of Pharaoh's army during the Passage of the Red Sea (Exodus xiv. 21-30) is shown at Salisbury, and, with an amusing economy of detail, on one of the bosses in the nave of Norwich. Moses striking the rock, which was a frequent subject in the Catacomb paintings, occurs as a type of the Wounded Side of Christ, in the east window of the Corona at Canterbury, and in a window now at St. Martin's, Stamford (Lincs), where the design has obviously been copied from the woodcuts of the *Biblia Pauperum*. Otherwise it is rare, and even rarer is the Burning Bush (Exodus iii) which appears in a window at Fairford.

Both the Passage of the Red Sea and the sending by Moses of Spies into the land of Canaan were used in the *Biblia Pauperum* as types of the Baptism of Christ. The artists followed faithfully the description, given in Numbers xiii, of how the Spies cut a bunch of grapes by the Brook of Eschol 'and they bare it between two upon a staff'. In the 13th-century east window of the Corona at Canterbury, and in those panels from the Sainte Chapelle in Paris which are so unexpectedly to be found in the east window of Twycross (Leics), as well as on late medieval misericords at Ripon and Beverley Minster, we see the two men carrying an immense bunch of grapes from a pole hanging upon their shoulders. The symbolical interpretation was complex; as the juice of the grapes symbolised the Blood of the Redeemer, so the grapes symbolised His body. Because one of the men, walking in front, turned his back upon the grapes, he was associated with the Jews, while his companion, who is shown at Twycross stretching forward his hand to touch the grapes, represented the Christians. The Spies also occur in carvings on the pew at Holcombe Rogus and a bench-end at Milverton (Somerset).

Another medallion on the cresting of the Holcombe Rogus pew shows the Israelites kneeling before the Golden Calf, set high on a pillar, and this subject, which typified the Fall of the Idols during the Flight into Egypt (see page 109), is very fully illustrated in the windows of Malvern. Here the designer has drawn upon an ancient Jewish legend which amplifies the Bible statement that Moses burned the Golden Calf and 'ground it to powder, and strawed it upon the water, and made the children of Israel drink of it' (Exodus xxxii. 20). The anonymous author of *Cursor Mundi*, who borrowed extensively from Petrus Comestor,[21] tells us that

> All the men that had the guilt
> They had their berdis (beards) all over-gilt. . . .

but if they were innocent

> The water proved them for clene
> There was no gold on their berdis seen.[22]

In the Malvern windows several of the men shown drinking from golden bowls have yellow beards, as has also a man kneeling to receive his death stroke in the massacre.[23]

Single figures of Moses may also be identified by horns on his head as on the Southrop font (PLATE 3). This latter attribute originated in a mistranslation in the Vulgate. In Exodus xxxiv. 30, which describes how, when Moses came down from Mount Sinai 'the skin of his face shone', the phrase was rendered *facies cornuta*, because the Hebrew word for 'shone' was also the root of the noun 'horn', and this false lead was followed by the artists. The finest British example of the horned Moses is the 12th-century statue from St. Mary's Abbey, York, which is now in the Yorkshire Museum. Some later medieval artists seem to have realised this error, for a window at North Tuddenham (Suffolk) shows Moses with rays of light coming from his ears as he turns his face upward to hear the commandment of the Lord.[24]

BALAAM (Numbers xxii).—The journey of Balaam, associated in the Theological windows at Canterbury with that of the Magi (see Fig. 5), is not often represented. A carving on the pew at Holcombe Rogus has many points in common with a woodcut of the block-book *Speculum Humanae Salvationis*, including the exaggerated pose of the arm wielding the whip (the reversal of the block in printing has made Balaam left-handed) and the small head of the accusing ass, twisted round to confront its rider.[25]

GIDEON (Judges vi. 36-40).—The miracle of the dew which fell only upon the fleece, while the rest of the ground was dry, was considered as a type of the Incarnation but is rarely represented. A window in Fairford is a fine example.

SAMSON (Judges xiii-xvi).—I know of no series of pictures of the life of Samson in a British church, but isolated incidents from it are common, particularly his rending of the lion's jaws. This symbolised Christ breaking open the gates of Hell, and its association with the idea of a door opened to salvation may have led the Norman carvers to represent it on the tympana of Stretton Sugwas (Herefs) and (probably) Highworth (Wilts). The theme of a battle between man and lion has appealed to artists in many ages, from Mesopotamian seal-cylinders of *c.* 3000 B.C. onwards, and it may have been some eastern tradition, perhaps connected with the Mithraic combat, which decreed that Samson should always be shown astride the lion, forcing its head back with his hands.[26] On a misericord in Bristol Cathedral Samson is identified by the jaw bone of an ass tucked into his belt, but this weapon is only shown in use in the conflict with the Philistines, carved upon the Kirkham chantry at Paignton (Devon).[27]

The carrying away of the gates of Gaza was a type of the Resurrection, and is carved in this connexion upon the south door of Malmesbury Abbey. It also occurs at Paignton. A misericord in Ripon Cathedral (PLATE 5) is closely copied from the mid-15th-century block-book *Biblia Pauperum* printed in the Netherlands (Fig. 4). The same pose, with one gate under his arm and the other on his shoulder, occurs on a boss in the nave of Norwich Cathedral, where two other bosses show Samson being bound by Delilah and the shearing of his hair. This binding of Samson, which was associated with that of Christ after His arrest, also appears on misericords in Gloucester and Hereford Cathedrals. Samson pulling down the pillars of the house is shown in the east window of York Minster.

SAMUEL.—Despite his historical importance, Samuel is only represented in British church imagery as the child whose presentation in the Temple at Shiloh prefigured that of Christ. This subject is very rare but it occurs in the typological windows of Canterbury, where an inscription explains the symbolical meaning of the 'bottle of wine' offered by Hannah (1 Samuel i. 24) when she presented Samuel. She is shown holding this bottle on a misericord in Worcester Cathedral, thus identifying the subject and also suggesting the interesting possibility that the artists of the Chapter House paintings followed designs akin to those used at Canterbury and Peterborough although the author of the Worcester verses did not interpret the symbolism of this detail.

THE TREE OF JESSE.—The father of David is chiefly represented in ecclesiastical imagery as a symbol recalling the prophecy of Isaiah xi. 1-2: 'There shall come forth a rod out of the stem of Jesse, and a Branch shall grow out of his roots: and the Spirit of the Lord shall rest upon him'. As early as the 3rd century Tertullian had expounded the association of this *virga de radice Iesse* with the Virgin Mary, and when she is shown enthroned her sceptre often takes the form of a rod tipped with a triple bud, as on the font at Cowlam (Yorks). The lovely carving on a tomb at Willoughby-on-the-Wolds (Notts) (PLATE 18) has elaborated this theme into the rose bush in the right hand of the Virgin, on which the Holy Dove is resting.

The development of this 'rod' into the branching Tree of Jesse, and its counterparts in the Far East, has been exhaustively studied [28] —we are only concerned here with its representation in medieval churches. From the loins of a recumbent Jesse springs a luxuriant growth, usually represented as a vine, whose branches frame the figures of kings and patriarchs, while the Virgin and Child are enthroned upon its topmost shoot. Despite the incalculable destruction of many centuries, a large number of examples survive, ranging in scale from the great Jesse window at Dorchester (Oxon) or the impressive figure at Abergavenny (PLATE 19) to ingeniously concentrated versions on a misericord in Lincoln Cathedral, a boss in Worcester Cathedral cloister, an image-niche at Llantwit Major (Glam) or a stall-end in Chester Cathedral. Stained glass was the ideal medium for the design, and whenever we see a fragment of old glass representing a figure surrounded by a coil of foliage we can assume the former existence of a Jesse window. Fine panels from 14th-century Jesse windows have been replaced in the north aisle at Lowick (Northants) and the east window at Merevale (Warcs). In the later medieval windows the kings no longer stand amid scrolls of foliage but appear as half-length figures rising from the blossoms of the tree. Both forms occur in the superb Jesse window at Llanrhaiadr (Denbighs) which bears the date 1533.

DAVID.—Although single figures of the king playing upon the harp occur fairly often, scenes from his life are rare. His victory over Goliath has been copied from block-book woodcuts in the windows of St. Martin's, Stamford (Lincs), and St. Martin-cum-Gregory at York. It was used as a type of Christ's Descent into Limbo, as was also David's battle with the lion (1 Samuel xvii. 33), which is difficult to distinguish from that of Samson. The identity of the fighter on the Norman tympanum at Highworth (Wilts) is uncertain, but the boyishness of David is cleverly represented on the supporter of a misericord at Sherborne (Dorset). The most interesting example is the 8th-century carved slab in the Cathedral Museum at St. Andrews (Fife) which shows David fighting the lion, with his sheep in the background, and other hunting elements. On this slab, and on other early Scottish carvings at Aberlemno (Angus), Aldbar (Fife) and Nigg (Aberdeens), David is standing in a frontal pose, with a diminutive, but realistic, lion leaping up to claw his thigh. Both this posture and the type of the lion have been considered as being perhaps derived from representations of the Assyrian, or Chaldean, god Gilgamesh, brought to Scotland on some imported treasure of wrought silver.[29]

The feigned madness of David was used as a type of the Last Supper in the Theological windows of Canterbury, but this medallion has been lost. The only surviving example I know is in the 13th-century glass of Lincoln Cathedral, where David is shown walking on his hands, with red-stockinged legs waving in the air, before the throne from which Achish, King of Gath, watches him contemptuously (1 Samuel xxi. 13). By over-literal translation the Greek expression meaning 'he feigned himself mad in their hands' was rendered *ferebatur in manibus suis*, and the tradition that David thus carried himself upon his own hands was strangely associated with the idea of Christ bearing His own Body when He broke bread at the Last Supper.[30]

SOLOMON is mostly represented giving judgment between the two mothers (1 Kings iii). This occurs as part of the great Judgment theme of the western windows at Fairford and on the misericords of

Worcester Cathedral and Henry VII's Chapel, Westminster, where the complex story has been spread over the supporters as well as the central corbel. A fragment of a 12th-century capital, now in the triforium of Westminster Abbey (PLATE 3), shows a sensitive appreciation of the contrast between the impassive figure of the false mother, clasping the doomed child, and the passionate supplication of the real one, prostrate at the feet of the king.

The visit of the Queen of Sheba to Solomon was sometimes considered as symbolising the conversion of the heathen who leave their errors to learn wisdom, and when she appears enthroned beside Solomon, as in a window of St. Michael, Spurriergate, York, she is a figure of the Church, or of that Mystic Spouse of Christ to whom, according to Isidore of Seville, Solomon addressed the Song of Songs. This interpretation explains the prominence given to statues of Solomon and the Queen of Sheba on French Romanesque cathedrals. Her journey, and offering of gifts to Solomon, shown in the Fairford glass, were also associated with the Epiphany.[31]

ELIJAH.—The translation of Elijah in the chariot of fire (2 Kings i), which was frequently shown in early Christian art, is associated in the east window of the Corona at Canterbury with three other types of the Ascension of Christ; the Ark of the Mercy Seat, the Burial of Moses and the Sundial of Ahaz.

DANIEL in the lions' den (Daniel vi) occurs on several early crosses in Ireland and Scotland. On the High Cross of Moone Abbey the sculptor has surrounded Daniel by seven lions, the number specified in the Byzantine Manual for Painters, but as a rule symmetry limits them to four.[32] I know of no representation in England earlier than the 12th-century relief on the west front of Lincoln Cathedral.

JONAH.—The story of Jonah and the whale was one of the first to be represented by Christian artists as a symbol of deliverance, and in the Middle Ages it was associated with Christ's Descent into Limbo and the Resurrection. At Ripon two misericords, based on woodcuts from the *Biblia Pauperum* (Fig. 4), show Jonah being swallowed by the whale and his subsequent escape.

This list of Old Testament themes makes no claim to be complete, even as to subjects, while many more examples could have been included. Its purpose is merely to indicate which subjects are most likely to be found, and in what context they were probably used.

CHAPTER 6

THE INFANCY OF CHRIST

W<small>E</small> have seen that the choice of the isolated subjects from the Old Testament represented in churches was generally determined by their prophetic relationship to the life of Christ. Just as the medieval masons transmitted the thrust of their high vaults, by successive stages of buttressing, to the unshakable foundations of earth, so the teachers sought to reaffirm the truth of each Gospel incident by showing how it had been foretold since the very darkness of Time. When we turn from this marshalled testimony of the Past to consider the Gospel imagery we shall find this rich in extra-Biblical details, some of them referring back to Old Testament prophecies, others drawn from the visions of medieval mystics who contemplated the scenes of Christ's earthly life in an ever-enduring Present and described them with the authority of actual participants. The carved alabaster tomb of William Rudhall at Ross-on-Wye (Herefs) (PLATE 18), which shows the dead man and his family as kneeling witnesses of the Annunciation, may serve to illustrate a mystical approach to the Gospels which inspired much medieval iconography.

The apocryphal Gospels which, since the 2nd century, had partly satisfied men's hunger for further details of the life of Christ, were now supplemented by such works as the *Meditationes Vitae Christi* of the Pseudo-Bonaventura, dating from the 13th century, and the Revelations of St. Bridget of Sweden who is shown, as a seated nun with an open book, upon the painted rood-screen of Horsham St. Faith (Norfolk). About 1410 the *Meditationes* were translated into English by Nicholas Love under the title *The Mirrour of the Blessed Lyf of Jesu Christ*.[1] The frequent appearance in imagery of details apparently derived from these works is proof of their widespread influence. It is my aim in this chapter to explain the derivation and meaning of some of these extra-Biblical details.

The A<small>NNUNCIATION</small> is one of the most frequent subjects and shows many interesting variations. In the Eastern Church the Virgin Mary is sometimes represented with a distaff in her hand to indicate that she was spinning the thread for the Veil of the Temple when the angel appeared,[2] but western artists mostly show her holding a book, or, later, kneeling at a prayer desk, since the Gospel of Pseudo-Matthew tells that she studied the Law of God and the Psalms. The finest British example of the early tradition, which shows both figures standing, is the pair of 13th-century statues which flank the doorway to the Chapter House of Westminster Abbey. On an early 13th-century font at Upavon (Wilts) are carved two standing figures, stately in spite of their damaged condition, and the subject is identified by the descent of the Holy Dove and the lily in a jar set between them.

This motive of the lily-pot originated in western Europe.[3] Émile Mâle ascribes the first French examples to the 13th century and says that it passed on into Italy,[4] but England can claim an earlier use of a motive which was later included in almost every Annunciation. Before considering such examples it is interesting to note that in the Anglo-Saxon poem of *Solomon and Saturn*[5] the evil spirit puts the question:

> 'Tell me which is the best and happiest of herbs?'

to which Solomon replies:

> 'I tell thee the lily is that herb for it denoteth Christ.'

On some early 12th-century capitals at the crossing in Southwell Minster, the Virgin of the Annunciation has a triple flower, placed in a jar, at her side, like an identifying attribute, and not between her and the angel as an intrinsic part of the scene. A fragment of Norman sculpture from St. Mary's Abbey, York, now in the Yorkshire Museum, clearly shows the lily-pot in its traditional position. The precise meaning of this symbol has not been established. Since the lily often has three blooms, it has been interpreted as symbolising the purity of the Virgin before, during and after the Incarnation, but M. Mâle suggests that the flower was not always a lily, and merely indicated that the Annunciation took place in the spring. John Mirk recounts a story of the Christian and the Jew discussing the Nativity with a wine pot between them. 'Then said the Christian man: "We believe that right as the stalk of the lily groweth and conceiveth colour of green, and after bringeth forth a white flower, without craft of man or impairing of the stalk, right so our Lady conceived of the Holy Ghost and after bringeth forth her son without stain of her body, that is the flower and chief fruit of all women." Then said the Jew: "When I see a lily spring out of this pot I will believe, and e'er not." Then anon therewith a lily sprang out of the pot, the fairest that ever was seen.'[6]

From the 14th century until the Reformation the lily of the Annunciation was sometimes shown bearing upon its stem a miniature figure of Christ crucified, as on the misericord at Tong (Salop) (PLATE 13), and for this also various explanations have been offered. These include suggested references to the special devotions to the Seven Joys and Seven Sorrows of the Blessed Virgin, and the belief that both the Annunciation and the Crucifixion took place on the same date, March 25th.[7] The explanation which I prefer is found in the *Speculum Humanae Salvationis* and which I quote from the only known medieval English translation.[8]

> Of Jesse root a ȝerd | in tyme to come shall springe
> out of that Rote a floure | upright is ascendinge.
>
> . . . .
>
> The ȝerd is oure Ladye | with fruyt be hevenysh dewe
> The floure hir Sonne yt sho | unto this werld shall shewe.

This flower contains seven gifts of the Holy Ghost, its touch assuaging swelling pride, its savour giving the gift of pity, its fruit calming anger, its leaves giving council against avarice, its juice the gift of intellect against gluttony and its taste the gift of sapience against lust while

> A man is strengthid noblye
> That he no payne may fele
> Nor have drede of laboure
> Of this floure, Crist-on-crosse,
> Behalding the coloure.

In early Christian art we always see the angel standing, but as the belief gained ground that the Virgin Mary conceived while hearing the words of the Annunciation, artists began to show Gabriel kneeling to honour one who was already the Mother of God. This belief also underlies the late medieval representations of God the Father sending down a ray of light from Heaven to reach the ear of the kneeling Virgin. Often the Holy Dove is shown flying down this ray, and in the 14th and 15th centuries artists occasionally represented a tiny Child, sometimes bearing His Cross, descending after the Dove. This motive, which appears in the east window of St. Peter Mancroft, Norwich, and on the tomb at Ross-on-Wye (PLATE 18), proved a potential source of error, suggesting that the body of Jesus was not formed in the Virgin's womb, but it was not until the 18th century that its use was finally condemned by Pope Benedict XIV.[9]

The VISITATION is rarely represented with details calling for explanation. In the *Magnificat* window at Malvern St. Elizabeth is shown touching the body of the Virgin, from which issue golden flames as though the divine Embryo was already surrounded with a glory of light. This is also shown in a window at Newark (Notts).

The NATIVITY very often includes details which we should question if they were less familiar. Why, for instance, is the scene so often represented as happening in the open air: a convention which appeared very early in Eastern art ? The scantly sheltering roof supported on posts, or the half-ruined, lean-to building, is not the stable implied in St. Luke's Gospel, or the desert cave of the apocryphal Gospels, but the 'diversorie' (a temporary shelter from rain placed between two buildings) which is described in the *Meditationes Vitae Christi*. In the English translation we read that in such a place 'Joseph, that was a carpenter, made them a closere, and a cracche for their bestes'. To the medieval artist a 'closere' evidently meant the fence of plaited osiers which we see in many 'Nativities', possibly because it was used in staging mystery plays. In medieval paintings this ruinous shed is sometimes incongruously supported upon a column with a richly carved capital because the *Meditationes* tell how, at midnight, when the Virgin gave birth, she leant for support against such a column.[10] This column does not figure in the English translation, and I do not remember seeing it in any British glass or wall-painting, but the penalty we pay for the ever-widening interest of studying iconography is the mortifying suspicion that we may have looked at significant details, while our eyes were still too ill-informed to notice them !

I wonder how many readers could say with immediate certainty whether the ox and the ass are mentioned in the Gospels. They are not. All we learn there is that the Child was laid in a manger, but the apocryphal Gospel of Pseudo-Matthew[11] describes how Mary left the desert cave in which the Nativity took place, on the third day, and hid from Herod's men in a stable, where she laid the Child in a manger, and the ox and the ass adored Him. Yet, in spite of this historical uncertainty, the two animals were regarded as essential witnesses from the 4th century onwards. On an early sarcophagus in Milan all that the sculptor has considered necessary to the message of his work is the swaddled child in the crib and the ox and the ass, one at each end of it,[12] as they appear underneath the Crucifixion on a Saxon cross at Sandbach (Ches). On the Norman font at Fincham (Norfolk) a great star above the crib shows that the main subject is the journey of the Magi, shown on the other sides of the font, and that this meagre hieroglyph of the Nativity merely expresses the portent of the Star.

The reason why the ox and the ass were so important that their presence enables us to distinguish a Nativity of Christ from any other birth scene, is that they express the fulfilment of a prophecy. 'The ox knoweth his owner, and the ass his master's crib: but Israel doth not know, my people doth not consider' (Isaiah i. 3). The words of Isaiah were interpreted as referring to the manger at Bethlehem, and the refusal of the Jews to acknowledge Christ was contrasted with the adoration of the animals. Commentators not only accepted the presence of the ox and ass but explained it: the sermon of the Pseudo-Augustine, the *Golden Legend* and the *Meditationes* all tell how they came there, but we shall realise better how this explanation reached the ordinary parishioners from John Mirk's Christmas sermon. After telling of the ordered taxation he tells how St. Joseph, 'for that he had no money, took an ox with him, for to sell and make him money of. But, for he durst not leave Our Lady behind, for she was nigh time of birth, he set her on an ass and took her with him.' On a boss on the north transept of Norwich Cathedral St. Joseph is shown leading the two beasts with the Virgin Mary following him. They had to shelter in 'a cave between the houses', where they found 'a cracche with hay and setten the ox and ass thereto' while St. Joseph went in search of a midwife. When the new-born Child was laid in the crib the animals 'anon knew Our Lord and fellen down on knees and worshippen Him, and ate no more of the hay'.[13] The *Meditationes* add that the creatures warmed the Child with their breath.

In early art the Virgin is often shown as an impassive recumbent figure, scarcely glancing at the Child whose crib is raised so high that He seems to be lying upon a sacrificial altar, but in the late 14th century there was a sudden change of tradition, and henceforth we generally see the Virgin kneeling in adoration of the naked Child who lies upon the bare earth, surrounded by a glory of light. The growing veneration of the Virgin had introduced the belief that, being without sin, she did not suffer pain in child-birth, and it was therefore almost heretical to show her in bed after the Nativity, but the decisive factor in this change was the vision seen by St. Bridget of Sweden while she was in ecstasy at Bethlehem in 1370. She beheld a virgin of extreme beauty come into a cave, accompanied by an old man leading an ox and an ass. He tied these to the manger and fastened a lighted candle to the wall before he withdrew. The Virgin took off her shoes, veil and mantle and knelt down in prayer. Then, 'suddenly, in a moment, she gave birth to her son from whom radiated such an ineffable light and splendour that the sun was not comparable to it, nor did the candle that St. Joseph had put there give any light at all. . . . When the Virgin felt that she had already born her child, she immediately worshipped him . . . saying: "Be welcome my God, my Lord and my Son".' [14] The instantaneous birth had already been described in the *Meditationes Vitae Christi*, but the kneeling Virgin and the glory of light proceeding from the Child were introduced into Christian art by St. Bridget, and it is a vivid illustration of the international structure of medieval thought that the vision of a single Swedish mystic should have changed the traditional iconography of the Nativity. A window in the nave of Malvern Priory shows St. Joseph kneeling in adoration, shielding the flame of his candle with his hand, but the Virgin has retained her mantle and head-dress (PLATE 7). The glazier probably copied a woodcut, perhaps from the *Speculum Humanae Salvationis*, which imperfectly reproduced the vision of St. Bridget.

While the Virgin adoring the Child appeared in most important works of art in the 15th century, the humbler artists continued to enrich the older type of Nativity with details from the apocryphal Gospels. The 2nd-century *Protevangelium* first tells us of the two mid-wives, and how the scepticism of one, Salome, was punished by the withering of her hand, until, having repented, she was healed at the touch of the Child.[15] On roof bosses in Worcester Cathedral and in both the Cathedral and St. Helen's Church at Norwich, we see one woman standing beside the Virgin's bed. In the glass of St. Peter Mancroft at Norwich she is warming the baby clothes at a fire while St. Joseph sits comfortably in an arm-chair, and a window at East Harling (Norfolk) shows two midwives. The bathing of the new-born Christ Child, which is sometimes represented, might have been derived from Byzantine Nativities, but is more probably due to the humanising influence of popular taste in the later medieval periods. It seems also to have been a special subject of devout meditation for women. Margery Kempe [16] tells how, in her visions, Christ thanked her for 'the many times that thou hast bathed me in thy soul, at home in thy chamber, as though I had been there present in my manhood'.

The ADORATION OF THE SHEPHERDS is often represented as a remote incident in the landscape background of a Nativity, but where it is the main subject the artists visualised it in contemporary realism. A wall-painting at Cocking (Sussex) shows one shepherd shielding his eyes from the blaze of a star which has whirling tongues of fire, while his dog shrinks back on its haunches and bares its teeth in fear. At Ashampstead (Berks) one of the shepherds is painted with a pipe in his hand, and elsewhere they are shown playing upon their pipes as they come to the stable of Bethlehem. The lines in a Coventry Corpus Christi play

> I have nothing to present with thi Chylde
> But my pype; hold, hold, take yt in thi hond. . . .[17]

suggest that craftsmen who made the windows of St. Peter Mancroft, or East Harling, or carved the boss at Salle (Norfolk), which all show this feature, were copying the plays, but the tradition that the shepherds were making music when the angel appeared is much older. On the 6th-century ampullae of Monza we see the shepherd with a flute, and a canticle used on Christmas Eve in the 9th century describes how the vision of the angelic host silenced the pastoral flutes.[18]

THE ADORATION OF THE MAGI.—These words immediately call up in our mind's eye three crowned figures, one old and bearded, one in the prime of life and often of African type, and the last a stripling, bringing their offerings to the new-born Saviour. We may even name them, Melchior, Caspar and Balthazar, before we pause to wonder how this information has been added to the bald statement in St. Matthew's Gospel that 'there came wise men from the east to Jerusalem' who, when they had worshipped the Child, 'presented unto Him gifts, gold and frankincense and myrrh'. Even their number is thus left uncertain ! It is in a text once attributed to Bede [19] that we first learn that the oldest of the Magi, Melchior, had long white hair and beard, and that he offered gold, the symbol of kingship; next, the beardless Caspar offered frankincense to mark the divinity of Christ, and lastly the dark, bearded Balthazar offered myrrh to the Son of Man who must die. The convention of showing Balthazar as a negro started in the 14th century, when theologians taught that the Magi had been prefigured by the three sons of Noah who divided the earth between them (they are shown in one of the Theological windows at Canterbury marking out the 'three corners of the world' upon a globe), and that they thus symbolised the three races of men coming to worship their Saviour.[20] Legends told of the return journey of the Magi and their baptism by St. Thomas, in India, and their heads were among the relics honoured in Cologne Cathedral, but, with the exception of the crowns which mark their apocryphal royalty, these legends are not illustrated in British churches. The angelic warning not to revisit Herod is shown in detail on a Norman doorway in Glastonbury Abbey, the vision of each seer being shown in a separate medallion.

THE CIRCUMCISION OF OUR LORD.—An interesting divergence from pure illustration occurs on a boss at Salle (Norfolk) (PLATE 16) and in the east window of St. Peter Mancroft, Norwich, where we see the Virgin seated on a low stool, suckling the Child, while the High Priest, seated on his throne, leans forward to perform the operation. St. Joseph, and another man and woman, watch in the background. The similarity of design, despite the difference of medium, suggests a common origin in some illustrated version of the *Meditationes Vitae Christi*, where the author describes with touching tenderness how the Child wept 'for the sorrow that he felt there through his flesh, for without doubt he had very flesh and kindly sufferable as have other children'. The Virgin wept for sympathy 'and so through the compassion of the mother the child ceased of sobbing and weeping. And then his mother, wiping his face and kissing him, and putting the pap in his mouth, comforted him in all the manners that she might, and so she did as often as he wept.' [21] This motive was probably derived from an early rendering of the Circumcision of Isaac as it is shown on a misericord in Worcester Cathedral (see page 93).

The PRESENTATION IN THE TEMPLE or the PURIFICATION OF THE VIRGIN is shown with little variation of iconography. The Child may be held in His Mother's arms, or stand, or lie, upon the altar, and in later medieval art Simeon is shown as a mitred bishop, although there is no indication in the Gospel that he was an officiating priest. In the *Ludus Coventriae* the officiant is alluded to as 'episcopus' and was probably so vested, wearing, perhaps, an archaic form of mitre to make plain that he was a Jewish, not a Christian, bishop, as we see the High Priest receiving the Virgin Mary in the Temple in PLATE 15. St. Joseph usually carries birds, either in his hands or in a basket, but not always the 'pair of turtle doves, or two young pigeons' (St. Luke ii. 24) prescribed by Jewish law. A single bird may be due to difficulties of design, but when we see three birds, as in the Malvern windows, the fault probably lies with the play writers, for in the Chester plays, Mary says:

> Receive my sonne nowe at me
> And to my offeringe birdes three.[22]

In the background we may see a figure bearing a candle, in allusion to the Candlemas procession of lights with which the festival of the Purification of the Virgin was celebrated. This was a custom borrowed from pagan rites and in the Candlemas sermon of Mirk's *Festial* we read how it was adapted from the Roman ceremonies in honour of their goddess Februa, mother of Mars.[23]

THE MASSACRE OF THE INNOCENTS.—This subject was rare in early

Christian art, but the common medieval convention of showing it taking place before the throne of Herod appears in the 5th-century mosaics of S. Maria Maggiore, Rome. In the 11th and 12th centuries the subject was included in the regular sequence of Gospel subjects, since it explained the meaning of Holy Innocents Day. Early 13th-century carvings of the subject occur on a voussoir from an arch in St. Mary's Abbey, York (now in the Yorkshire Museum), and on the doorway of the Lady Chapel of Glastonbury Abbey. The 15th-century roof bosses of the north transept of Norwich Cathedral show an unusually rich series of illustrations of the life and death of Herod. These include his interview with the Magi, his consultation with the priests, the violent gesticulations of his fury when these fail to return, and his instructions to his soldiers, as well as the actual massacre.

THE FLIGHT INTO EGYPT.—The carvings upon the High Cross of Moone Abbey (Kildare) and the Ruthwell Cross (Dumfries) are unusually early examples of a rare subject. In the background of later representations we sometimes find motives derived from apocryphal Gospel of Pseudo-Matthew. A palm tree bowing low as though before a storm reminds us how Mary longed to eat of the fruit of a tall tree beneath which the Holy Family rested, and how Jesus commanded the tree to bow down to His mother's hand and later to give them of the water concealed beneath its roots. When they set out once more Jesus said to the palm: 'I give thee this privilege that one of thy branches shall be . . . planted in my Father's garden. And henceforth all who win contests shall be told that they have won the palm of victory.'[24] The finest example I know of this subject is in the east window of the Lady Chapel at Fairford (Glos), where the foliage of the stooping palm seems to glow like a dark emerald down the vista of the aisle. Among its branches is an angel, minister of the Christ Child's will, and in the foreground the Virgin sits upon the earth feeding her Babe with fruit. The still rarer subject of the dragons coming out of their dens to worship the Holy Child upon His journey is shown in one of the carvings of the Lady Chapel at Ely.[25]

A small figure tumbling from a pillar alludes to the legend that when the Holy Family entered the city of Sotinen (sometimes they are shown following a man into the city gates) they lodged in a temple containing 365 idols, which all fell to the ground as the Child came in. This fulfilled the words of Isaiah (xix. 1): 'Behold the Lord rideth upon a swift cloud, and shall come into Egypt : and the idols of Egypt shall be moved at his presence'. The 13th-century wall-paintings at Brook (Kent) show the Flight into Egypt, with a slightly bent tree in the background, in one medallion, and in the next, a single idol tumbling from its pedestal. The earlier paintings at Hardham (Sussex) show four idols standing in niches, one of which falls forward.

CHRIST AMONG THE DOCTORS.—The miniature in the Canterbury Gospels, now at Corpus Christi College, Cambridge, which dates from 6th or 7th century, shows Jesus seated between two doctors, while the Virgin stands on the left, but in the Middle Ages a design became traditional which placed Christ in the centre, on a high seat, surrounded by learned men who sometimes wear the robes of contemporary doctors. In the windows of Malvern the Jewish sages wear black caps and gowns with fur-edged hoods, as though the debate were taking place in the hall of a medieval University, while at East Harling (Norfolk) an attempt at an Oriental flavour has given the doctors fantastic headgear.

This subject brings us to the end of the normal cycle of illustrations of the Infancy of Christ. The miracles performed by the child Jesus, as they are described in the apocryphal Gospels, are rarely shown in churches, although a most interesting series of Chertsey tiles representing several of them is now in the British Museum.[26] A 15th-century wall-painting at Shorthampton (Oxon) has been interpreted as alluding to the legend of how Jesus made clay birds on the Sabbath, and, when reproved, He clapped His hands and the birds became living sparrows which flew away.[27]

CHAPTER 7

THE MINISTRY OF CHRIST

BECAUSE one main purpose of medieval imagery was to explain the significance of the great Church festivals, we rarely find illustrations of episodes in Christ's adult life before His Passion, for very few of these were associated with any particular festival.

The BAPTISM OF CHRIST appears fairly often, because of its sacramental associations, and some features of its representation recall early baptismal customs. I cannot remember a British example of Christ standing ankle-deep in water, as He is shown in the Catacombs, but in several cases the water is strangely heaped about his body to indicate a deeper immersion. M. Émile Mâle attributes this curious invention to an Oriental indifference to the laws of perspective among early Syrian artists.[1] This watery pile can be seen on the font at Castle Frome (PLATE 4) and more clearly on a Norman capital at Adel (Yorks) and the 12th-century font at Bridekirk (Cumb). In all these cases the Baptist only lays his hands upon Christ, but later representations show him pouring water from a jug, bottle or shell, following an occasional liturgical usage.[2]

It has been suggested that the presence of angels at the Baptism derives from an early 6th-century book on the Divine Hierarchy attributed to Denys the Areopagite.[3] In art, both the ampullae of Monza, c. 600, and the ivory throne at Ravenna show attendant angels with their hands veiled, a mark of respect correctly reproduced in the flying angels of Bradford-on-Avon (Wilts). Later western craftsmen, unfamiliar with eastern ceremonial, transformed this veil into a cloak, or the tunic held by the angel upon the Norman font at West Haddon (Northants).[4] It may also have been through misunderstanding of this veil that the carver at Castle Frome, where there are no angels, has given the Baptist a maniple, or possibly a stole, over his right arm. The fishes often shown swimming in the waters of Jordan symbolise the souls of Christians (*pisciculi* as they sometimes called themselves) whose spiritual life depended upon the saving waters of baptism as the earthly life of fishes is dependent on their native element.

The MARRIAGE AT CANA was frequently represented in the Catacombs, though sometimes reduced to a mere hieroglyph, but medieval artists either ignored the subject entirely or represented it realistically. An interesting presentation occurs in a 15th-century window at East Harling (Norfolk), where the be-turbanned bride is seated between Christ and her groom. In the foreground, the Virgin Mary, already crowned as Queen of Heaven, directs a servant to fill the water-pots, and opposite her stands a nimbed man holding a palm.[5] The anonymous 'Ruler of the Feast' is here treated as a saint, and some very rare legend may have told of his later conversion and martyrdom.

THE TRANSFIGURATION.—This is rare in the Western Church until the mid-15th century, when the Feast of the Transfiguration was observed. There is a fine window in the south chapel at Fairford (PLATE 14), and a wall-painting was recently uncovered at Hawkedon (Suffolk). It is also painted on three panels of the screen at Westhall (Suffolk).

THE MEAL IN THE HOUSE OF THE PHARISEE.—Although the Eastern Church never accepted the identification of the woman 'which was a sinner' who washed the feet of Christ as he sat at meat in the house of the Pharisee (St. Luke vii. 37-50) with Mary Magdalene and also with Mary, the sister of Martha and Lazarus, Gregory the Great taught that they were one person and this belief is implicit in medieval imagery, where the Magdalene's hair generally flows loose, like a penitent, and she holds a box of ointment in her hand. The actual washing of Christ's feet is rare, but occurs on a Norman capital in Leonard Stanley (Glos) and a medallion of 13th-century glass at West Horsley (Surrey).[6] The most interesting representation of the Magdalene is that on the Ruthwell Cross (Dumfries), not only because of the emotion conveyed by the forward sweep of her hair, the bowed intensity of her head, but because its inclusion in an iconographical scheme where every principal subject seems to be connected with contemplation in desert places (the accepted practice of the Celtic Church), suggests that the legend of Mary Magdalene ending her life as a desert hermit was known in 7th-century Britain.[7]

THE RAISING OF LAZARUS.—On early sarcophagi Lazarus is shown as a swathed mummy standing in the doorway of a mausoleum, but this does not appear in British churches. The most famous British representation of the scene is on one of the much debated Chichester reliefs (the other shows the even rarer subject of Christ entering the house of Martha and Mary). Here Lazarus stands erect in an open grave while the servants release the grave clothes from his legs, or rest on the levers with which they have opened the tomb. On the font at Lenton (PLATE 9) Lazarus is represented as a swaddled corpse, and only by the lifting of his head does he indicate his obedience to the command of Christ, who stands above the tomb with hand raised high in the gesture of speech. The servant raising the lid of the tomb and the kneeling figures of the two sisters make a design of compelling force which was perhaps inspired by some foreign treasure belonging to the Cluniac Priory of Lenton (Notts), for which this font was made.

The RAISING OF JAIRUS' DAUGHTER, sometimes used as an alternative symbol of resurrection in early Christian art, is very rare in England, but at Copford (Essex) it inspired one of our most important 12th-century wall-paintings.[8] The bold and flexible composition has a central feature which suggests the walls and doorway of Jairus' house. On one side of this the mother is shown mourning the dead girl, while on the other the agitated gestures of the father express his entreaty 'My daughter is even now dead: but come and lay thy hand upon her, and she shall live' (St. Matthew ix. 18). The great figure of Christ towers above him, the eyes gazing into infinite distance and the hand raised in the gesture of speech as though He were already uttering the words of resurrection.

Rare subjects which are probably isolated remnants of unusually full series of Gospel illustrations may sometimes be noted in stained glass, as, for instance, the two panels at North Tuddenham (Suffolk) which show Christ with the woman of Samaria and with Nicodemus, but their iconography calls for no special comment.

A medallion in one of the Theological windows at Canterbury which shows the calling of Nathaniel by Peter, as he sat under the fig tree, may be mentioned as introducing the scanty illustrations of Our Lord's teaching which we find in medieval imagery. Upon His description of the Judgment Day (St. Matthew xxv) were based many of the painted Dooms and also the representations of the Seven Works of Mercy (pages 134, 165), but the vivid parables which often inspired later artists were relatively little used by those of the Middle Ages. An exception to this rule is the parable of the Wise and Foolish Virgins, since the image of a gate open only to those who have kept faithful watch was particularly appropriate for the decoration of church doors.[9] Charmingly virginal little figures are set in the mouldings of the 13th-century Judgment Door of Lincoln Cathedral, the foolish ones holding their lamps upside down to prove their emptiness, but the theme did not achieve the importance in Britain which was

I

accorded to it on the Continent. The tracery lights of the Seven Sacrament window at Melbury Bubb (Dorset) represent both Wise and Foolish Virgins and the dialogue between them, with the concluding exhortation to vigilance, is shown upon inscribed scrolls.[10]

The parable of Dives and Lazarus was regarded by the designers of the Norman west front of Lincoln Cathedral as sufficiently important to fill two of the panels of figure sculpture representing the New Testament in the frieze which runs across the façade. One shows Dives at table with his cup-bearer at his shoulder and the other the soul of Lazarus being received by an angel while that of Dives is plunged into Hell. A 12th-century tympanum, now in the Yorkshire Museum, which shows demons seizing the soul of a dying man, is thought to represent the death of Dives. The parable is illustrated in two scenes in the stained glass at Great Milton (Oxon), and some indistinct 13th-century wall-paintings at Ulcombe (Kent) are said to have shown it with realistic details, such as a servant carrying the beggar's bowl back to him with every appearance of contempt. Traces of another 13th-century wall-painting can be seen at Findon (Sussex).

The remaining parables occur too rarely to need much comment. The Sower (PLATE 6) is shown in two medallions at Canterbury which are among the most beautiful examples of early glass in the country. We know from the recorded titles of these windows that many other parables were originally shown: the Leaven, the Net, the Tares, the Lost Sheep, the Unjust Debtor, the Wedding Garment and the Good Samaritan, but all these are lost.[11] The single panel of the Prodigal Son in Lincoln Cathedral may have formed part of such another series, but even if there were once many more such exceptional windows in the greater churches, the general rule would still be that Our Lord's parables did not form an essential part of the Picture Book of the Churches.

CHAPTER 8

THE PASSION AND RESURRECTION

THE ENTRY INTO JERUSALEM begins the cycle of scenes depicting the Passion of Our Lord, just as its celebration, on Palm Sunday, marks the beginning of Holy Week. Its iconographical tradition has varied very little since its first presentation on 4th-century Roman sarcophagi. Christ approaches the city gates, almost always riding from left to right, a man climbs a tree in the background and other figures spread garments before the ass or throw flowers from the battlements. In the east window at Malvern these figures are shown as children, either literally interpreting the account given to Pilate in the apocryphal *Gospel of Nicodemus* of how 'the children of the Hebrews' rejoiced at the coming of Christ,[1] or as an allusion to the boys often stationed on the roof of a church porch to greet the entry of the Palm Sunday procession with flowers and song.[2] In the east window at Fairford the figures on the battlemented gate hold a scroll inscribed with the opening words and music of an antiphon sung by the cantors inside the church and the choir outside, before this procession entered the church.[3]

At Aston Eyre (Salop) a Norman tympanum shows Christ riding a very elongated ass, with its colt (rarely shown) running behind, and another early carving occurs on the font at West Haddon (Northants).

THE LAST SUPPER.—The oldest surviving representation in a church is perhaps the 6th-century mosaic at S. Apollinare Nuovo at Ravenna. By then the bread and fish associated with the miraculous feeding of the multitudes, and with the post-Resurrection appearances of Christ, had symbolised the Eucharist for so long[4] that when the Last Supper became part of every full cycle of Passion illustrations the Lamb of the Passover was rarely represented. Although St. Augustine had written 'The roasted fish signifies the crucified Christ',[5] many medieval people were probably unaware of the origin of this early Christian symbolism, for we find explanations that Our Lord substituted fish for the Lamb, because fish did not share in the curse of the Fall since, in the words of the *Golden Legend* (i. 175), 'the trespass was of the fruit of the earth and not of the water'.

The moment illustrated is always that of the identification of the traitor, not of the Communion of the Apostles, and Judas very often stretches out his hand to seize the fish lying upon the table. This taking of the fish was probably intended to emphasise Christ's words, 'He that dippeth his hand with me in the dish, the same shall betray me', by showing the traitor grasping an accepted symbol of the Saviour, but later medieval craftsmen probably did not understand this early symbolism, for Judas is shown hiding the fish under the tablecloth in the Malvern windows and in wall-paintings at Ashby St. Ledgers (Northants), which rather suggests some theatrical 'business' expressive of his general knavishness. If so, the playwrights may have drawn this motive, together with much other material, from *The Northern Passion*[6] which tells that Judas

> . . . stole out of his Lordis dish
> The best Morsel of his fish.

Roman social conventions influenced the earliest representations of the Last Supper, in which Christ is seated at the dexter point of a horseshoe table, the accepted post of honour. The second most honoured person sat at the opposite point and the rest of the company ranged in order from his right hand, so that the youngest sat next to the principal, who might accord to a favoured friend the privilege of leaning in front of him.[7] Thus St. John by 'leaning on Jesus' bosom' was only assuming a position normal at a Roman dinner-table, and misunderstanding of this probably gave rise to the familiar pictorial tradition that he was asleep. A straight table accommodating all the Apostles along one side could only be represented on long, narrow panels, as round the font at St. Nicholas, Brighton, or on the stone reredos at Somerton (Oxon). Where space was restricted, the Last Supper was shown with a round, or square table, as on roof bosses, at Salle (Norfolk) or Tewkesbury (Glos). At Madley (Herefs) a 13th-century glazier has solved a similar problem by showing only three Apostles, including St. John sleeping on His Master's breast to make identification certain.

Judas is often represented on the near side of the table, with his back to the spectator. I can remember no case in which he looks out at the spectator and the medieval artists thus obeyed (albeit unconsciously) the Byzantine tradition which forbade such a position for any image representing an evil person. This was based upon the belief that if the eyes of a faithful image met those of the worshippers some actual communion was set up between them and the original of the image.[8]

CHRIST WASHING THE FEET OF THE APOSTLES was represented by a simplified formula upon 4th-century sarcophagi,[9] only St. Peter, and occasionally another Apostle, being shown, but from the 6th century onwards tradition placed Jesus on the left, stooping to wash the feet of Peter, behind whom were grouped the other Apostles. It is thus that we see the subject on the Saxon stone at Wirksworth (Derbs) (PLATE 2) and on the early 12th-century capitals in Southwell Minster. The kneeling posture of Christ was introduced in the 13th century, and in the English version of the *Meditationes Vitae Christi* we read 'For what was that to see the king of bliss and that high lord of majesty kneel to all others that seten about'.[10] The subject occurs rarely in later church decoration.

THE AGONY IN THE GARDEN.—The traditional arrangement shows the Saviour kneeling in the middle distance with the Apostles asleep in the foreground. The 'Cup' is placed upon a bank before Him, or is held by an angel. Sometimes this angel holds the Cross instead, and on a late carving on the pulpit at Bosbury (Herefs) both symbols are shown. The Gospels do not speak of an angel, nor of an actual appearance of the 'Cup' (which is sometimes shown as a chalice with the Host above it), and the convention of representing it thus may have originated in the religious drama. In 15th-century wall-paintings at Shorthampton (Oxon) and Ford (Sussex) the whole background is '*semé*' with drops of blood and it has been suggested that these paintings may have been associated with altars dedicated to the Holy Blood.[11]

The BETRAYAL OF CHRIST is rare as an isolated subject, and the fine alabaster panel at Hawkley (Hants) was probably once part of a retable of Passion scenes. The kiss of Judas naturally forms the central feature, but the incident of St. Peter striking off the ear of the servant, Malchus, is almost equally ubiquitous and it is the device of a drawn sword with an ear upon its blade which represents the Betrayal on the Cornish bench-ends at Poughill and Launcells. The modern observer may wonder whether the emphasis was placed upon the desperate courage of St. Peter or the healing mercy of Christ, and the ordinary medieval parishioner probably understood only the historical allusion, but the scholarly medieval interpretation was quite different. A note appended to a text from St. Ambrose in Graham's *Decretum* runs thus: 'Peter cut off Malchus' ear and Christ restored it to him. From this we may see that if a man hear not (the Church) his ear must be spiritually smitten off by Peter; for it is Peter who hath the power of binding and loosing.'[12]   Thus this passage, divorced from Christ's own rebuke 'all they that take the sword shall perish with the sword' was considered as giving authority for merciless strictness.

The DENIAL OF ST. PETER, often featured in early art, perhaps bringing a message of hope to those who despaired of forgiveness since the Founder of the Church had been forgiven for so terrible a sin.   The scene is usually identified by a cock standing at St. Peter's feet, or perched on a column, and a porphyry column crowned by a bronze cock, which once stood in the Lateran Palace, was popularly believed to be that from which the cock of the Passion had crowed. Since the Gospels do not mention such a column it has been suggested that its acceptance in early Christian art indicates that the cock-on-the-column was an appropriate pre-Christian symbol, a possible proto-type occurring on the Panathenaic amphorae, given to winners in the Games at Athens as early as the 5th century B.C.   On these the goddess Athene is shown standing between two columns surmounted by cocks.[13]

As St. Peter became regarded more exclusively as the Founder of the Church, and the Magdalene took his place as the ideal penitent, the Keys rather than the cock became his attribute, but the connection between the cock and the column continued, albeit with a changed significance, among the Emblems of the Passion.   The carving on a bench-end at Sefton (Lancs) and the screen at Llanrwst (Denbighs) (PLATE 20), show the bird standing on a short column round which is coiled the rope which shows that the craftsman had in mind the pillar of the Flagellation.

The devotional woodcut reproduced in Fig. 3 shows the way in which these emblems expressed the whole story of the Passion, so I shall here confine myself to its less abstract illustrations.   In these we shall note a marked difference of outlook between the early Christian artists, who hardly ever represented the Passion scenes, or did so only with austere symbolism, and those of the mid-13th century onwards who included an increasing complexity of realistic or symbolical details often drawn from extra-Biblical sources.

The FLAGELLATION is rare in early art, and the first miniatures representing it show Our Lord fully clothed.   In 1216 a porphyry column, which had been revered in Jerusalem since the 4th century as part of the Pillar of the Flagellation, was brought to S. Prassede, at Rome, where it still remains,[14] and this may have helped to make the Flagellation a more frequent subject of mystical contemplation. The artistic development of the subject during the 14th and 15th centuries showed an increasing savagery, particularly in northern Europe. The executioners were made hideous, to bespeak their evil passions, their bodies contorted with cruel effort and the artist lays emphasis not so much upon Christ's nobility of pose and expression, as on the multiplication of His wounds. We should, however, be wrong to attribute this treatment to the coarse-fibred imagination of the craftsmen, since the writings of contemporary mystics show us whence they drew their inspiration. Margery Kempe tells how she saw in her contemplation 'Our Lord Jesus Christ bound to a pillar and His hands were bound above His head. And then she saw sixteen men with sixteen scourges and each scourge had eight pellets of lead at the ends and every pellet was full of sharp prickles, as if it had been the rowel of a spur. And those men with the scourges made covenants that each of them should give Our Lord forty strokes.'[15]

The CROWNING WITH THORNS shows us a similar change in approach. A 2nd-century fresco in the Catacomb of Prestatus in Rome shows Christ crowned with leaves rather than thorns, and a soldier touching His head with a long, leafy reed, to illustrate the words of St. Mark (xv. 19) 'and they smote Him on the head with a reed'. In 1238 financial straits forced the Emperor of Constantinople to pledge a relic, reputed to be the true Crown of Thorns, to Louis IX of France, and its journey to Paris had an interesting effect on medieval iconography.[16] The relic was not in fact a crown of *thorns* at all, but a wreath of rushes bound together by twisting ties, and for approximately sixty years after its transit artists showed Christ wearing a spiral fillet round His brows. It was during this period that the Angel Choir of Lincoln was built and in its western bay we see one angel holding such a Crown and another with a spear,[17] presumably the Holy Lance which had also been brought to Paris. The 13th-century glass in the north Rose at Lincoln shows the Crown of Thorns as a green wreath of twisted stems with small trefoil leaves. As English designers perhaps forgot the true appearance of the relic, they began to show the Crown of Thorns with the spiral ties exaggerated into a double twisted cable, and after 1300 the thorns are shown projecting from this with increasing emphasis (PLATE 20). From this date also we see, with few exceptions, the crucified Christ shown wearing the Crown of Thorns, whereas earlier He was often bare-headed upon the Cross, or crowned with a royal diadem.

The mystics who described visions of the Passion and the preachers and actors who reproduced them, all contributed to an increasing brutality of representation. John Mirk's description of how 'after

they had wrythen a crowne of thornys and setten upon His head, and
so betyn it on with staves of reeds that the thornys pierced His brain' [18]
also occurs in a sermon manuscript in St. Albans Cathedral [19] and in
the text of the Towneley plays. From such sources it passed into the
idiom of the artists and we see men pressing down the thorns with
staves in the glass of St. Peter Mancroft, Norwich, on alabaster panels,
and in the carvings on the porch at Tiverton (Devon).

THE BEARING OF THE CROSS.—The early iconography of this
subject shows two conflicting traditions, corresponding to the accounts
given in the Gospel of St. John, where Christ is described as bearing
His Cross, or in the Synoptic Gospels which tell how Simon of Cyrene
was charged with it.[20] A 10th-century stone carving in the church at
Leek (Staffs) which shows a nimbed figure bending beneath the weight
of the Cross is an early example of the tradition which is most frequently
represented. The *Meditationes Vitae Christi* developed the theme of
how Christ fell beneath the load and the medieval playwrights contributed further incidents to enrich its iconography. On the alabaster
reredos at Yarnton (Oxon) the soldiers press upon the Cross to make
it heavier to bear, while a fragment of alabaster at Blunham (Beds)
shows the Virgin trying to share her Son's burden.

The VERNICLE, or kerchief, bearing the portrait of Christ, is often
included among the Emblems of the Passion, but it is only in late
medieval art that we see the legend of its origin in connection with
the Bearing of the Cross represented in churches, as upon the reredos
at Yarnton. M. Émile Mâle attributes this fact to the influence of the
playwrights who supplemented the meagre description of the passage
to Calvary given in the Gospels by introducing legends previously
associated with Our Lord's Ministry.[21] These included several different
accounts of how Christ granted to His followers the portrait which
they deeply desired by imprinting His likeness upon a cloth which
had touched His face.[22] In one version the recipient of the *Vera Ikon*, or
True Picture of Christ, is identified with the woman healed of an issue
of blood and is made one of the 'daughters of Jerusalem' who followed
Christ to Calvary (St. Luke xxiii. 27-8). In this way the legend was
formed of 'St. Veronica' handing Christ the veil from her head to
wipe His brow and receiving it back with His portrait miraculously
imprinted upon it. A fine example of this Vernicle, among the
Emblems of the Passion carved on the bench-ends at Altarnum (Cornwall), seems to recall the older legends by the serene face of Christ
and the absence of the Crown of Thorns.[23]

THE FASTENING TO THE CROSS.—On the Saxon cross shaft in the

church of St. Andrew Auckland (Durham) Christ is fastened to the Cross by ropes, and this feature (which is thought to be of Syrian origin) may have suggested the medieval tradition of the executioners straining Our Lord's arms on to the Cross with ropes because the holes for the nails had been drilled too far apart. This horrible scene in the Chester plays may have been based upon the visions of St. Bridget, or on *The Northern Passion*, a poem translated from a French original in the 14th century.[24] Preachers and playwrights alike probably helped to make this theme accepted as fact and we see it represented on a boss in the transepts of Norwich Cathedral and in a fragment of glass at Stockerston (Leics).

We need not dwell upon the brutal details depicted in some of the Passion pictures in our churches, but we must realise that both the ecstatic love of the visionaries and the crudity of the playwrights were characteristic of the medieval approach, and so both find expression in the art of the Church.

THE CRUCIFIXION.—It is naturally in this subject of supreme solemnity that we find the greatest variety of symbolical detail. It was represented only by abstract symbols in the early Christian art, one of the oldest direct portrayals being the carving on the 5th-century wooden door at Sta Sabina, at Rome. On the 8th-century Saxon grave cover at Wirksworth (Derbs) (PLATE 2) the Lamb of God is carved in the centre of the Cross, a form of representation forbidden by the Eastern Church in 692 but which was used in Britain until at least the 10th century when we find it on the head of the Oswald Cross in the cathedral library at Durham.

When Christ crucified was represented in human form the artists faced a difficult choice between showing Him as the Son of God, not subject to death or pain, but glorified through voluntary sacrifice, or as the Son of Man, dying at the hands of sinners, in atonement for men's sins.[25] Until the 11th century artists mostly represented a living, triumphant Saviour, robed and sometimes crowned, standing in front of the Cross rather than suspended from it. There are two Saxon Roods set on the porch of the church at Langford (Oxon). On the east wall we see the headless figure of a Christ wearing a long straight robe, and with His arms spread horizontally, with no indication of suspense.[26] In another early Rood group above the south door Christ's arms have a curious downward curve which is usually attributed to the stones having been reversed at some later resetting, and this explanation is also put forward to account for a similar curve on the scarred outline which is all that remains of the Saxon Rood at Breamore

(Hants).[27] If the coincidence of such reversal in both places seems too strange, we might associate the meditation of St. Anselm (1033-1109) on the ineffable sweetness of Christ crucified, His head bent as if to kiss, His arms spread wide as though He would embrace all mankind [28] with these Saxon carvings which give to the outspread arms of Christ the curve of protecting wings.

It was not until the 13th century that western artists adopted the convention of the dead Christ, hanging heavily from His arms, although Byzantine designers had used this much earlier, and one feature in this change of iconography provoked passionate controversy. If we are to see medieval religious art through contemporary eyes we must remember that the change from such a Rood as that at Langford, which shows Christ robed, with His feet fastened by two nails, to the type of crucifix, later accepted as normal, on which His crossed feet are pierced by one nail, was thought to involve actual heresy. Luke, Bishop of Tuy, Spain, denounced the new convention, saying of those who favoured it: 'In derision and scorn of Christ's Cross they carve images of Our Lord with one foot lain over the other, so that both are pierced by a single nail, thus striving to annul or to render doubtful men's faith in the Holy Cross and the traditions of the sainted Fathers, by superinducing these diversities and novelties'.[29] Yet in spite of such denunciations the change in imagery was accepted because it corresponded to a change in religious thought.[30]

From the invulnerable grandeur of Divinity, expressed in abstract symbolism, mystics of the 14th and 15th centuries turned to contemplate the physical agony of sacrifice, and the artists visualised Christ's emaciated body, hanging in an arch of pain from almost vertical arms. This last characteristic was exaggerated by the late medieval glaziers since they could thus represent Christ upon the Cross within a single light.

Although it had no Scriptural authority, the belief that the Cross could not have been made from ordinary wood gave rise to a wealth of legends.[31] In the Creation window at St. Neot (Cornwall) we see the first scene of this strange symbolical saga, Seth placing the pips from the Apple of the Fall, given to him by the Angel guarding the gates of Eden, beneath the tongue of the dead Adam. From these pips grew three trees, of which, after many vicissitudes, the Cross of Christ was made. The making of the Cross is shown in the glass from Dale Abbey which is now at Morley (Derbs), as part of the legend of the Invention of Holy Cross by the Empress Helena, a theme which is illustrated in greater detail in a window at Ashton-under-Lyne (Lancs).

Sometimes the dead Adam is shown inside the Hill of Golgotha, indicating that the Cross was raised on his grave. Carved on the rood-screen at East Harling (Norfolk) is a Crucifixion in which the Cross is a tree springing from the body of a recumbent man, but this is more probably Jesse than Adam.[32]

Following the authority of the Gospels the Virgin and St. John are always shown standing beneath the Cross, but during the early Middle Ages they appear rather as statues, in a formalised Rood Group, than as living, suffering, actors in the scene of cosmic tragedy.[33] With the increasing emphasis on pathos in the 14th century we see the Virgin swooning amid a group of other women, as on the font at Salle (Norfolk), but the imagery remaining in our churches does not usually lay that emotional stress upon her sufferings which characterises much later Continental painting and which we see in the 16th-century Flemish carving upon the pulpit at Feering (Essex).

The presence of the Virgin Mary and St. John beneath the Cross is a matter of historical record but both St. Ambrose and Isidore of Seville [34] also explained it symbolically. The Blessed Virgin represented the Church because she alone never lost faith in the Resurrection, while Gregory the Great associated St. John with the Synagogue because of the text: 'the other disciple did outrun Peter and came first to the Sepulchre, yet went he not in '(St. John xx. 4-5).[35] Thus, even where the Church and Synagogue are not actually personified in scenes of the Crucifixion, the contrast between them would have been presented to the thoughts of a medieval scholar [36] while the simpler mind of an ordinary parishioner would have found in the presence here of the Virgin and St. John a renewed assurance that they would also appear at the Last Judgment to intercede for men's souls, and they were thus represented in most Doom paintings.

In all detailed representations of the Crucifixion we see two figures, one holding a lance, the other a reed topped with a sponge, and tradition named the soldier who pierced Christ's side Longinus (from λόγχη, the Greek word for his spear), and the man with the sponge Stephaton.[37] The importance of their inclusion lies in the words of St. John xix. 36, 'For these things were done that the Scripture should be fulfilled'. Longinus always stands on the dexter side of the Cross, for although the Gospels give no guidance and realism would suggest a thrust aimed directly at the heart, the inflexible tradition of the Church dictated that the blood and water, symbols of the Holy Sacraments, issued from the right side of Christ.

Often Longinus points to one of his eyes, an allusion to the legend that he was blind when he aimed his spear at Christ but was healed by the Holy Blood. In a wall-painting at Peakirk (Northants) the eye to which he points is open while the other remains closed.[38] Some artists confused Longinus with the centurion, and an alabaster carving at Drayton Parslow (Bucks) shows both men on horseback.[39] But in the east window of East Harling (Norfolk) the two are correctly identified: Longinus points to his eye and a scroll inscribed '*Vere filiu' dei erat* is placed near the figure of the mounted centurion.

The difference between the two thieves was clearly indicated. The good thief is always on the right hand of Christ and gazes towards Him; sometimes he is given a nimbus. The bad thief averts his head. On the font at Lenton (Notts), in the glass of Hingham (Norfolk) and on a painted panel at Fowlis Easter (Perthshire) an angel is shown bearing the soul of the good thief to Heaven while a demon flies to Hell with that of his companion.[40]

In the sky above Golgotha the sun and moon are often represented, either naturalistically, as on the fonts at Coleshill (Warcs) and Honington (Suffolk) and in glass at Llandyrnog (Denbighs), or by two demi-figures. In a panel of medieval glass recently brought to Stoke d'Abernon (Surrey) the sun and moon are set below the transom of the Cross where personifications of the Old Law and the New are generally shown. Unless this panel has been incorrectly built up from fragments it would seem that the glazier was expressing this symbolical opposition by placing the refulgent sun on the right of Christ and the waning sickle of the moon on His left. This was probably the meaning which many medieval worshippers would have attached to the sun and the moon in such a context, unless they followed the account given in *The Southern Passion* of how the sun was unnaturally eclipsed and the moon withdrew her light from the earth because they 'might not shine, when the Lord of Sun and Moon suffered such pain'.[41] It has been suggested that the ultimate origin of the motive was in the mystical imagery of Babylon or in Mithraic shrines where the sun and moon were often shown in scenes of Mithras slaying the bull.[42]

DESCENT FROM THE CROSS.—Some features which characterise medieval renderings were derived from versions of the apocryphal *Gospel of Nicodemus*: Joseph of Arimathea supporting the body while Nicodemus draws the nail fastening the left hand and the mourning Virgin kissing the right hand which already hangs free. Further details of dramatic poignancy were derived from the visions of later medieval mystics whence also came the ultimate simplification of the scene; the men have vanished, even the Cross is not shown, and he worshipper's field of vision is narrowed to the tragic figure of the Mother with her dead Son lying across her knees. Although this subject is usually called by the Italian term a Pietà, Dr. Kunstle [43] claims for the early 14th-century sculptors of Germany its original conception. It was very often carved in the round, a fact which probably made British examples particularly vulnerable to the icono-clasts and explains their rarity. An alabaster figure (c. 1350) at Breadsall (Derbs) and a battered wooden figure from Battlefield (Salop) alone survive as free-standing statues, but an unscathed relief appears upon the font at Orford (Suffolk).

THE HARROWING OF HELL.—The apocryphal *Gospel of Nicodemus* describes how two recently deceased Jews rose from the dead with Christ, and returned home to give their testimony. They told how a great light shone in Hell before Simeon, followed by John the Baptist, came thither to tell of their earthly knowledge of Jesus.[44] On the Norman tympanum at Quenington (Glos) (PLATE 4) a large sun is shown behind the figure of Christ forcing open the Hell Mouth and represents this 'Dayspring from on high' which pierced even the eternal darkness. Most medieval artists represented Hell in the form of a monstrous head with gaping jaws, a conception possibly derived from the description of Leviathan in Job xli : 'Who can open the doors of his face ? His teeth are terrible round about.' It also explained the dialogue between Satan and Hell, given in the apocryphal Gospel, for if Hell was to answer Satan, it must have a mouth ! The Harrowing of Hell was a favourite subject with 12th-century artists ; we find it on Norman tympana at Beckford (Worcs) and Shobdon (Herefs) and other early carvings occur at South Cerney (Glos), Jevington (Sussex) and on a grave cover in Bristol Cathedral. The cross with which Christ is shown forcing open the Hell Mouth is not the plain instrument of His Passion but the tall processional cross with a floating banner. These two features, the Hell Mouth and the *vexillum*, added by medieval tradition to the original theme, became the most important elements in its iconography, for the first expressed the fulfilment of an Old Testament prophecy and the second added a solemn association to the processional crosses. On one of the bench-ends of Poughill (Corn-wall) a combination of these two emblems was considered adequate to represent the Harrowing of Hell.

THE RESURRECTION.—The first Christian artists shrank from portraying the sublime mystery of the Resurrection and only indicated it by showing the three Maries and the angel at the Sepulchre. On the Norman font at Lenton (Notts) (PLATE 9) we see the Resurrection both prefigured by the raising of Lazarus and attested by the appearance of the angel to the three women. The Sepulchre is here shown with a domed roof supported on columns, recalling a classical mausoleum or perhaps the actual appearance of the tomb chamber in the Church of the Holy Sepulchre at Jerusalem as it was restored by the Crusaders.[45] In the 13th century artists began to show Christ rising from a tomb which was more like a Gothic altar tomb with panelled sides. Since many actual tombs in British churches were used as Easter Sepulchres it was natural for the artists to visualise the Holy Sepulchre in these terms although the Gospel account makes clear that it was a chamber large enough to contain several people. In the glass at Fairford (PLATE 14) the artist has compromised by placing an altar tomb in the entrance to a cave.

In the 14th century several British churches were enriched by elaborately carved Easter Sepulchres intended only for use in this liturgical drama.[46] The most notable examples are those at Heckington (Lincs) and Hawton (Notts) and Fig. 2 shows the simpler form at Patrington (Yorks). In all these cases the lower panels are carved with the figures of sleeping guards, but in 15th-century illustrations of the Resurrection the soldiers often start up in dismay and Christ sometimes steps upon one of them as He leaves the tomb. The influence of the plays is to be seen here, both in the startled gestures which correspond to the lines provided for these soldiers in the plays, and in the practical advantage of giving an actor a human stepping-stone to enable him to 'rise' from a deep tomb-chest with apparently effortless dignity.

The POST-RESURRECTION APPEARANCES OF CHRIST are relatively rare in what remains of our medieval imagery. The *Golden Legend* (i. 96) mentions the first appearance of the risen Lord to His Mother in the house of St. John with considerable reserve, as something which surely should have happened rather than a proven event, so we are lucky to find an illustration of such a rare subject in a window at Fairford (PLATE 14). The background of this panel shows the 'chapel' mentioned by Margery Kempe as the scene of this appearance, and the salutation on the scroll breathed forth by the figure of Christ; *Salve sancta parens* (Hail Holy Parent) is the introit of the Mass of Our Lady from Easter to Pentecost.[47]

The APPEARANCE OF CHRIST TO MARY MAGDALENE occurs in several churches. On the misericord of the Dean's stall in Lincoln Cathedral, the central carving shows the Resurrection and the supporters represent the Magdalene with her pot of spices and Christ wearing a loosely fitting robe and a large hat, and holding an iron-shod wooden spade. There can be little doubt that the carver had seen Him thus portrayed in some play before the actor threw off his disguise at the moment of recognition.

THE INCREDULITY OF ST. THOMAS (St. John xx. 24-9).—This was introduced into composite alabaster retables but does not very often occur as a separate subject. It is shown in a window in All Saints, North Street, York, and a 13th-century wall-painting at Rotherfield (Sussex). On the bench-end at Launcells (Cornwall) (PLATE 12) it is symbolised by a hand touching the wounded Heart which is supported on the *vexillum*.

THE MIRACULOUS DRAUGHT OF FISHES (St. John xxi. 1-13).—There are 12th-century examples of this in the glass at Canterbury and on a capital from Lewes Priory now in the British Museum. Two later examples can be seen in the glass of the Stapleton chantry at North Moreton (Berks) and on a vaulting boss in the transepts of Norwich Cathedral. It has no particular points of iconography which call for comment.

THE ASCENSION.—There were two different traditions in the early iconography of this subject.[48] In one Christ is shown striding up a mountain peak to grasp the Hand of God stretched down to receive Him, in the other he floats upwards in a mandorla surrounded by wings, from which project the heads of the emblems of the Evangelists, or carried by angels. He is often seated upon a segment of a circle, within the mandorla. The prophecy of the 'men in white apparel' that Jesus should come again 'in the like manner as ye have seen him go' (Acts i. 10-11) was so faithfully observed by the medieval artists that many medieval Dooms could be transformed into scenes of the Ascension by the substitution of a group of upward-gazing Apostles for the figures of the Dead rising to Judgment.

In the 11th century a new type of Ascension picture showed Christ disappearing into a cloud so that only His feet and the hem of His garment remain visible. We know that in some churches on Ascension Day an image of Christ was drawn up into the vaulting where it disappeared into a ring of curtains [49] and the highly conventionalised 'clouds' in some later British examples, as on a misericord in Lincoln Cathedral, suggest that the craftsman was visualising the event in terms of such dramatised ritual. Sometimes two footprints are shown upon the rock beneath the feet of the ascending Christ, as on the bench-end at Launcells (PLATE 12) and these refer to the footprints shown to pilgrims in the Church of the Ascension on the Mount of Olives. The apocryphal *Epistle of the Apostles* makes these footprints an affirmation of Christ's bodily Resurrection, for there He bids His disciples mark whether His feet press the earth 'for it is written in the prophet, a phantom of a devil maketh no footprint on the earth'.[50] The number of the Apostles represented at the Ascension varies; there may be as few as ten or as many as twelve, regardless of the fact that Judas's place had not then been filled.

THE PENTECOST (Acts ii).—Some early representations of the Pentecost are so closely linked with the Ascension that it would seem as if the artists were illustrating Christ's promise of the Comforter, spoken, according to St. Luke (xxiv. 49), immediately before His Ascension, rather than the actual Descent of the Holy Ghost. The 13th-century east window of the Corona at Canterbury shows Christ seated upon the rainbow, while rays of fire descend from the cloud under His feet to touch the heads of the Apostles, but such renderings, which show the gifts of the Holy Spirit coming directly from the hands of Christ, are rare and the accepted convention of all later artists showed the Apostles grouped together, with either the Virgin Mary or St. Peter in the centre, while the Holy Dove hovers above them in a downward-darting glory of fire.[51]

CHAPTER 9

HEAVEN AND HELL

ONE of the major differences of outlook between modern and medieval people concerns their belief in Heaven and Hell as concrete places, existing in space and peopled by spirits who influence the daily lives of humankind. We cannot tell how far an educated person in the Middle Ages visualised Hell in terms of the Doom paintings in churches or pictured Heaven according to the imagery of the Apocalypse, for things beyond the power of human minds to conceive, whether in mathematics or religion, can only be expressed in symbols, and the value of such symbols lies in the universality of their acceptance rather than in their realism. Narratives of supposed travellers to the Underworld, and the Fifteen Signs by which the imminent approach of the end of the world could be recognised were widely studied, but the former belong rather to the study of literature and the latter are now only illustrated in the famous 'Prikke of Conscience' window in All Saints, North Street, York,[1] so I will here confine myself to the sources from which medieval artists drew most of the images of Heaven and Hell: the Apocalypse, the teaching of Christ and the vagaries of their own imaginations.

The first pictures of the Apocalypse recorded in any British church are those which Benedict Biscop placed on the north wall of Monkwearmouth but these have long since vanished and, in spite of this early introduction, full illustrations of the Apocalypse are rare, while the ubiquitous Doom is largely composed of motives drawn from other sources. Some Apocalyptic symbols are, however, among the most familiar themes of medieval imagery.[2]

THE AGNUS DEI.—Since the Lamb of God is rarely shown with the seven horns described in the Book of Revelation (v. 6) (an exception occurs on a boss in the Norwich cloisters)[3] we cannot usually tell whether the artists were thinking of the Apocalyptic Lamb or of the words of St. John the Baptist. The Lamb between censing angels in the 12th-century wall-painting above the chancel arch at Hardham (Sussex) almost certainly represents the Adoration of the Lamb which

K   129

figured in the most solemn imagery of the early Church. The same theme is more crudely expressed on many Norman tympana which show the Agnus Dei adored by human figures, or by other animals, as at Langport (Som.) and Aston(Salop). It should be noted that in all cases the Lamb faces to the east.[4]

THE EMBLEMS OF THE EVANGELISTS.—The four creatures described in the Book of the Revelation as having the faces of a lion, a calf, a man and an eagle respectively,[5] were associated with the four Evangelists by the Early Fathers, and iconography makes it clear that these emblems were derived from the Apocalypse rather than from Ezekiel (i. 10) since they never appear with four faces each, as in the prophet's vision.

It was not until the 5th century that their individual associations became accepted and even then the reasons given for these varied. Some writers based their identifications on the opening verses of each Gospel. St. Matthew begins with the earthly descent of Christ (the man), St. Mark with the 'voice crying in the wilderness' (the lion); St. Luke with the sacrifice of Zacharius (the calf), while St. John takes us into the very presence of the Divinity like the eagle soaring up to the sun. Another explanation which appears in the gloss attached to some 13th-century copies of the Apocalypse [6] associates the lion with Christ's Resurrection (see page 174), the calf with His sacrifice, the man with His humanity and the eagle with His divinity, each Evangelist being particularly associated with one of these themes.

The author of *Dives and Pauper* seems to have ignored this symbolism, for when Dives asks why these creatures are painted at the ends of the Cross he is told that the eagle is king of all fowls, the lion of all wild beasts, the ox of all domestic animals, while the man is king of all things visible. In these capacities they attend upon Christ who is king of all things visible and invisible.

While the Apocalypse merely states that the third beast had 'a face as a man', Christian artists at all times depicted the emblem of St. Matthew as an angel. The curious iconographical motive, which we find on such Anglo-Saxon carvings as the crosses at Ilkley (Yorks) and Sandbach (Ches) or the grave cover at Wirksworth (Derbs) (PLATE 2), of showing the Evangelists with human bodies but with the heads of their respective emblems, may derive from the pictorial traditions of paganism for the beast-headed gods of Egypt, and the lion- or bird-head-dresses worn by officiants in the rites of Mithraism offer most plausible prototypes. There was also a Hebrew pictorial tradition of showing persons of a heavenly nature with animal heads.[7] Up to the

12th century the four Creatures usually retain their Apocalyptic association, appearing as attendants upon Christ in Majesty, but in later medieval art their status degenerates into that of identifying attributes of the Evangelists, sometimes serving them in menial capacities, supporting a book or holding an ink-pot.

The WOMAN CLOTHED IN THE SUN with the moon under her feet (Revelation xii) became merged with the Assumption of the Virgin in the imagery of medieval churches. The *Speculum Humanae Salvationis* explains that the crescent moon betokens:

> The steadfastest stableness of Mary perpetual.
> The moon lasts never in one, in fulness nor wasting,
> Tokening this world changeable, and all other earthly things
> Whilk Mary under her feet treads down ilk one, alway.[8]

An unusual example of the Woman Clothed in the Sun occurs in the 15th-century glass of St. Michael, Spurriergate, York, where the Child is bearded, presumably in an attempt to express the text 'she brought forth a man-child who was to rule all nations'. The lower part of the window shows Lucifer among the demons, perhaps reminding us that the 'war in Heaven between Michael and the Dragon' follows immediately on the vision of the Woman Clothed in the Sun, or alluding to the widespread power of the Virgin. A sermon on the Assumption, preserved in the British Museum, associates this vision with the birth of the Virgin and adds that the sign stretcheth down into the depths of Hell, for all the devils there dread the name of this glorious Virgin and are subdued to her power, and she letteth them to tempt her servants to the utterest limit of their malice![9]

M. Émile Mâle [10] has described the debt of early sculptors in southern France to the illuminated manuscripts of a commentary upon the Apocalypse written by Beatus, Abbot of Liebana. A double-page painting of Christ in glory, surrounded by the Four Beasts and with the twenty-four Elders enthroned below Him, served as the prototype of the tympana at Moissac and elsewhere. The Norman tympanum of the west door of Rochester Cathedral is more like this prototype than any other in Britain, being, in iconography as in style, closer to the French architectural tradition. Christ stands in an oval vesica, surrounded by angels and the Emblems of the Evangelists, while the figures of the Elders were probably shown upon the lintel, now sadly weather-worn. At Malmesbury the subject is spread over the whole interior of the south porch; Christ in Majesty, in a vesica supported by angels, is carved over the south door and on the tympana of the east and west walls are groups of enthroned figures. Above their heads great angels sweep in level flight who might fitly sound the Trumpets, or let flow the Vials of the Wrath of God. Christ in Majesty, borne in a mandorla by flying angels, or surrounded by the four Beasts is represented on several Norman tympana, as, for instance, at Elkstone (Glos) or Pedmore (Worcs), but these village carvers did not elaborate further the imagery of the Apocalypse.

It is probable that, in the 12th century, many churches contained wall-paintings of the Apocalypse, but few have survived. At Kempley (Glos) only patient looking will reveal the Golden Candlesticks upon the chancel roof, but at Copford (Essex) the 19th-century restorer has been disastrously industrious. On the apse of St. Gabriel's Chapel, in the crypt of Canterbury Cathedral the Christ in Majesty still appears in the centre of the vault together with Seraphs and the towers of the Heavenly Jerusalem. On the soffit of the arch are the Seven Stars, the Seven Golden Candlesticks and the Seven Angels, together with a figure of St. John writing down the Revelation.[11]

From the later medieval period two magnificent series of illustrations to the Apocalypse have survived, the cloister bosses of Norwich Cathedral and the east window of York Minster. The window was made *c.* 1405 and the bosses are contemporary, or a little earlier. Norwich has the wider range of subjects, since the many bosses of a lierne roof offered greater freedom to the carver, while the glazier concentrated chiefly on subjects of didactic importance, such as the Judgment of the Dead. There may be about a hundred bosses at Norwich illustrating the Apocalypse but the identification of some of these depends only upon their context. Thus a carving of an angel with a trumpet, seen elsewhere, would have no special significance, but here it may recall the 'great voice as of a trumpet' (Revelation i. 10).

When an extensive series of rare subjects is represented in a great church it is natural to suppose that the craftsmen copied the miniatures of a manuscript and at Norwich we can come one step nearer to identifying their model. A boss at the west end of the south alley shows St. John telling of his vision to a group of five figures, and Dr. M. R. James considered that this prelude to the series of Apocalyptic subjects related the carvings to a group of East Anglian Apocalypse manuscripts of which an outstanding example is in the British Museum, Royal MS. 15. D. ii.[12] To show what use the craftsmen could make of such models, we may compare the drawing of the Angel with the Second Trumpet (Fig. 7) from the manuscript belonging to Trinity

Fig. 7. THE ANGEL WITH THE SECOND TRUMPET. TRINITY APOCALYPSE

College, Cambridge,[13] with the roof boss illustrated on PLATE 17. The Angel blowing his trumpet over the sea whose waves are heaped high in one place to indicate the fall of the flaming mountain, the ships in the foreground sinking vertically while their occupants fall into the water and those whose craft are still afloat make gestures of despair, all these elements have been fitted into the restricted circle of the stone boss without either overcrowding or weakening the design.

The second boss illustrated on PLATE 17 shows the Vision of the Son of Man with the Seven Stars and the Seven Candlesticks, but unfortunately the sword issuing from the mouth of 'He who sitteth upon the throne' has been broken away. Faithful following of the lurid imagery of the text sometimes produced unexpected details. Two bridled horses are shown on a boss representing the Vintage of the Earth and in the Trinity Apocalypse we see them with their reins hanging down to touch the streams of blood which 'came from the winepress even unto the horse bridles' (Revelation xiv. 20). The same imagery is repeated at York. Comparison with several manuscripts enabled the restorers of the York window to recognise that several fragments of a monster, scattered in various panels, were the Hell Mouth into which the victims of the Rider on the Pale Horse should be drawn.[14]

The Doom which was represented in almost every church borrowed little of its imagery from the Book of Revelation, for the obscure symbolism of the Apocalypse was both less effective for the instruction of a semi-literate congregation, and less authoritative, than Our Lord's description of the Day of Judgment to come.

The most complete example of a Doom painting, somewhat restored, is that in St. Thomas' Church, Salisbury (PLATE I), dating from the late 15th century. In this we can see how the artists, like the preachers, were relating contemporary social abuses with the idea of ultimate condemnation. The Dominican preacher, John de Bromyard, described how, on the left hand of the Judge shall stand 'the harsh lords who plundered the people of God with grievous fines . . . the wicked ecclesiastics who failed to nourish the poor with the goods of Christ . . . the usurers and false merchants who deceived Christ's members'. The victims accuse their oppressors in words adapted from those of Christ. 'We have hungered and died of famine and those yonder did detain our goods that were owing to us' or 'We were in prison and those yonder were the cause, indicting us on false charges and setting us in the stocks', and the excuses put forward by the rich are swept aside by the Judge.[15] The artists show the souls of the great (dis-

(Middlesex), Lenham (Kent) and South Leigh (Oxon) to name only a few examples. On a tomb at Harewood (Yorks) the rosary hangs on one scale of the archangel's balance, although the figure of the Virgin is not shown. In the great Doom paintings the Blessed Virgin is shown kneeling in supplication to her Son.

This chapter would be incomplete without some mention of those denizens of Heaven and Hell who play such an important part in the imagery of our churches, yet whose appearance is so familiar that few people wonder how angels, or devils, came to be thus represented. The Jews seem to have pictured the Cherubim as winged, human-headed animals, deriving partly from the Egyptian sphinx, and the Seraphim as serpent-like creatures with wings.[22] Winged human figures had been common in classical art and the Winged Victory of Samothrace represents the ultimate glorification of many humbler genii. In Christian art seraphs are sometimes shown with only a face and six wings, but most angels were conceived anthropomorphically from the beginning. Since 'the angel of the Lord' in the Old Testament was often mistaken for an ordinary man, the earliest angels were wingless, but in British churches even the oldest Saxon angels, at Breedon-on-the-Hill (Leics), Bradford-on-Avon or Winterborne Steepleton (Dorset), have wings *and* arms, in defiance of anatomical possibility.

The famous censing angels of the triforium of Westminster Abbey, or those of the Angel Choir at Lincoln, are sexless beings, aloof and eternally young. Their long robes fall in delicate folds and are simply girdled at the waist, but the accoutrements of later angels are more complicated and were probably derived from the costumes of actors in the Gild plays. These also account for the angels in feathered tights with bare hands and feet. Particularly elaborate costumes are shown in the carvings of the Beauchamp Chapel at Warwick [23] and on the rood-screen at Southwold (Suffolk).

The conception of the 'Nine Orders of Angels' is based upon texts in Colossians i. 16, 'By him were all things created . . . whether they be thrones, or dominions, or principalities', and Ephesians i. 21, 'far above all principality, and power and might and dominion'. In Wycliffe's translation 'might' was rendered as 'vertu', and from these two texts came the five categories which, with Cherubim and Seraphim, angels and archangels made up the Nine Orders. The *Golden Legend* (v. 184-7) gives an elaborate description of these Orders as grouped in three hierarchies. The highest Orders, Cherubim, Seraphim and Thrones 'assist God and be converted to Him'. The Dominions, Virtues and Potestates 'dominate and govern the university of people in common'. The third Hierarchy, the principates, archangels and angels have a more limited rule, archangels governing particular nations or cities while with the angels 'their service and ministry is limited unto one man'. Usually the Nine Orders are shown as subsidiary figures, in the tracery lights, but at St. Michael, Spurriergate, York, a whole window is devoted to them. The seraphs are distinguished by their six wings, the Thrones are crowned and one of them holds the scales of Justice; Principalities and Dominions are shown as knights in contemporary armour, and one of them has the arms of Holy Trinity (Fig. 1) blazoned on his shield. The Powers are less war-like but one of them holds a birch-rod as a symbol of government. Among the varied forms of angels in the bottom panels is one with feathered legs who stands among ripe corn, the Apocalyptic Reaper of the Harvest of the Earth.

In no other country have the plastic possibilities of angels' wings been so richly exploited as in England. Their long pinions sweep forward to fill the spandrels of arcades, or are squared above the shields they hold, with the Emblems of the Passion, or the heraldry of benefactors, blazoned upon them (PLATE 18). Heaven's eternal song of praise is represented by angels with musical instruments; the bosses above the High Altar of Gloucester Cathedral show an orchestra of angel musicians, holding examples of most of the instruments known to the Middle Ages.[24] In the tracery of many windows the angelic musicians are interspersed with others holding scrolls, on which are inscribed the opening words of canticles, or phrases from the liturgy, to emphasise the connection between the Church festivals and those events in the life of Christ, or of the saints, which were once illustrated in the lower lights.[25] Lastly, but most impressive of all, perhaps, we have the great angel roofs of East Anglian churches where winged figures are carved upon every projection of the hammer-beam roofs; tier above tier of wings soaring up into the darkness of the rafters.

The evolution of devils was naturally less orderly, being chiefly directed by popular fancy. What we might call 'the basic devil' was probably derived from the faun of classical mythology, for this creature, half goat, half human, was associated by the early Christians with the devils, elves and fallen angels who all inhabited the wild woods. In the medieval Hell Lucifer preserved no trace of his fatal beauty, and the only instance I remember in which a carver seems to allude to the angelic past of a demon is on a misericord at Gayton (Northants). Only the talons upon hands and feet distinguish this amiable feathered being from an ordinary angel, but the fact that he grips a man and a woman, one of whom holds a conspicuous rosary, shows us that we have here one of the few devils whose precise function in the world of evil we know. This subject, which also occurs on a misericord at Enville (Staffs) and on a boss at Wakerley (Northants) and a corbel at Berkeley (Glos), finds its clearest illustration on a misericord at Ely. It refers to the story told in the sermon manual 'Jacob's Well',[26] of how a devil was seen writing down all the idle talk he overheard in church and having to draw out his scroll with his teeth, because it was all too short for his purpose.

CHAPTER 10

THE LIFE OF THE VIRGIN MARY

THE iconoclasts fell with particular fury upon images of the Madonna; few important carvings escaped grave damage and of the thousands of windows which must have represented the Virgin and Child only a few remain intact. Natural decay as well as deliberate damage has obliterated most wall-paintings, but the exquisitely tender 13th-century roundel of the Virgin and Child in the Bishop's Palace at Chichester remains as one of the accepted masterpieces of British painting. A few early carvings escaped; on the Saxon crosses at Shelford (Notts) and Nunburnholme (Yorks) and an 11th-century fragment at Inglesham (Wilts) which shows the Virgin and Child beneath the Hand of God. The 12th-century tympanum at Fownhope (Herefs) is distinguished not only by its barbaric vitality but as an unusually early example of the Virgin and Child being shown in that position. If we wish to find an undamaged carving of the Madonna from the later medieval periods we must seek it on bosses or capitals, beyond the reach of hammering fanatics, or in hidden places, as between the folded hands of the effigy of Lady Alicia de Mohun at Axminster (Devon). Some Lords of the Manor may have protected the imagery of their family tombs, for a stone Virgin still watches over the effigy of Sir John Lyon at Warkworth (Northants) and the crowned Virgin-with-the-Rosebush on a tomb at Willoughby-on-the-Wolds (Notts) is intact, although the upturned face and arms of the suckling Child have been broken (PLATE 18). There are thus too few examples to illustrate the different iconographical traditions, such as the 'Madonna with the writing Child' [1] or 'The Suckling Madonna', [2] and I will concentrate upon the surviving illustrations of the Life of the Virgin and of her posthumous miracles. [3]

Early Christian artists did not single out the Virgin Mary for special reverence, and it was not until after the Council of Ephesus had condemned the Nestorian heresy (which maintained a distinction between the divine and human natures in Christ and opposed the use of the title *Theotokos*, Mother of God) that she was represented enthroned and crowned. The dedications of ancient British churches reflect this mounting tide of honour; among those mentioned by Bede only three were dedicated to Saint Mary, but her dedications among the later medieval churches outnumber those to any other saint.[4]

M. Émile Mâle considers that the carvings of the Adoration of the Magi which appear on the 12th-century tympana of several French churches, such as Saint-Gilles and Neuilly-en-Donjon (Allier), were expressions of this growing reverence since they represent her as Queen of Heaven enthroned and crowned.[5] The 'Adoration of the Magi' is probably carved on the Norman tympanum at Bishops-teignton (Devon), although the figure of the Blessed Virgin has lost the Child, and on the Norman font at Cowlam (Yorks) the three Kings do homage before a throne and both the Virgin and Child wear lofty diadems. This subject also appears on the early font at Sculthorpe (Norfolk).

While theologians thus exalted the meek Virgin to transcendental majesty, the simple folk tried to draw her nearer to their own apprehension of life by craving to learn more of her earthly life and benevolent intervention on behalf of those who truly honoured her, however ignorant, or sinful, they might have been. As the Evangelists said nothing of the parentage and early life of the Virgin Mary, it was natural that the oldest apocryphal Gospel, the 'Book of James' (later called the *Protevangelium*),[6] should have supplied this lack and it is here that we first learn the names of her parents, Joachim and Anne. The Book of James is certainly as old as the 2nd century in which was also written the Gospel of Thomas, which covers the next big gap in the Gospels, from the Flight into Egypt until the dispute with the Doctors in the Temple. At some time between the 6th and 7th centuries those two texts were combined in the *Liber de infantia B.V. Mariae et Saluatoris*, or Gospel of Pseudo-Matthew, from which the medieval artists drew many of the subjects which we must now consider.

The ornate arcading round the interior of the Lady Chapel at Ely once comprised a full series of carvings based upon the apocryphal Gospels and the miracles of the Virgin, but unfortunately the soft clunch of which it is made was particularly liable to damage, and few of the figures are undamaged. The late Dr. M. R. James was, however, able to identify most of the carved groups and upon this sequence I will base my outline of the life of the Virgin as it was portrayed in the Middle Ages.[7]

The first two groups show us the rejection of Joachim's offering and the angel appearing to him when he had retired, in lonely shame, to watch his flocks upon the hills. The angel's annunciation to Anne, that she should bear a child, comes next and one of the two figures in the background of this group probably represents Judith, the handmaiden who mocked her mistress's childlessness. In a window at Malvern which illustrates this subject we see the nest of sparrows in the laurel tree which called forth the anguished lamentation of Anne: 'I am not likened unto the fowls of the heaven, for even the fowls of the heaven are fruitful'.[8]   The meeting of Joachim and Anne at the Golden Gate was a popular subject from the 13th century onwards, because it was believed that the conception of the Virgin Mary took place at that moment. The pictorial tradition varies little, husband and wife being always shown in profile, embracing each other in front of a city gate.

The Birth of the Virgin, which rarely has any details of particular significance, is usually followed by the Presentation of Mary in the Temple (PLATE 15). This subject became increasingly popular after the institution of the Feast of the Presentation of Mary, in 1372,[9] and the mere mention of it calls up memories of paintings showing the child Virgin ascending a massive flight of steps in the dignified loneliness of predestined sanctity. The prominence given to these steps, even when the Temple is represented as a Gothic church, unlikely to have such an approach, was not fortuitous, for they were associated with the Fifteen Gradual Psalms and one version of the Pseudo-Matthew described how the child Mary recited these psalms as she climbed the stair and never looked back. In the Coventry plays this episode is developed at length.[10]   The next carving at Ely shows Mary in the Temple, receiving in a boat-shaped dish the food which an angel brought to her daily. A hanging drapery prominent in the background of this carving probably represented the Veil of the Temple, for which Mary spun the purple and scarlet thread.

Dr. M. R. James identified a wall-painting at Croughton (Northants) as Joachim bringing the Virgin Mary to the High Priest to be betrothed. This divergence from the apocryphal Gospels, which tell that she remained in the Temple until her betrothal,[11] may have been inspired by the drama for it also occurs in the Coventry plays.[12]   Perhaps the great popularity of the subject of 'St. Anne teaching the Virgin to read' suggested this rearrangement in order to justify a later sojourn of Mary in her parents' house? The cult of St. Anne had become widespread by the later Middle Ages and the obvious way to identify her images was to show her with the child

Virgin. The reading lesson, which is still represented in all its touching beauty in many churches, avoided any risk of appearing to treat the figure of the Virgin Mary as an attribute. The pages upon which mother and daughter concentrate their attention bear different inscriptions in various windows. At Queenhill (Worcs) it is A B C, at Stanford-on-Avon (Northants) the opening words of the Office *Domine labia mea aperies*, and in the east window of All Saints, North Street, York, which has perhaps the most charming example of all, *Domine exaudi orationem meam.*

Three panels in the north aisle at Malvern illustrate the rare subject of choosing a husband for the Virgin Mary. An inscription identifies a scene of the Virgin standing before an altar, with two other maidens, as Mary's refusal to break her vow of virginity when the High Priest ordered husbands to be found for all virgins brought up within the Temple. The next panel perhaps represents the priests' prayer for guidance in answer to which an angel bade them command all suitors of the House of David to bring rods into the Temple, since the rod of the divinely chosen husband should blossom and a dove descend upon it. A third panel at Malvern shows Joseph as an old man receiving from the High Priest a short golden rod tipped with a flower, above which a dove hovers in glory, following the account given in the *Golden Legend*, v. 102-3. The betrothal is shown at Ely and Croughton, but the clearest illustration I know of these early scenes from the life of the Virgin Mary is the 16th-century Flemish window now at Elford (Staffs) (PLATE 15). Here the steps of the Temple form the central feature of a design cleverly conceived in the dimensions of both time and space. Joachim and Anne are prominent in the foreground, while the child Virgin is ascending the steps towards the altar where the High Priest awaits her coming. On each side of him are groups of figures, smaller as though still remote in the future: one shows the disappointed suitors holding their barren rods while Joseph turns away to gaze at his, transformed into a flowering lily; the other shows the betrothal before the High Priest. The choice of Joseph, with the Virgin kneeling before an altar, is also shown in a fragment of 13th-century glass in the north rose of Lincoln Cathedral.

Most of the incidents associated with the Nativity and Infancy of Christ have already been discussed, but one more, particularly connected with the Virgin Mary, may be mentioned here. Dr. M. R. James identified some small figures in the background of the carving at Ely which represents St. Joseph leading the pregnant Virgin to Bethlehem, as the unique illustration in western art of the laughing and weeping people whom Mary then beheld, and who foreshadowed the future joy of the Gentiles and the grief of the Jews.[13]   The next carving at Ely shows an angel leading Mary into the desert cave of the early Nativity tradition, while Joseph stands by the ass.

The next subjects which we must consider are those connected with the festivals by which the Church celebrated the death (or Dormition) of the Blessed Virgin and her Assumption.   A full series of such illustrations usually begins with the appearance of an angel to the Virgin, announcing her impending death and bringing a palm branch (this was shown in the Croughton wall-paintings) which she later gave to St. John, commanding him to bear it before her funeral procession.   This second scene is represented in St. Peter Mancroft, Norwich, by a copy of the original glass, now at Felbrigg Hall (Norfolk), and the tradition of it probably accounts for the palm borne by figures of St. John upon tombs at Tong (Salop) and Harewood (Yorks) (PLATE 8) (see also page 154).   The miraculous gathering together of the Apostles from all parts of the world is illustrated in the glass at St. Peter Mancroft by five demi-figures riding upon clouds and this rare subject was also represented in the wall-paintings at Croughton, and perhaps at Cold Overton (Leics).   In most cases this miracle is merely implied by showing all the Apostles grouped round the death-bed, with Christ in the centre, beyond the bed, holding in His arms the little figure which symbolises His Mother's soul.

The funeral procession is often represented because of the legend of the Jew who tried to overset the bier and whose impious hands withered away and remained attached to the pall, until he confessed faith in Christ and that He was the son of the Blessed Virgin, whereupon they were healed.[14]   In the paintings at Croughton several figures seem to be attacking the bier, as in some versions of the apocryphal narrative, but most artists followed those texts which speak only of one mighty Jew.   The glass in St. Peter Mancroft shows him as a man in armour with his hands fast upon the pall, and a second man lying on the ground is probably the glazier's way of expressing two moments of time on the same panel.[15]   This miracle was also illustrated in the Eton wall-paintings, in a carving below the south window of the choir at Dorchester (Oxon) and in glass at Gresford (Denbighs) North Moreton (Berks) and Stoke d'Abernon (Surrey).   A fragment also remains in the south transept of Lincoln Cathedral.   With the exception of this last all these date from the 14th century, or later.   On the Continent the miracle of the Jew only appears in these later periods, but in Britain we have an exceptionally interesting example on the

8th-century grave cover at Wirksworth (Derbs) (PLATE 2). The figure of St. John bearing the palm branch, and the fallen Jew whose hand still touches the bier identify the group in the top left-hand corner, and the six heads surrounded by a solid ring immediately above the bier recall a verse in the text according to the pseudo-Mellito (chap. xii) : 'There appeared a very great cloud over the bier, like the great circle that useth to be seen about the splendour of the moon : and an host of angels was in the cloud sending forth a song of sweetness'.[16]

The scene of the burial may have been represented on wall-paintings at Chalgrove and Broughton (Oxon) and at Croughton (Northants), but most artists passed directly to the Assumption of the Virgin, showing her borne up by angels in a mandorla, and frequently anticipated her Coronation by showing her already crowned. At Broughton the painting of the Assumption includes an allusion to the legend of the Virgin casting down her girdle from Heaven to convince St. Thomas, who had arrived too late to witness it.[17] The clearest reference to this legend I know is the boss in the porch of Peterborough Cathedral which shows the ascending Virgin holding a thick strap in her hands.[18] This girdle was honoured at Prato as a most holy relic.[19] At Ely a small figure kneeling upon a hill, in the background of the Assumption, may represent St. Thomas beholding it from afar (according to another version of the text), or the still rarer subject of the Virgin withdrawing to the Mount of Olives to pray after the visit of the angel.

In his sermon on the Assumption John Mirk describes how Our Lord called His Mother to Him, with that lyric simplicity which also characterises many of the early medieval renderings of the Coronation of the Virgin, a subject which is heralded by the form of the Son's greeting.

> Come my sweet, come my flower,
> Come my culver [dove] mine own bower,
> Come my Mother now with me
> For Heaven's Queen I make thee! . . .

and so with all this mirth and melody they bare Our Lady into Heaven, both body and soul, and so Christ set her there by Him on His throne, and crowned her Queen of Heaven, Empress of Hell and lady of all the world.[20]

The theme of the Coronation of the Virgin seems to have developed in western Europe during the 12th century, and England can perhaps claim the earliest surviving illustration of it in monumental art, on a capital from Reading Abbey, now in the Victoria and Albert Museum.

Another 12th-century carving of the subject occurs over the south door at Quenington (Glos). At first the Blessed Virgin was shown sitting beside Christ upon a long seat, meekly bowing towards him as he placed the crown upon her head, as we see them on the beautiful 13th-century boss from the choir of Lincoln Cathedral (PLATE 16). In the 15th century a more elaborate iconography, originating probably in northern Europe, showed the Virgin crowned by all Three Persons of the Holy Trinity, as in the east window of Holy Trinity, Goodramgate, York. Here the Three Persons are represented by identical human forms, but more often the Holy Dove hovers above the Father and the Son, while the Virgin kneels before them. This three-fold crowning of the Blessed Virgin, or else her triple empire, is symbolised in the windows of St. Denys, Walmgate, York, and East Brent (Somerset) by a crown like the papal tiara. The Coronation appears on vaulting bosses more often than any other presentation of the Blessed Virgin, perhaps because, taking place in Heaven, it was considered peculiarly appropriate to roof decoration, or merely because the subject, once equally favoured in more vulnerable positions, was here beyond the reach of vandals.

Posthumous miracles of the Blessed Virgin were recorded as early as the 5th century, but it was the period between the 11th and 15th centuries which saw their most rapid multiplication. Some of the oldest legends are of eastern origin and as the period of their rapid increase coincides with that of the Crusades, they were perhaps brought back by returning Crusaders, whose inaccurate memories may account for their multiple versions. Some of the legends originating in western Europe are localised by the names of places, or people, while others are clearly adapted from existing folk stories.[21]

The legend most popular with medieval artists was that of Theophilus of Adana, who sold his soul to the Devil in order to recover a high ecclesiastical office.[22] When the Devil had paid the price, Theophilus repented bitterly and spent forty nights in fasting and prayer. At last he fell asleep and was visited by a vision of the Virgin who gave him back his infernal contract and bade him confess his sin to the bishop. In the 13th-century glass of Lincoln Cathedral four panels are devoted to this legend, the figure of Theophilus being identified by an inscription. The Jewish magician introduces Theophilus to the demon who buys his soul; the Virgin is shown recovering the contract from a yellow, woolly devil with a red beak and horns and the penitent finally shows this contract to his bishop.[23] The subject is also shown in the Canterbury windows, in carvings at Ely and on the altar-screen of Beverley Minster. The importance attached to this miracle in medieval minds can be gauged by the fact that a 12th-century carving, which was originally the tympanum of the church portal at Souillac, France, is quoted by M. Émile Mâle as the first work of monumental art dedicated to the Virgin alone, not in connexion with her Son.[24]

Another early eastern legend is that of the Virgin raising a warrior saint from the dead to do battle against the Emperor Julian the Apostate, in response to the prayers of St. Basil. Originally told of St. Mercurius, the legend was frequently applied to St. George in English art. The arming of St. George is shown in the glass at Madley (Herefs) and St. Neot (Cornwall) in a wall-painting at Astbury (Ches) and on a poppy-head in St. George's Chapel, Windsor. There are further scenes from the legend in the carvings at Ely, but the fullest sequence of illustrations is shown on the cloister bosses at Norwich.[25] Here are shown St. Basil with the offering of bread which the Emperor rejected as an insult, the Virgin appearing in answer to the saint's prayer, the arming of St. George and the victorious combat of the saint, who is protected by an angel while a devil tries in vain to assist his own champion.

Another boss in the Norwich cloisters shows the legend of the Jew of Bourges whose child went to Mass and received the Sacrament from a beautiful lady whom he beheld standing by the altar. When he told his parents, his father threw him into an oven, but when his mother's cries brought Christian helpers to the scene they found the child unhurt, playing with the flames and eager to tell how the same beautiful lady had wrapped him in her mantle. This legend also appears in the glass of Lincoln Cathedral and a carving at Ely. Traces of it remained in the paintings of the College Chapel at Eton [26] where the restored paintings also show the miracles of the knight who sold his wife to the Devil (the Virgin took the poor woman's place as she knelt in prayer, and thus confounded the fiend) and of the woman who assisted, in a vision, at High Mass on Candlemas Day with all the saints and the Blessed Virgin herself, and who retained a portion of the candle there given to her, when she awoke. This was the Holy Candle treasured at Arras.

Another panel at Eton shows one of many legends describing the compulsion applied to the Virgin by some supplicants. A woman whose son is a captive, seizes the Child from the arms of an image of the Virgin and only replaces it when her own son is miraculously restored to her. The Virgin's protection of the ignorant priest who could only say the Mass of Our Lady is painted there and also in Winchester Cathedral.[26]   Most of the panels on the south wall at Eton show scenes from the legend of the Empress unjustly accused, which also furnished the subjects for many bosses in the Bauchun Chapel, Norwich Cathedral.[27]   This is an example of the adapted folk story into which the role of the Virgin has been introduced, and a slightly different version of it is given by Chaucer in the *Man of Law's Tale*.

The Emblems of the Blessed Virgin are often introduced into the decoration of the churches.   Her crowned 'M' appears on East

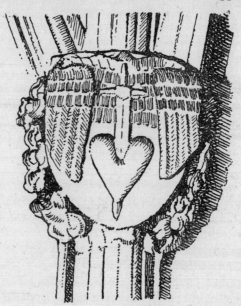

FIG. 8.   THE BADGE OF THE BLESSED VIRGIN MARY

Anglian churches, inlaid in stone upon the dark wall surface of cut flint, and the rose and the lily are carved on capitals and bench-ends. These emblems need no explanation but her heraldic badge is more complex.   A boss in Bristol Cathedral (Fig. 8) shows this badge clearly: the sword transfixing the heart refers to the prophecy of Simeon, 'Yea, a sword shall pierce through thy own soul also' (St. Luke ii. 35), and the wings recall the angel of the Annunciation.[28]

Although the Joys and Sorrows of the Blessed Virgin had been subjects of devout meditation before St. Dominic (1170–1221) associated with the 165 beads of the Rosary the saying of one Paternoster, ten Aves and one Gloria for each of the Five Joyful, Five

148

Sorrowful and Five Glorious Mysteries of the Blessed Virgin,[29] it was not until the late 14th century that the latter were more particularly celebrated. On the Continent late medieval artists expressed the Seven Dolours of Mary by showing the Virgin standing with seven swords radiating like an aureole from her heart, and this subject occurs in foreign glass in St. Mary's Church, Shrewsbury. A window at Butcombe (Somerset) shows the winged heart with seven drops of blood upon it, to express the same meaning.[30]

The verse from Ezekiel xliv. 2, 'This gate shall be shut, it shall not be opened, and no man shall enter in by it ; because the Lord, the God of Israel, hath entered in by it . . .' made The Closed Door a very ancient type of the Virginity of Mary. On misericords at Lincoln, Norwich (PLATE 23) and Holy Trinity, Coventry, there are carvings of fortified gateways, made about the same time that John Mirk was writing the sermon in which he interprets the Gospel for the Feast of the Assumption (which tells of the visit of Christ to the house of Martha and Mary) as a symbolical glorification of the Blessed Virgin. She was the castle into which Christ entered at His incarnation and, unlike most weak women, she was 'strong as a castle and withstood the assaults of the fiend . . . for right as a castle wall hath a deep ditch . . . so hath Our Lady a ditch of meekness so deep down into the earth of her heart that there might never no man go over it'. Her tears, shed during the Passion, were likened to the water which filled that ditch and her discreet obedience in accepting the Annunciation was the drawbridge which she lowered across it. The castle has a double ward ; the front part is low to signify her patience and her wedlock, while the high inner ward symbolises her virginity. A gate in this wall betokened faith, for 'whereas it was seemingly impossible that she should conceive without union of man . . . she by teaching of the angel, believed, and so came Christ and entered by this gate of belief into the body of Our Lady'.[31] The double ward is clearly shown in the carving at Norwich and the inner ward is topped by a roof with chevron markings like the base of a leaded church spire, reminding us that the Virgin often personified the Church upon earth. Between the outer and inner walls there are trees, so the designer probably also had in mind another type of the Virgin, suggested by the Song of Solomon (iv. 12), 'A garden inclosed is my sister, my spouse'.

Mirk's *Festial* cannot be considered as typical of the sermons preached in parish churches throughout Britain, and in this sermon he was probably rationalising the purely pictorial features of some image of The Closed Door which was familiar to him. Nevertheless, his words exemplify the symbolical meanings which could have been associated with such a carving by a parishioner of a mystical turn of mind, while to another, as to the majority of churchgoers to-day, it appeared only as a well-designed representation of a medieval walled town.

CHAPTER II

THE SAINTS

THERE are more books written about the lives of the saints and their attributes than on any other single aspect of medieval iconography, ranging from the monumental *Acta Sanctorum* of the Bollandists to several concise popular handbooks.[1] So, instead of attempting to summarise this information as it applies to the saints who occur most frequently in our medieval imagery, I will discuss the context in which medieval parishioners probably regarded them.

Saints are like the mountain peaks of human nature and, like other mountains, they differ in kind. Some are as authentic as the Alps and inspire us by their lofty steadfastness; others have arisen like a mirage from the deserts of ignorant and superstitious minds, and there are also many who were probably real men and women but whose lives now seem cloud-hidden and remote. The authors of many medieval 'Lives' of the saints embroidered the few known facts with so many miracles and legends, generally borrowed from other 'Lives', that their compilations often have little historical value. Yet real stories of heroism may lie behind their borrowed motives, or those based upon misunderstanding of ancient symbols. St. Denis, or St. Osyth, are most unlikely to have walked about, carrying their own heads, after they had been decapitated, but our rejection of this picturesque legend need not imply that they did not faithfully endure the martyrdom to which earlier artists were alluding when they showed such saints with their severed heads in their hands, as we see St. Denis in a window at Methley (Yorks) and St. Osyth in the glass of Long Melford (Suffolk).[2] The evil which the saints overcame was none the less real because it did not take the form of the symbolical dragon from whose belly St. Margaret burst forth, or which St. Armel haltered with his stole as is shown by his statue in Henry VII's Chapel, Westminster, and an alabaster panel at Stonyhurst College (Lancs).

In the later Middle Ages these lives of the saints were read aloud in religious houses during meals, while the laity knew them either from their private reading or from the lections in the Breviary which

were read in the churches at Matins on the saint's day. In addition
to the general collections of 'Lives', some religious communities collected biographies of saints more particularly connected with their
house, and, from the 14th century onwards more collections of lives
of English saints were written [3] which corresponds to their increasing
representation in sculpture and glass. By far the most famous of such
collections of 'Lives' is the *Golden Legend*, which was compiled by
Jacobus de Voragine, Archbishop of Genoa *c.* 1275, from such earlier
authorities as St. Jerome's *Lives of the Fathers* and the *Ecclesiastical
History of Eusebius*, together with contemporary legends and traditions.
In William Caxton's translation the ordinary reader will find most of
the legends which explain the scenes from the lives of saints represented
in medieval imagery.[4]

It seems to me the best way to focus upon a few pages this vast
theme is to follow the arrangement, at once so familiar and so solemn,
of the *Te Deum*, which has been sung in Christian churches ever since
the 4th century. So let its stately words help us to picture the windows
of a medieval church aglow with the figures of saints in richly coloured
robes, paintings of their lives and martyrdoms upon the walls and
their images carved on reredos and tomb, and stalls, so that those who
attended Mass saw everywhere reminders that their act of worship
was one with the eternal homage of the saints in Heaven.

'The glorious company of the Apostles' is rarely represented as a
group, except in such Gospel scenes as the Last Supper or Pentecost,
but in stained glass we very often find a series of single figures, each
breathing forth a scroll on which appears a phrase of the Apostles'
Creed. The tradition that all the Apostles combined to compose the
Creed is mentioned *c.* 400,[5] but it is in a sermon attributed to St.
Augustine of Hippo, although probably later, that each article of that
Creed is associated with a particular Apostle.[6] 'Creed Windows' were
once common in British churches, to judge by the remaining frag-
ments,[7] and the Fairford windows have shown us how each Apostle
was associated with a member of 'the goodly fellowship of Prophets'.
To St. Peter, whose figure in the south aisle windows proclaims:
'I believe in God the Father Almighty, maker of Heaven and Earth',
Jeremiah answers from the north, with two quotations merged into a
single prophecy, 'Thou shalt call me, My father' (iii. 19) and 'Ah Lord
God ! behold thou hast made the heaven and the earth by thy great
power' (xxxii. 17). St. Andrew's phrase, 'and in Jesus Christ, His only
Son, Our Lord', is foreshadowed by the verses from the second Psalm
of David, 'The Lord hath said unto me, thou art my son ; this day

have I begotten thee'. The texts allotted to the prophets are not always correctly assigned ; a verse from Zephaniah iii. 9 is attributed to Micah, not only in the Fairford windows and on the 15th-century painted screen at Thornham (Norfolk), but also in Queen Mary's Psalter.[8] The fault may have lain with some scribe who miscopied his original text as the passage from another pseudo-Augustinian sermon, in which the preacher calls upon the Jewish prophets to testify how the coming of Christ was foretold, was gradually developed into the liturgical drama, the *Prophetae*. (The full Creed sequence is given in Appendix 3.)

In spite of occasional errors, the great figures of the Old and New Testaments seem to march abreast in their testimony, like the parallel piers of a great arcade, and in some places they are also associated with the Sibyls, expressing the belief that classical antiquity had also known foreshadowings of Christ. A 15th-century Dominican, Filippo Barbieri, wrote a treatise in which he assigned such prophecies, and also attributes referring to them, to each of twelve sibyls, and his text was a frequent source of inspiration to late medieval artists. The sibyls are painted on the Devon screens at Ugborough, Heavitree, Exeter and Bradninch, and isolated figures, the remains of similar series, occur on the screen at Ipplepen (Devon) and in the east window at Coughton (Warcs). The allocation of attributes to the sibyls is variable, which makes certain identification very difficult, when their names are not given. The Sibylla Persica generally holds a lantern in which the light glimmers feebly, because she foretold the Saviour, albeit obscurely, while Samia has a cradle because she prophesied that a child should be born of a poor maiden, and the beasts of the earth should adore Him.[9]

Apart from the full series of Apostles, generally associated with the Creed, surprisingly few of them appear singly. Their relative popularity as patron saints of churches also shows an apparent capriciousness which raises interesting problems, but these lie outside my scope. Most of the Apostles are shown as noble, bearded figures with no individuality except that conferred by their attributes, or such a detail as the spectacles given to the statue of St. Matthew in Henry VII's Chapel, Westminster, referring to his clerical occupation before he was called. The exceptions to this rule are interesting.

The physical appearance of both St. Peter and St. Paul seems to have been determined by ancient tradition. St. Peter always has a square bushy beard, and a ring of thick hair surrounding a bald crown, like the Roman tonsure. In the *Golden Legend* (iii. 52) we read that 'when St. Peter preached the first time in the city of Antioch, the paynims sheared him upon his head above, like a fool, in despising Christian law. And because this was done to St. Peter to do him despite and shame, it was sith established that the clergy should have his crown shaven in sign of right great honour and authority.' St. Paul always has a bald forehead and a long pointed beard, and holds the sword of his martyrdom. These two saints very often appear in association, a link forged in the earliest days of the Church in Rome. In the wall-paintings at Clayton (Sussex) and on the Norman tympanum of Siddington (Glos) Christ delivers the Keys to St. Peter and the book of the Law to St. Paul. St. Paul is rarely represented apart from St. Peter, either in church dedications or in imagery, the rule of rarity as regards scenes from his life being proved by a most magnificent exception in the 12th-century painting of 'St. Paul and the Viper' in Canterbury Cathedral.

The youthful appearance which distinguishes St. John the Divine has already been mentioned, and also the probable reason why he sometimes holds a palm as well as the poisoned chalice which is his particular attribute (pages 116 and 144) (PLATE 8). *Dives and Pauper* explains correctly why the saint is shown 'with a cup in his hand and an adder therein, in token that he drank deadly venom and through virtue of the cross it lost its malice and did him none harm', but is probably rationalising a misunderstood symbol when it goes on, 'And in his other hand he beareth a palm in token that he was a martyr, and had the palm of martyrdom, although he was not slain; for his will was to die for God's sake'. The 'adder' is usually shown as a small black dragon emerging from the chalice.

Because of the immense fame of his shrine at Compostella as a place of pilgrimage, St. James Major is usually shown in the dress of a pilgrim. The scallop shell on his hat and scrip was the special badge of those who had made this pilgrimage, and it is probable that the slender rod sometimes shown lashed to the pilgrim's staff, as on a Vernon tomb at Tong (Salop), had similar associations.[10]

St. Andrew, holding the cross saltire which, curiously enough, is not mentioned in his 'Acts' as the instrument of his martyrdom, is often seen in imagery, and he was among the most popular dedication saints. His special connexion with Scotland dates from the 8th century when some of his bones are said to have been secretly transferred from Greece to St. Andrews.

The position of St. John the Baptist, being unique, makes it appropriate to consider him directly after the Apostles, and as a patron saint he was preferred to all save St. Peter and St. Andrew. Since his feast, on June 24th, coincided with the celebrations of Midsummer, the Baptist probably took over both the sites and customs associated with the pagan solar festival. Dr. Hildburgh has suggested [11] that an association with the solar year may account for the arrangement of the saints around the many alabaster 'Heads of St. John' of which there is a very fine example in the church at Amport (Hants) (PLATE 13). The flanking figures are almost always those of SS. Peter and Thomas of Canterbury, although large panels sometimes add other saints. At the base is carved the figure of Christ in the Sepulchre and at the top an angel bearing a soul to Heaven in a napkin. The feast days of the three saints and the traditional date of the Crucifixion correspond closely with those of the solstices and equinoxes. Another explanation associates the alabaster carvings with the Corpus Christi Gilds, particularly those of York, for in some York service books the fourth lesson of the Feast of the Decollation of St. John tells that 'Caput Johannis in disco : signat Corpus Christi.[12]

Many of the carvings show a wound, painted or carved, above the saint's left eyebrow, a detail relating to the frontal bone of St. John, presented to the Cathedral of Amiens in 1206, and which has a hole at that point. This was accounted for by the legend (carved on a screen in the choir aisle at Amiens) that Herodias, when she received the head on a charger, pierced the tongue which had rebuked her sin with a pin from her hair and stabbed at the forehead with a knife.[13] A fragment of carved alabaster in Ripon Minster shows Herodias holding the head on a charger in one hand while in the other she holds something which might have been the hilt of a dagger.

St. John the Baptist was one of the most popular patron saints among gilds and craft associations, and the reasons why he was thus chosen may serve to illustrate the general principles of such choice.[14] Because his images are identified by the Agnus Dei lying on the book in his hand, all those connected with the wool trade, also all domestic animals and those in charge of them, were held to be under his special protection. Because he wore a garment of camel hair girt with a leather girdle, he was the patron of those who worked in cloth, leather or pelts; because his head was struck off with an axe, all those who made, or used, incisive instruments, such as cutlers or carpenters, claimed his patronage. Those who worked with needles or awls remembered the legend of Herodias and the pin; the chandlers recalled the fact that the word lucerna was applied to the Baptist in the liturgy, while his incarceration may perhaps have endeared him to the bird-catchers. In order that there should be no mistake as to the material from which his shaggy robe is made, figures of St. John are often shown draped in the whole skin of a camel with its head hanging down in front. This motive is chiefly confined to northern Europe, the main area of the wool trade, and appears first in 14th-century glass, as at St. Denys, at York, or Grappenhall (Ches). Stone images which show the camel's skin very clearly are preserved in Hereford Cathedral and Tewkesbury (Glos).

'The noble Army of Martyrs' is the most numerous group of saints represented in imagery, for men revered those who had suffered the supreme ordeal as the most powerful intercessors before the throne of God, and divine assurance that their intercession would be effective is recorded in the legends of many saints frequently represented. St. Catherine, before she was beheaded, prayed to God that any who should 'remember my passion, be it at his death, or in any other necessity, and call me . . . shall have by thy mercy the effect of his request and prayer'. A voice from Heaven welcomed the soul of the virgin martyr and added 'to them that shall hallow thy passion, I promise the comfort of Heaven' (*Golden Legend*, vii. 25). The same celestial assurance is recorded in the legends of three other virgin martyrs familiar in imagery: SS. Barbara, Dorothy and Margaret of Antioch, and also in that of St. George. St. Dorothy's dying prayer, as told in the *Golden Legend* (vii. 46-7), was that any household in which her life was read should be protected from storms, fire and sudden death, and similar powers were exercised by St. Barbara. St. Margaret of Antioch, who appears more often than any female saint except St. Catherine, was granted the request that any woman who invoked her name in childbirth should be safely delivered (*Golden Legend*, iv. 71). Liturgical invocations, and hymns celebrating her power to protect, show that this belief was widely accepted,[15] and some of her surviving images may have been thank-offerings for a safe confinement. Historically St. Margaret is a shadowy figure; but the legend described in Mirk's *Festial* was widely known: 'anon there came out of an angle in the prison a great, horrible dragon and yawneth upon her, so that his mouth was upon her head and his tongue extended down to her heel, and he would have swallowed her. And when he had her all in his mouth Margaret made the sign of the cross, and anon the dragon burst asunder. . . . Herefore is Margaret painted, or carven, with a dragon under her feet and a cross in her hand, showing how, by virtue of the cross she gat victory of the fiend.'[16] On the misericord at Sherborne (Dorset) (PLATE 21) the saint seems to be sitting comfortably on her dragon, but on the font at Cotham (Yorks), a capital at Bretforton (Worcs) and a bench-end at North Cadbury (Somerset) the tail of her robe is still disappearing into its jaws while the upper part of her figure bursts from its belly.

St. Dorothy is identified by the basket of roses, or apples, sent from Heaven after her martyrdom to convert a scribe who had mocked her hope of entering Paradise. She is often painted on East Anglian rood-screens, such as Eye (Suffolk) or Walpole St. Peter (Norfolk), is carved on a bench-end at Fressingfield (Suffolk) and appears in glass at Langport, Mark and Middlezoy in Somerset.[17] St. Barbara carries a small tower and appears in many windows, including one at Awliscombe (Devon), and on painted screens as at Ranworth (Norfolk).

In what remains of our medieval imagery it is rare to find a series of subjects illustrating the life and miracles of a single saint. The outstanding exception is in the Chapel of St. Thomas in Canterbury Cathedral, although only the windows showing his posthumous miracles have survived. A window in the nave of York Minster shows us nine scenes from the life of St. Catherine, including her conversion of the pagan philosophers and their subsequent martyrdom, her ordeal by the spiked wheels and eventual beheading. The Nottingham alabaster panels in the Roman Catholic Chapel at Lydiate (Lancs) add to these subjects the rarer scene of her burial on the summit of Mount Sinai by angels, with the miraculous springs of oil gushing from the tomb. It is possible that her burial was also suggested in the wall-paintings at Little Kimble and Little Missenden in Buckinghamshire. Two early scenes from the life of St. Margaret remain in the glass of North Tuddenham (Norfolk) and several later episodes at Combs (Suffolk). Far more often we see only single figures of the saints, each with some attribute referring to their martyrdom which is often fantastically formalised. Thus, on a cusp of the Percy tomb in Beverley Minster, St. Catherine holds a small spiked wheel at the end of a stick, like the modern firework.

Such formalised attributes were probably familiar to many humble worshippers who had never seen the legend of the saint fully illustrated, or even heard it told. Like the Cross of Christ, these gruesome instruments of torture became symbols of victory, a transformation which justifies the otherwise curious medieval reasoning that, because St. Blaise holds the iron comb with which his flesh was torn in his martyrdom, he would regard with special favour those who used similar implements in their daily toil. The wool-combers claimed him as their patron and a wooden statuette of him still stands on the Spring chantry at Lavenham (Suffolk). He also appears on the painted screen at Eye (Suffolk) and in a window at Payhembury (Devon).

By the same reasoning St. Bartholomew, who, because he was flayed, holds a skinning knife and sometimes his own skin over his arm (as on the statue in Henry VII's Chapel, Westminster), was the patron of all tanners. St. Erasmus was invoked by sufferers from internal complaints because his entrails are shown wound round a windlass, and the tooth which St. Apollonia holds up in a pair of pincers, as on the painted screen at Ashton (Devon), led to her invocation for toothache, with the result that this obscure saint is more often represented than many others with far nobler claims to commemoration. Because St. Lawrence was identified by the gridiron on which he was roasted, as on a tomb chest at Harewood (PLATE 8), men invoked his protection against the flames of Purgatory or Hell. His single figure often appears in windows, but the glass at Ludlow which shows many scenes from his life is a rare memorial to this 3rd-century Roman martyr.

Martyrdom by shooting with arrows was held to confer powers of protection against disease and sudden death, which, according to primitive belief, were caused by the shafts of angry spirits. In early German paintings God the Father, or Christ, is shown aiming the arrows of Pestilence, Dearth or War against sinful men, some of whom seek shelter under the cloak of the Blessed Virgin Mary.[18] Saints who had been miraculously healed from arrow-wounds, like St. Sebastian, or shielded from them, like St. Christopher, were credited with the power of protecting those who did them honour from infection and sudden death. In medieval Britain this belief seems more particularly to have referred to St. Christopher, and the inscription on the wall-painting at Wood Eaton (Oxon), KI CEST IMAGE VERRA LE JUR DE MALE MORT NE MURRA (who looks upon this image, that day shall not die an ill death, i.e. without the rites of the Church), explains why every church in Britain probably once had some representation of him. C. E. Keyser lists 186 wall-paintings of St. Christopher,[19] far more than those of any other saint, and almost all of them placed where they could be seen from the threshold of the main door. Many of these paintings are so much alike, both in general design and such details as the lantern held by the hermit on the bank, that they suggest a common original. One of the earliest known woodcuts (Fig. 9), dating from 1423, shows the holy giant who sought to serve the mightiest of all Lords by carrying travellers across the stream. He grasps the staff which miraculously became

ristofori faciem die quacumq; aueris ∴
illa nempe die morte mala non moueris ∴

Millefimo cccc
xx° anno ∴ſ∴

FIG. 9.   ST. CHRISTOPHER

'like a palmier bearing flowers, leaves and dates' (*Golden Legend*, iii. 9), and an orb in the hand of the Christ Child symbolises the burden which made the giant feel as if he had all the world upon him. Ships and mermaids, as well as fishes, may show the depth of the river which only reaches mid-way up his calves. Such woodcuts, widely distributed by those who wished to carry an image of their protector always with them, probably crystallised the tradition of his representation.[20] Scenes from the passion of St. Christopher are rare but appear in small panels flanking the large central scene at Shorwell (Isle of Wight) and may have been represented at St. Keverne (Cornwall), where an allusion to the legend that St. Christopher was originally dogheaded, of the race of Cynocephali, has been tentatively identified.[21]

'The Holy Church throughout the World' is most often represented by the four Doctors of the Latin Church: SS. Gregory, Jerome, Ambrose and Augustine of Hippo. They are carved upon the pulpit at Trull (Somerset) (PLATE 8) wearing the robes of a Pope, Cardinal, Bishop and Doctor respectively. They also appear on the painted pulpits at Burnham Norton and Castle Acre in Norfolk, and on the doors of several East Anglian screens, placed there, presumably, because their teaching opened men's minds to the meaning of Holy Scripture. At Castle Acre each figure is accompanied by a Latin inscription referring to such teaching.[22] The Four Doctors also appear in windows and on fonts and tomb chests. On the Bruce Cenotaph at Guisborough (Yorks) St. Ambrose is shown with a beehive, to recall the legend that, when he was a baby in his cradle, a swarm of bees flew in and out of his mouth and then ascended to Heaven (*Golden Legend*, iii. 111). The other Early Fathers are rarely found except in cathedrals and places of learning, as for instance in the windows of New College Chapel, Oxford, where an interesting series includes the unique figure of St. Athanasius.[23]

The international character of the medieval Church is illustrated by the wide range of Continental ecclesiastics who are shown as saints. Of the founders of the great monastic Orders, St. Benedict is the only one often represented; he appears on screens at Burlingham St. Andrew, North Elmham, Great Plumstead and Smallburgh, all in Norfolk. A 12th-century panel of glass in St. Denys' at York shows him beating the devil with rods. St. Bernard is rare despite the great influence of the Cistercian Order. The window in St. Mary's, Shrewsbury, which illustrates his miraculous extermination of the flies infesting a new church, is of German or Flemish origin and belongs to the same series as those in Marston Bigot (Somerset).[24] The Stigmatisation of

St. Francis is shown on the screens at Bradninch (Devon) and Hemp-
stead (Norfolk) and his preaching to the birds in wall-paintings at
Little Kimble (Bucks) and Wiston (Suffolk). The painting at Little
Kimble is on a window splay and opposite is the figure of a nun
holding a book which may be the unique representation of St. Francis'
devoted disciple, St. Clare.[25] The appropriation of British parishes
to foreign religious houses probably explains the inclusion of some
foreign saints in the imagery of their churches, as well as their dedications to foreign saints, but lacking space to discuss such interesting
importations I must pass on with only a mention of the foreign
ecclesiastic most held in popular affection in Britain, and to whom two
of our earliest churches were dedicated, St. Martin of Tours. The
episode of his cutting his cloak in half to share it with a beggar appears
in the glass of Canterbury Cathedral, Christchurch, Oxford, and
St. Martin-cum-Gregory at York. It is also carved on a reset misericord at Fornham St. Martin (Suffolk).

Of the outstanding figures of English history represented as saints
I can mention very few. King Edward the Confessor can be recognised
by his attribute of the ring which he gave in alms to St. John the
Evangelist, in the guise of a beggar, and which the saint gave to some
pilgrims in the Holy Land, bidding them announce to the king his
approaching death (*Golden Legend*, vi. 26-8). His figure is carved on a
tomb-chest at Harewood (PLATE 8). The chief female saint of Saxon
England was St. Etheldreda, Abbess of Ely, whose life is illustrated
by carved capitals beneath the lantern of that cathedral and whose
statue stands on the west front of Wells Cathedral. Great churchmen,
such as St. Wilfrid of Ripon or St. John of Beverley, are mostly
honoured in the districts where they served and ruled, but every
church in the country probably had some image of St. Thomas of
Canterbury until the deliberate campaign waged against his cult by
Henry VIII destroyed most of them. A boss at Exeter Cathedral, a
wall-painting at South Newington (Oxon) and two alabaster panels
at Elham (Kent) (PLATE 21) are among the most interesting survivals.

Passing from the greatest churchmen to the most obscure we find
in the dedications of churches in Wales and the western counties our
only source of information about many of the lesser teachers who
established Christianity in Britain in the years after the Roman with-
drawal, for which we have no written records, but their figures are
very rarely represented.[26]

The reasons why a church was dedicated to a particular saint are
rarely recorded except in cases like St. Bartholomew the Great,

London, when we know that the saint appeared to its founder, Rahere, and commanded him to build it. The reasons for choosing the saints represented in imagery are still more conjectural. Memorials of St. Nicholas, who protected sailors, occur chiefly in coastal areas and may express supplication or gratitude. Some representations of St. Leonard with his attribute of fetters may be thank-offerings for safe deliverance from captivity,[27] while images of St. Roch, who laboured among the sick, probably multiplied in times of pestilence. His statue appears with that of St. Sebastian upon the Kirkham chantry at Paignton. St. Sitha, the holy waiting-maid of Lucca, had the power of finding lost articles, and her image appears, with keys at her belt, in the windows of Mells (Somerset) and carved on a tomb-chest at Croft Castle (Herefs). The choice of saints represented in our churches may have been determined by any one of a wide variety of factors, but we can do little more than guess at them.

In conclusion I can think of no better way in which to epitomise the outlook of the average medieval parishioner than by quoting the words of St. Ambrose:

The angels must be entreated, who have been as guards to us ; the martyrs must be entreated, for we claim their patronage by the pledge, as it were, of their mortal remains. They can ask pardon for our sins who, if they had any sins, washed them away in their own blood. Let us not be ashamed to ask them to intercede for our weakness, for they knew the frailty of mortal flesh, even though they overcame it.—*Widowhood*, ix. 55.

CHAPTER 12

THE MIRROR OF MORALS

T HE imagery which we have so far considered expressed the lessons of the Past by reminding worshippers of Man's Fall and of how the Old Testament prophecies of a Redeemer to come had been fulfilled by the Incarnation and Passion of Christ, while the Future was represented by paintings of the Judgment to come. That ceaseless battle between good and evil which constitutes the Present of humanity has not been mentioned, but those who designed medieval imagery were not guilty of such an omission. Even a subject of such cosmic magnitude did not dismay the fearless, yet humble, artists of the Middle Ages; fearless, in that they attempted to portray universal themes by a few naïve symbols painted on a plastered wall or carved upon architectural details, humble in their realisation that, so long as the *meaning* of these symbols was recognised, their inevitable inadequacy of expression did not matter. The literary origins of some of the allegorical diagrams which they used is a subject of which I hope to write more fully in a future book, so I will here only describe very briefly their part in the Picture Book instruction of the churches.

The scientific analysis of sin, and the threatening horror of its eternal punishment, absorbed the intellectual energies of scholars, and overshadowed the mental horizon of ordinary men and women, to an extent perhaps most closely paralleled to-day by the problems and terrors of nuclear fission. The modern psycho-analyst has not devised more complicated pedigrees of spiritual disorders than those which are preserved in such medieval texts as *The Ayenbite of Inwit*,[1] written by Dan Michael, a 14th-century monk of Canterbury, or its northern counterpart, *The Prykke of Conscience*.[2] Yet both these books were intended by their authors to serve as works of popular edification. Dan Michael explains that

> This book is made for lewd men,
> For father for mother and for other kin,
> Them for to save from all manner of sin
> That in their conscience no foul thought remain. . . .

Since a large proportion of the nation could not read, the artists were called upon to summarise such teaching by pictorial allegories or by symbolical diagrams.

The PSYCHOMACHIA, or Battle of the Vices and Virtues, is the most important of these allegories,[3] and although Tertullian compared the vices and virtues to combatants in an arena, its direct literary source is a long poem by Prudentius. He describes how the armed Virgins, which represent the Virtues, each engage in single combat with an opposing Vice, both employing arms and tactics which are symbolically appropriate. The details of these battles do not concern us for, with the doubtful exception of the 12th-century wall-paintings at Claverley (Salop), British artists showed the Virtues already triumphant, trampling on their prostrate foes. The Psychomachia is represented on the south porch of Malmesbury Abbey, where the carvings are now almost indecipherably weathered, and, much more clearly, upon the 12th-century fonts of Southrop (Glos) and Stanton Fitzwarren (Wilts).[4] The carvers of these fonts were obviously directed by literate employers, for the Latin names of the Vices and Virtues are incised upon the backgrounds, or round the arches which frame each pair of figures. Above this arcade at Southrop (PLATE 3) there is a decorative design of small domed buildings, perhaps alluding to the Heavenly City which, according to Prudentius, was built by the united efforts of the Virtues after their several victories. Even these fonts, however, show that the carvers imperfectly understood their theme. At Southrop, Patentia most improperly uses a whip to chastise the cowering Ira, having taken over the instrument with which Pudicitia should scourge Libido. Was the Stanton Fitzwarren font carved first, one wonders, and did the original designer, perhaps a monk, trust the carver to reproduce correctly at Southrop the impassive figure of Patentia holding the shield which defied the assaults of Ira until, despairing of success, the Vice plunged her futile sword into her own breast? He should have realised that impassivity, if the reason for it is not understood, seems dull compared with the dramatic curves of an upraised arm and falling lash!

These allegories had to be dramatic if they were to grip the imagination of the people, and it was probably from the similes of popular preachers that the later artists derived their inspiration. The Virtues appear as noble ladies overcoming all sorts of familiar scalliwags on the 13th-century door of the Chapter House at Salisbury, and although most of the heads are restored, the less prominent details are original, and show the new form given to the old lesson. Falsehood has her tongue pulled out by Truth, with a very large pair of pincers, and Chastity hangs Lust upon a miniature gibbet. Graceful as these Virtues are, a comic element has invaded their combat which becomes more evident in later medieval examples. In the 15th century the dignified Virgin Virtues give place to the Seven Works of Mercy, derived from the words which Christ put into the mouth of the Supreme Judge : 'For I was an hungred, and ye gave me meat : I was thirsty, and ye gave me drink : I was a stranger, and ye took me in : naked, and ye clothed me : I was sick, and ye visited me : I was in prison, and ye came unto me' (St. Matthew xxv. 35-6). To these six manifestations of mercy was added the Burying of the Dead, which is mentioned as a work of piety in Tobit i. 17-18. This last work is omitted from the 15th-century window of All Saints, North Street, York (PLATE 11), which is our finest surviving illustration of the Seven Works of Mercy. Here we see a man of noble mien distributing food, drink and clothing from his home and welcoming four travellers as his guests. The remaining panels show him visiting a sick man and three prisoners in the stocks. At Combs (Suffolk) two panels from a similar window show a man and his wife ministering to the hungry and thirsty under the supervision of an angel, and we know from records that in lost windows showing the Works of Mercy at Lammas, Guestwick and Quidenham, and in a wall-painting at Wickhampton, all in Norfolk, the merciful person was a woman. Perhaps this point was determined in each case by the sex and number of the donors. At York the pictures are left to tell their own story, but in some of the East Anglian windows scrolls are inscribed with a brief dialogue between the needy person and the merciful one. Thus the two panels at Combs are inscribed :

> For mercye I hungyr me.
> Brodyr have mete anow

and

> I am thrysty ful drye y wysse.
> Have her' drynke p'y for hym y^t doth.

Other fragmentary inscriptions remain of which one clearly refers to Christ's words 'Inasmuch as ye have done it unto one of the least of these my brethren, ye have done it unto me'.[5]

The Lay Folks Catechism,[6] which was written by Archbishop Thoresby in the 14th century, urged men to perform the works of mercy, even as Christ did them unto us.

First men should willingly feed poor hungry men and thirsty
For in that they feed Jesu Christ as he himself saith in the Gospel.
And also Jesu Christ gives body and soul, life and catel (chattel) for this
    end.
And feeds us with His flesh and His blood in the sacrament of the altar. . . .

Also skilfully we ought to clothe naked poor men
Since Christ gives clothes to this end.
And He himself was stripped naked
And beaten, and suffered much cold for our need.
And if we do this well He will clothe our souls
With virtues and grace in body and soul
With the stole of undedlyness and bliss of heaven. . . .

Since Christ for our need died on the Cross
To bring us out of sickness and sin, and keeps us out of bodily sickness;
We should help other sick men and by this help deserve the bliss of
    Heaven. . . .

Thus the representations of the Seven Works of Mercy which we
know from fragmentary remains must originally have formed the
subject of many windows, wall-paintings and carvings, not only urged
men to make practical profession of that loving mercy which characterises true Christianity, but directly associated such actions with the
Passion of Our Lord. Even when the theme had been reduced to its
simplest elements, a figure stooping beside a sentry-box simulating
'prison', or a group of three figures standing above a shrouded corpse,
as on the arm-rests of the bench-ends at Feltwell (Norfolk), or the
single figures in bed, or fast in the stocks, on the poppy heads of
the benches at Blythburgh (Suffolk), its relation to the wider design
of religious education was unchanged.

In such minor works of sculpture the irony of the caricaturist is
evident in the personification of the Seven Deadly Sins. At Blythburgh Hypocrisy peeps slyly through devoutly folded hands, Gluttony
hugs a distended paunch, while Pride struts in rich robes, and so
lively are these carved poppy heads that one seems to hear again the
chuckle with which the carver's contemporaries may have identified
their originals. Sometimes parallels were sought in the animal kingdom
and the vices were shown mounted upon appropriate beasts. Gluttony,
tankard in hand, almost rolls off the back of a sow, on one misericord
in Norwich Cathedral, while others show Anger, with half-drawn
sword, mounted on a boar, and Lechery upon a goat. Some arm-rests
on the Norwich stalls show half-length figures emerging from

monstrous jaws, and although these lack identifying attributes, there is little doubt that they were meant to portray the Seven Deadly Sins as we see them on the bench-ends of Wiggenhall St. German (Norfolk). Here Lust is represented by a couple embracing, and Gluttony is shown pouring wine into his cup from a bottle. These figures all stand within the jaws of monsters, and while the simple interpretation that such sins lead directly to Hell is essentially correct, I think the carvings reproduce parts of larger designs, and are the lethal buds from the Tree of Pride, that sinister allegory which we must now consider.

The words of Christ: 'A good tree cannot bring forth evil fruit, neither can a corrupt tree bring forth good fruit. . . . Wherefore by their fruits ye shall know them' (St. Matthew vii. 18-20), probably suggested to early writers and artists alike the use of a tree-simile to illustrate the interrelation of vices or virtues and the common roots from which each sprang.[7] In the *Liber Floridus Lamberti*, an illustrated encyclopaedia written *c.* 1120, the *Arbor Bona* (here used as a symbol of the Church) is rooted in *Caritas*, and the *Arbor Mala* (the Synagogue) springs from *Cupiditas*, but the 12th-century manuscripts of the *Speculum Virginum* illustrate the tradition followed by most medieval wall-paintings of making Humility the root of all virtues and Pride the stem of sin.[8] The artist illustrating a learned text had a relatively easy task, for he only needed to name the half-length figure of Humility, or Pride, upon the stem of his tree in order to make clear its nature, and the many leaves sprouting from its six main branches could each bear the name of a subsidiary characteristic. This was much too complicated for a wall-painting in a parish church and in these Pride (which is more often shown than Humility) generally has a human body with scrolls, or dragons, issuing from it and ending in bestial heads, within whose gaping jaws are small groups of figures illustrating the various sins. The scrolls spring from that part of the body most likely to be concerned with the relevant sin. Thus at Little Horwood (Bucks) a jagged scroll from the mouth of Pride (here represented by a figure over 6 feet high) ends in a dragon's head within the jaws of which Gluttony is drinking from a bowl, while the scroll from her right hand reaches to Avarice, fighting with a demon for the possession of money-bags.[9]

One of the outstanding illustrations of this allegory, which is known as the Purging of Pride, was painted above the nave arcade at Raunds (Northants), but it has darkened so much that only by familiarity with early drawings can one now make out its general outline.[10] Pride is here shown as a crowned woman dressed in the fashion of *c.* 1460, with a demon on each side of her head and a Hell Mouth beneath her feet in which a lost soul is shown among the flames. Dragons issue from various parts of her body and vomit forth figures typifying sins. Above these there were smaller figures holding explanatory scrolls, but these have perished. On the right hand of Pride stands Death, a cadaver, who pierces her side with his spear. This motive, which is also recorded at Padbury (Bucks) and Alveley (Salop), suggests an infernal counterpart to the piercing of Christ's side upon the Cross. At South Leigh (Oxon) a faded painting in the north aisle still shows the dragon scrolls holding the sins, but the central part only dimly indicates a writhing serpent form. This may have been akin to the painting, above the nave arcade at Ruislip (Middlesex), of a bat-winged monster emerging from the flaming cauldron of Hell.[11] Above its head Pride sits enthroned, with attendants holding articles of adornment on one side and a leaping demon on the other, and in the mouths of subsidiary dragons we see two men fighting with swords (Ira), a woman asleep (Accidia) and a man counting money at a table (Avaritia). In this church the Seven Works of Mercy can be seen faintly, through later paintings, on the opposite wall, but the clearest painting of this theme is at Trotton (Sussex), where a male figure of *Caritas*, surrounded by medallions illustrating the Seven Works of Mercy, is opposed to a Pride in human form, with dragons issuing from it.

The use of beast heads in this connexion may be explained by a passage in *The Ayenbite of Inwit*, by which Dan Michael states that the seven heads of the Beast in the Book of the Revelation are the Seven Deadly Sins and that everyone falls into the throat of one or other of them. A masterly compression of this theme on to a single misericord can be seen in the Chapel of New College, Oxford. The central corbel is carved with the Apocalyptic Beast, while the significance of its seven heads is explained upon the supporters by the devil quitting a man who kneels in confession, and a penitent scourging himself.

Sometimes a wheel pattern was used instead of the Tree, or the human figure. At Ingatestone (Essex) a Wheel of Pride was discovered, but whitewashed over, between the spokes of which were groups of figures showing the types of people most likely to be affected by each sin. Envy was illustrated by men apparently swearing false witness before a judge and Sloth by a man in bed with a traceried window in the background, perhaps suggesting a monastery.[12] Medieval preachers often emphasised the temptations particularly menacing various types of men and women, and when the Deadly Sins were described as being the Hounds of the Devil, each was allotted its particular prey.

Wheel patterns were also painted on the walls at Kempley (Glos) and Leominster (Herefs), each of which had ten spokes ending in medallions. The words *me decepit* surviving at Leominster served to connect this painting with a miniature in the Arundel Psalter in the British Museum representing the Wheel of Life, with the head of the Almighty at the hub of the wheel and each of the medallions illustrating one phase of human life. Explanatory verses surround these medallions, of which the last two end with the words '*vita me decepit*'.[13]

Another allegorical diagram sometimes found in churches is the Wheel of Fortune. On a pier in the choir of Rochester Cathedral Dame Fortune sits in the centre of her wheel, controlling its revolutions, and the figures of men struggle upwards towards the triumphant figure at the top. The sinister side, which showed their fall, has been obliterated. A set of nine floor tiles excavated among the ruins of St. Mary's Priory, Nuneaton (Warcs), evidently formed part of such a wheel, but most of their details have been worn away,[14] and as the subject is rare in church imagery and its meaning familiar to all, we need consider it no further.

'Vanity of Vanity—all is Vanity.' Had the Preacher been a medieval one he might have described these words as marking the rhythm to which the Wheel of Fortune turns, and this was certainly the lesson repeated, in a grimmer form, by the paintings of the Three Living and the Three Dead.[15] Even within the relatively short space of time during which matters of medieval iconography have been thought worthy of record, some thirty examples of this allegory have been recognised in British churches, but many have been whitewashed over again, have faded away, or fallen in flakes from the crumbling plaster, so that only about a dozen paintings, mostly incomplete, still typify the importance of this subject in the Picture Book of the medieval Church.

It has been suggested that the legend was of eastern origin,[16] but most medieval artists knew of it through 13th-century French poems; the best known being that composed by Baudoin de Condé, a minstrel at the Court of Margaret II, Countess of Flanders in 1244–80. He describes the meeting of three gay young courtiers with three Deaths. The first youth flees, the second hails the apparition as one sent from God, and the third discants upon the horrors of decay. The first

Death proclaims that, even as they now are so shall the courtiers be; the second Death reminds them that rich and poor alike must die, and the third Death emphasises that none may escape his summons. Some of the remaining wall-paintings show by varied gestures that the reaction of the Living was differentiated, as in the poems. In the little chapel of Widford, near Burford (Oxon), the youth is intent upon his hunting and does not see the Dead, the middle-aged man tries to draw his attention to them and the old man shields his eyes from the horrible sight. At Charlwood (Surrey) the Kings were shown on horseback, a motive commoner in France than in England. In this subject a pictorial tradition has grown up independently of literary authority, for the meeting of the Three Living and the Three Dead is always associated with a hunting scene, although neither this fact, nor the royal status accorded to the Living, is derived from the poems. A forest setting is generally suggested, if only by a single tree, and the one King who remains in the wall-painting at Paston (Norfolk) has two small huntsmen in attendance, one of whom touches him to point out the Deaths. Professor Tristram thought that the Three Dead were here represented as hanging which, in an age when laden gibbets were not uncommon sights, must have added a sinister realism to the allegory, but too little now remains to decide this point. At Hurstbourne Tarrant (Hants) the remains of a wall-painting glow with an incongruously cheerful colouring; even the fleshless bones of the Dead are painted in a warm golden tint, but at Peakirk (Northants) the horror of the vision is enhanced by a background covered with flies, beetles and other insects which feed upon corruption.[17]

The painting of the Three Living and the Three Dead at Raunds (Northants) is on the same wall as that of the Purging of Pride, and we can thus imagine the sequence of admonitions which these paintings were meant to express. At the west end of the wall, above the nave arcade, the little group of sins in the dragons' mouths portray acts whose extreme familiarity inclines men to condone them, yet, as the eye travels down those branching dragons' bodies into the giant form of Pride, and through her limbs to their true place of origin, in Hell, these petty vices are seen in the awful perspective of eternity. A few paces eastwards and our glance falls upon the second allegory, seizing first upon the rabbit and the hunting dogs, still clearly visible and then discovering upon the darkened plaster above them, first the Kings, in their careless enjoyment of the chase, and lastly their horrible vision of the Deaths, unheralded and inescapable ! The figure of St.

Christopher, also painted on this wall, offers a limited protection against unshriven death, but even his legendary power extends only to the day in which we have gazed upon his image, and only the vanished Rood, which has left a pale scar above the chancel arch, brought to medieval parishioners a hope of escaping from the terrors of eternal damnation.

The last allegory which we must consider is the Dance of Death, which may originally have been a morality play or a mimed sermon, in which actors representing various ranks of society were summoned in turn to quit the stage of this world.[18] Illustrations of this allegory were once painted around the cloister walls of Pardon Churchyard, near St. Paul's Cathedral, perhaps in emulation of the famous series in the Cimetière des Innocents in Paris, but the English paintings were destroyed in 1549 and no other complete series remains. One misericord in St. George's Chapel, Windsor, shows three subjects from the Dance of Death. In the centre the cadaver summons the rich man from his table laden with cups and flagons, while chests or coffers make further allusions to his wealth. On the supporters Death calls a labourer from his digging and a thresher from the flail.[19] The subject was naturally appropriate to chantry chapels and a scene from it is painted upon two panels of the early 16th-century chantry of Robert Markham in the parish church at Newark (Notts). On the de la Warr chantry chapel at Boxgrove (Sussex) the carver has copied the marginal decorations of early printed books, probably from the presses of Thielmann Kerver or Simon de Vostre, in Paris.

On detached screen panels at Sparham (Norfolk) there are paintings of late date and unusual character. One pair shows the interior of a church with a fine font, and a shrouded skeleton standing up in its grave in the floor. The other pair represent a man and a woman, both skeletons but fully clothed; the man holds a torch inscribed: *sic transit gloria mundi* and the woman holds a bunch of flowers. Above them are scrolls bearing the legend:

> Natus homo de muliere brevi tempore parvo
> Nunc est nunc non est quasi flos qui crescit in arvo.[20]

These figures are not derived from the Dance of Death but, like the ghastly cadavers which were often carved on late medieval tombs, they are part of the same haunting obsession with the idea of death which made the Church appear as man's only hope and refuge, dazzling by contrast with the world's dark background of fear.

These allegorical designs were in effect pictorial homilies whose characteristics recur in many medieval sermons. The subdivisions of sin, in Tree or Wheel, are merely simpler, broader statements of the preachers' analyses, just as the racy grotesques, or the representations of domestic brawls which we find in detail sculpture (particularly on misericords) recall their vivid *exempla* and vitriolic denunciations of women. I have therefore chosen to end this chapter with a mention of a wall-painting at Broughton (Bucks) which is the most direct illustration that I know, of a sermon theme. The painting dates from *c.* 1400 and shows the dead Christ in the Virgin's arms, His right hand and foot severed from the limbs and His bones showing through His flesh. Round the central figures are shown gaily dressed young men holding the severed hand and foot, a heart, or various bones, while, at the bottom, two other men quarrel over a gaming board. This bizarre design is unquestionably intended as a warning to blasphemers, for a contemporary sermon preserved in St. Alban's Cathedral denounces the 'greet swereris that dismembre Crist, sweringe by his eȝen armys, naylis, boonys, herte, blode and soule. Hem thinkith that the cursid jewis deden him not turment y-nouȝ, but if thei with her grisli oothis al to drouȝ Cristis lymys from lymys (as crowis plucken a careyne).' [21] This was not a single preacher's simile, but a generally accepted theme, for we find it repeated, almost word for word, by Chaucer, in the *Pardoner's Tale*. A similar wall-painting at Walsham le Willows (Suffolk) has been destroyed, but the surviving parts of another, at Corby (Lincs), show us a demon in attendance on each heedless youth and, in one case, holding him by the exaggeratedly long tips of his fashionable shoes.[22] These paintings must be associated with the lost window from Heydon (Norfolk) which represented gamesters, and other profligates, with their blasphemous invocations of Christ's limbs and blood inscribed on scrolls, and made their future fate clear by showing such sinners amid the flames of Hell.[23] At Walsham-le-Willows the blasphemies were associated with daily toil, rather than gaming, for anchors, axes, scales and other implements, alluding to about thirty trades, were prominently represented. Such implements also appear surrounding a standing figure of Christ showing the wounds of His Passion at Breage (Cornwall) and in about a dozen other churches. It was at one time thought that this so-called 'Christ of the Trades' was an allusion to Piers Plowman,[24] but further research has associated these figures with a similar 15th-century wall-painting in San Miniato, Florence, where an inscription explains that the pains of Hell await the man who disregards the sanctity of the Sabbath. This is the 'Christ of the Unending Passion', His wounds hourly renewed by the sins which men commit, their strife and blasphemies, and their disregard of the Sabbath when they wish to use their tools for gain. The wall-painting at Broughton may therefore stand as a memorial of the Church's unending struggle against men's unending heedlessness.

CHAPTER 13

THE MIRROR OF NATURE

Although the exquisite carvings in the Chapter House at South-well (Notts) represent many types of naturalistic foliage, the wayward fashion in which their carvers have combined the fruit of one tree with the leaves of another, shows clearly that decoration, and not symbolism, was their chief concern.[1] I will therefore discuss only animal forms in this chapter and, since more than sixty different creatures, real or mythical, can be identified in the detail sculpture of British churches (see Appendix 4), I will describe only a few of those which most clearly illustrate the medieval use of animal symbolism.

The animal subjects in church imagery fall roughly into six categories:

(1) The emblems and attributes of particular persons.
(2) Subjects derived from the *Physiologus*, or Bestiary.
(3) The characters of Beast Epics, and other satires.
(4) Heraldic animals.
(5) Domestic animals figuring in genre scenes.
(6) Human abnormalities.

These categories are not mutually exclusive, for some animals figure in more than one, according to their context. Thus, the lion is the emblem of St. Mark, and also a type of the Resurrection, because the Bestiary tells that its cubs are born dead, but are brought to life after three days, when their father breathes upon them. This subject is rare but occurs on a boss in the Canterbury cloisters.[2] The fact that lions were said to sleep with their eyes open made them appropriate guardians for church doors and probably inspired the carver of the Norman font at Eardisley (Herefs) to show a lion with one eye open, the other shut. When the pillars of a doorway rest upon a lion's back, a feature common in the south of France and in Italy but of which the door at Sutton-by-Castor (Northants) is a rare British example, the animal represents the Evil One overcome by the might of the Church. The evil lion is sometimes shown holding a lamb, but when it fights with the dragon it is a good beast. On a misericord in St. George's Chapel, Windsor, the lion is shown eating a dead monkey, which the Bestiary tells us it does when sick and so cures itself, but I have not yet found a definite illustration of the lion obliterating its own spoor with its sweeping tail, a legendary habit which the *Physiologus* associated with Christ, who concealed His divinity when He entered the Virgin's womb, although the markedly bushy tails of some medieval lions would have been very good for this purpose. Lions were also prime favourites among heraldic fauna, and their natural appearance was sufficiently well known to be reproduced with reasonable accuracy.

The Agnus Dei and the Evangelistic symbols have already been mentioned and lists of animal-attributes are given in many reference books of saints. We can therefore turn directly to the Bestiary, which was one of the richest sources of medieval imagery.[3] The book is first heard of in the 5th century and it is thought that a Greek monk, living in Alexandria, was the original *Physiologus*, or natural historian, whose statements about the habits of animals, and their religious significance, were copied up to the end of the Middle Ages. In compiling his book he used the references to the clean and unclean beasts found in the Bible, and the writings of SS. Ambrose, Basil and Eustathius upon the Six Days of Creation. St. Gregory's *Moralia* and the *Etymology* of Isidore of Seville provided him with material, and he may also have been influenced by the fables of Aesop. Even had relatively accurate information been available the *Physiologus* would probably have preferred to repeat the legendary material which better served his purpose, showing how the truths of Christian teaching were reflected even in the lives of wild beasts, and how the most grotesque perversions of the human form could exemplify the greater glory of God.

The Bestiary was declared heretical in the 6th century but its popularity did not decline and texts written in many languages, from Ethiopic to Icelandic, testify to its wide circulation. Most surviving texts are in Latin or French, but it is thought to have been an Englishman who, in the 12th century, rearranged the entries and added much new material, less fantastic in character. Among the later medieval encyclopaedists who contributed to the general acceptance of the Bestiary stories I would particularly mention Bartholomaeus Anglicus, a 13th-century Franciscan, whose book *De Proprietatibus Rerum* explained the properties of natural phenomena mentioned in the Bible so as to furnish preaching friars with similes likely to impress their congregations.[4]

It seems odd that in a largely illiterate age, when men lived much closer to Nature than they do to-day, the influence of a book full of obvious untruths should have overridden the evidence of personal observation, but this was often the case. Since the *Physiologus* said that the hart pants for cooling streams because of the thirst engendered by the fiery breath of the dragons, or serpents, which it fights and devours, the carver of a 14th-century misericord in Ely Cathedral (PLATE 24) had no scruples in showing a stag placidly munching a snake, although he must have known that deer, which still abounded in England, do no such thing. He had probably seen a manuscript which, like Queen Mary's Psalter,[5] illustrated a hart eating a serpent, and copied it without further question. It is generally upon the choir stalls of cathedrals and great collegiate churches that we find the most accurate representations of rare Bestiary subjects because the carvers, or those who furnished them with designs, had access to illuminated manuscripts. Further afield we find carvings which suggest a crafts-man's rather hazy memories of such miniatures with no true under-standing of their meaning, and so, through widening circles of dis-tortion, the scholarly symbols become grotesque baberies.

The chapters of the Bestiary generally begin with some Biblical reference to the animal, followed by what the *Physiologus* said about it and the spiritual significance of the creature's habits is then ex-plained. These habits are rarely true to life, and mythical creatures greatly outnumber animals which were familiar to the carvers: there are more pelicans than poultry, more unicorns than cows, in the detail sculpture of our churches ! So I will illustrate the sort of teaching found in the Bestiary by describing how it was applied in the legends of these two creatures.

The PELICAN is never represented in its natural form, but as a dove-like bird. It symbolised Man's Fall and Redemption through the Passion of Our Lord, because the parent bird was said to slay its fledglings in a moment of irritation at their importunity, and then, after three days, to bring them back to life by tearing its own breast so that the blood flowed upon them. A misericord in Lincoln Cathedral (PLATE 23) is the only case I know in which the first phase of this story is perhaps indicated, for on one supporter the parent bird seems to be literally 'biting the head off' the fledgling ! One of the most beautiful examples of English medieval wood-carving is the misericord of the Pelican-in-her-piety in Wells Cathedral.

The UNICORN is described as a beast so powerful and tameless that no hunter could subdue it, but if a pure virgin should sit alone in the forest, then the great beast would lay its head gently in her lap, and fall a prey to the hidden hunters. This fable, which is represented on misericords at Chester, Lincoln, Stratford-on-Avon and Tewkesbury, symbolised the Incarnation of Christ who laid aside His divine immunity from pain and death when He entered the Virgin's womb. British artists simply show the unicorn kneeling before the seated virgin, with the hunter lurking in the background, and do not stress the symbolical interpretation. We must turn to the Flemish, or northern French, window now in King's College Chapel, Cambridge, to find a representation of the 'Holy Hunt' in which the Archangel Gabriel is shown, with *Justicia, Veritas, Misericordia,* and *Pax* as his four hounds, driving the Unicorn (Christ) down from Heaven to the lap of the Virgin Mary.

The *Physiologus* described the unicorn as a great beast with a terrible bellow, having the body of a horse, the feet of an elephant, the tail of a stag with a horn four feet long and so sharp that it pierced everything which it touched. The 'unicorn horns', sold for vast prices in the Middle Ages (really the tusks of the arctic whale), were credited with the power of detecting poison, and eminent persons, including Queen Elizabeth I, had drinking cups made of one.[6] The real animal behind this legend was probably the rhinoceros and Marco Polo suggests the grim impact of truth upon symbolical fiction when he writes of the rhinoceros of Java: 'They are not of that description of animal that suffer themselves to be taken by maidens, as our people suppose, but are of a contrary nature'. On a misericord in St. George's Chapel, Windsor, the carver seems to have attempted a realistic rhinoceros but most medieval artists made the unicorn an elegant animal with the body of a stag, a goat's beard and the narwhal's spiral horn.

THE TIGER.—Another strange hunting custom recorded in the Bestiary was given a symbolical interpretation. If a man would capture a tiger-cub he must ride off with it in the absence of the parent beasts and, if the tigress seemed likely to overtake him, throw down little mirrors in which she would see the reflection of her own face. Mistaking this for the lost cub, she would stop to fondle the mirror while the hunter made good his escape. This subject is carved in full on a misericord in Chester Cathedral, with the rider stooping low to throw down the mirrors, and also on a wooden boss at Queen Camel (Somerset). Most carvers were content to show the tigress fondling the mirror in order to illustrate how the deceitful attractions of the world hinder a man's pursuit of goodness. At Lakenheath (Suffolk)

(PLATE 24) the tigress has an appropriately taut and agile appearance, but at Wendens Ambo (Essex) it is only the mirror that identifies the lumbering beast which seeks therein the reflection of its flat, hideous face.

The ELEPHANT was the subject of many symbolical legends. It was said to typify the Fall of Man because it bred only once in a lifetime of 300 years, when the naturally passionless male was induced by the female to eat of mandrake roots, and also because, having no joints in its legs, it took its rest leaning against a tree, and fell helpless to the ground when this tree had been partly sawn through by the cunning hunter. It could rise only when a young elephant (Christ) came to put its trunk under the fallen one. Bartholomaeus Anglicus tells us that 'Between elephants and dragons is ever-lasting fighting, for the dragon with his tail bindeth . . . the elephant's legs and maketh him to fall, but the dragon buyeth it full sore . . . for the elephant falleth upon him and slayeth him.'[7] On the Norman font at Dunkeswell (Devon) the head of an elephant can (with some difficulty) be perceived emerging from a jungle of indeterminate forms perhaps representing the coils of the dragon, for a serpent's head is clearly visible below.

The elephant is often shown bearing a castle upon its back which reaches considerable elaboration of military architecture on a finial of the stalls of Ripon Minster and on a misericord in Manchester Cathedral, and the Bestiary explains that Indians and Persians go to war in such fashion. Sets of richly carved chessmen had their Castles of this form, the alternative name for this piece, 'rook', coming from the Persian word for an elephant. The likeness between the unusually accurate elephant carved upon a 13th-century misericord in Exeter Cathedral and a drawing made by Matthew Paris of the elephant presented to Henry III in 1255 by the King of France, suggests that the carver had also seen this creature, but in most cases it is painfully clear that all the carvers knew about elephants was that they had long noses, the structure of which was a matter for guesswork. I have chosen to illustrate the poppy head at South Lopham (Suffolk) (PLATE 24) because it is the worst elephant I know ! Its bird-like head with what looks like a flabby, corrugated beak, and its slim legs with horse's hooves bear no resemblance to the real beast, and yet this long nose, and the castle which sits like a tea-cosy on its back, definitely identify the carver's intention, and the spiritual interpretations of the subject would not have been obscured by his lack of skill. Recognition of the fauna of medieval art never depends upon realism, but on the presence of certain accepted attributes.

The CAMEL was also popular with the carvers in spite of their complete ignorance as to its true form. Its habit of kneeling down when being loaded was associated with the humility of Christ who stooped to take upon Himself the burden of men's sins and the best illustration of this occurs on a misericord at Boston (Lincs) (PLATE 24). For the most part the carvers were content to apply a hump, sometimes shown as a heavy tuft of hair, to the backs of animals which resemble horses, or even cats, far more than camels.

Perhaps the most interesting Bestiary carvings are those on the Norman door at Alne (Yorks) where the carver has not only included some very rare subjects but has carved their Latin titles upon the frame of each medallion. These subjects are as follows :

The WOLF is described as a bloodthirsty beast, yet capable of living on wind if food is lacking; it licks its feet before approaching a sheep-fold, to make them tread more softly, but if, in spite of this precaution, a twig should snap, the wolf administers a sharp bite to its own offending foot. This licking, or biting, of its feet is usually the distinguishing mark of a wolf.

PANTHER.—With superb disregard for truth the *Physiologus* describes the panther as a gentle beast which typifies the Resurrection of Christ, for, after having slept for three days, 'he crieth, and out of his mouth cometh right good air and savour, and is passing measure sweet : and for the sweetness all beasts follow him. And only the dragon is a-feared when he heareth his voice and fleeth into a den, and may not suffer the smell thereof . . .'[8] At Alne the panther confronts a dragon emerging from its den, and on a boss at Tewkesbury it is surrounded by other animals.

The EAGLE which has grown old and blind soars upwards until the scorching sun burns away its faded plumage and the film upon its eyes; then it dives into a fountain of fresh water and emerges rejuvenated. If a strange egg is placed in an eagle's nest it will cherish the fledgling until it discovers that this, unlike a true eagle, cannot gaze directly at the sun, after which the intruder is cast forth from the nest. At Alne, and elsewhere, the eagle is shown with its head bent sharply round to glance over its own back, so this may have been an accepted convention for representing its unusual powers of sight.

HYENA.—The Bestiaries usually show the hyena dragging a corpse from its grave, and the carver of the wooden bosses at Queen Camel (Somerset) has reproduced such a miniature, but at Alne it merely holds a large bone, for the classical writers mention the powerful jaws with which the hyena cracks bones.

CALADRIUS.—This carving at Alne is the only certain representation of the white bird, described in the Bestiaries as dwelling in the courts of kings. Guillaume le Clerc's rhymed Bestiary tells us that: 'When a man is so deadly sick, | that they despair of his life, | then is this bird brought in. | If he is to get better | and recover from that sickness | the bird turns its face to him | and takes upon itself his infirmity; | And if he may not regain his health | the bird turns the other way | and will not have a look at him.'[9] At Alne it is shown above a sick person in bed.

DRAGONS of every shape and kind abound in church decoration, but although the Bestiaries enumerate twenty-five sorts of dragon the artists were not so scientific, and apart from the two-legged heraldic wyvern, their dragons are merely generalised symbols of Evil.

The TERROBULI, described in the Bestiaries as male and female stones which burst into flames when brought together, are represented at Alne and on another 12th-century door rich in Bestiary subjects at Dalmeny (West Lothian), by half-length human figures amid flames. They stressed the perils of man's association with women.

The ASPIDO CHELONE, or sea-tortoise, was often confused with the whale and is generally shown as a very large fish, because no medieval artist knew what it did look like ! At Alne, and on one of the Queen Camel bosses,[10] the carvers refer to the story told in the Bestiaries, of a ship anchoring to the back of the monster as it sleeps on the surface of the sea. When the sailors awaken the Aspido by lighting a fire on their supposed island, it dives, carrying them all to destruction. It thus typifies the Devil who wins men's trust in order to destroy them. At Queen Camel a smaller fish swimming just below the gaping, sharp-fanged jaws of the Aspido Chelone alludes to the statement of the *Physiologus*, that the monster has such sweet breath that small fishes swim in shoals to meet destruction in its jaws, but the larger, and wiser fishes, avoid it. It is typical of medieval lore that a correctly observed fact of nature should be explained, not by the structure of the whale's throat, but by the supposed wisdom of the larger fish, symbolising the spiritual strength of those who can resist the wiles of the Evil One. The carvers often made still greater nonsense of the tale by showing the whale swallowing a fish almost its equal in size.

GOAT.—The only animal on the Alne door which does not have its Latin title is a goat feeding upon a branch. The *Physiologus* tells us that the word *caper* is derived from *carpendo*, gathering, and that the goat is so called because it gathers food from the tops of bushes.

In spite of its sculpturesque appearance the goat is rarely represented in carvings and almost always in connexion with foliage, as on one of the capitals of the Chapter House at Southwell (Notts).

Although the *Physiologus* attached a spiritual message to each creature, and thus often furnished similes for the preachers, it would be rash to assume that such associations were known to the carvers of the animals we recognise on capitals, bosses and choir stalls. At all ages of life and periods of history men have delighted in highly coloured travellers' tales and the medieval story-teller had the great advantage that, since so much of the globe was still unknown, almost anything *might* be true. It is only in the realm of science that we can still experience the thrill of contemplating limitless possibility, such as our weird animal carvings may faintly recall. *We* know that Sir John Mandeville's *Travels* were a work of fiction, but few medieval craftsmen would have questioned his statement that a griffin was 'stronger than eight lions and more stalwart than a hundred eagles' as they carved those monsters, with the forepart of an eagle and the hindquarters of a lion, which still abound in church art. Early Greek and Latin writers had described how griffins guarded treasure in strange lands and it has recently been suggested that the legend may have originated in the ancient Jewish conception of the Cherubim which guarded the Ark of the Covenant.[11]

Before we mock the medieval craftsmen's passive acceptance of grotesque legends we should remember that we unthinkingly perpetuate this lore in some familiar idioms. The carving on a misericord at Stratford-on-Avon which shows a leggy bird holding a horseshoe in its beak should make us question why 'the digestion of an ostrich' is supposed to be better than that of a sparrow, and our answer would come from the Bestiary which tells that the ostrich can eat iron.[12] It is also said to run as swiftly as a horse or deer, and the artists often allude to this fact by showing the bird with hooves. Again, when we say that we have quailed before 'the basilisk eye' of some hostile person, how many of us associate the phrase with the monster, half-cock, half-serpent, which is carved upon misericords at Malvern and Worcester, and which appears, superbly ferocious, upon a bench-end at Stonham Aspal (Suffolk)? The Bestiary told that this offspring of a cock's egg incubated by a toad upon a dunghill, had the power of slaying by its mere glance those who had not the foresight to reflect back the lethal beam from a mirror, or a polished shield.

Medieval artists also reproduced grotesque human abnormalities derived from the Bestiary. The attitude of the Early Fathers towards these latter is interesting. St. Augustine devotes a whole chapter of *De Civitate Dei* [13] to the question whether Adam's sons 'begat any monstrous kinds of men'. He enumerates many such: the Cyclops with a single eye in their foreheads, the hermaphrodites, the race which have their feet reversed, the pygmies and 'some that have but one leg and bend it not, and yet are of a wonderful swiftness, being called Sciopodes because they sleep under the shade of this their foot; some neckless with the face of a man in their breasts. What shall I say of the Cynocephali, that had dogs' heads and barked like dogs?' He quotes cases of abnormal births to prove the possibility of such creatures existing and, while admitting the fact that such stories of monsters may be 'plain lies', he does not condemn them out of hand as he does the 'fable of a people that inhabit that land where the sun rises when it sets with us, and go with their feet towards ours . . .'. The 13th-century *Mappa Mundi* in Hereford Cathedral [14] shows several of the monsters mentioned by St. Augustine among the fauna of lands which fringed the known world and isolated examples occur sometimes in detail sculpture.[15] On a bench-end at Dennington (Suffolk) the sciapod is shown lying under the shade of his feet (the carver has incorrectly given him two) and the Blemyae, whose faces are in their stomachs, are carved upon misericords at Ripon and in Norwich Cathedral.

By far the commonest of human abnormalities, if indeed we include him among them, is the woodwose, or hairy wild man, who is frequently shown fighting with lions. On some of the great East Anglian fonts lions and woodwoses alternate around the shaft of the font. The wild man thus seems to have been considered as a good beast, although in classical literature he is associated with fauns, the prototypes of devils. The late Mr. G. C. Druce found a possible explanation of the exalted status given to the woodwose in a French Bestiary of *c.* 1300 [16] which describes how the wild men living in parts of India fought with the Sagittarii, and how they went naked unless they had slain a lion, after which they wore its skin. The writer explained that the Sagittarius represented man's body and the wild man his soul, which warred against each other; and as the wild man slew the lion and wore its skin, so the soul slew the body and destroyed the vain delights of the world. The battle between the woodwose and the Sagittarius is crudely carved upon a 12th-century font at West Rounton (Yorks) and in the 14th century we often see the woodwose fighting, or having mastered, a lion. One misericord in Norwich Cathedral shows the woodwose holding two lions in leash and on the stalls of Lincoln Cathedral and Holy Trinity, Coventry, the carver (perhaps the same man in both cases) has shown the wild man bestriding a lion which he controls by a collar and chain (PLATE 23).

Sometimes the wild man is not wild by nature but by ascetic devotion, and there are many versions of the legend of the Hairy Anchorite,[17] including some which identify him with St. John Chrysostom. I know of only one illustration of such a legend, the fine 14th-century wall-painting in the little chapel at Idsworth (Hants)[18] where it is curiously combined with scenes from the life of St. John the Baptist. The painting shows an old man, covered with hair all over his body, but with a halo, emerging on all fours from some bushes. Huntsmen and dogs, in attendance on a crowned bowman, complete the scene which evidently represents the discovery of the anchorite by the king whose daughter he had murdered seven years before, a crime which he still sought to expiate in crawling nakedness. One is tempted to speculate whether the painter has seen a miracle play on the lines of *Jehan le Paulu*[19] and, confusing the long hair of the anchorite with the Baptist's robe of camel hair, had taken the theme to be an incident in the desert life of that saint. But such speculations together with other factors of theatrical use, or heraldry, which made the woodwose so popular in the later Middle Ages, would take us too far from my theme and must be ignored.[20]

The preference of the medieval craftsmen for picturesque fables rather than sober truth was as marked as that of their descendants for 'glorious technicolour' romances rather than documentary films, but occasionally their work was true to Nature. The most popular subject embodying correct observation is that of the mobbed owl and the misericord in Norwich Cathedral which represents the bird of prey, dazzled by its accidental emergence in daylight, attacked by a crowd of small birds, is one of the masterpieces of English wood-carving. I doubt whether the carvers of mobbed owls were much concerned by the Bestiary explanation that these typified the Jews who preferred the night of their ignorance rather than the fair day of Christian belief, and they certainly ignored the parable (stressing the importance of men's unity), which told how bats cling together until, one having let go, all are scattered. Bats are frequently shown in carving, but only singly. A lively carving of a long-eared bat on a misericord at Edlesborough (Bucks) shows clearly the carver's approach to his model. The unusual (and therefore interesting) features of its anatomy, the long ears and the marked 'keel' on its breast-bone, have been exaggerated but, taking the structure of its wings for granted, the carver has made nonsense of their bony 'fingers' which appear as meaningless lines radiating from the arm-bone like a bird's feathers. The carver of some of the Wells misericords is more humbly observant of the beautiful logic of natural forms than most of his fellows and shows the curious junction of the wing membrane to the sides of the bat's tail in one carving while a pair of parrots on another misericord are delicately naturalistic.

One short chapter cannot do justice to the varied interest of animal carvings; the illustrations of the Beast Epics and other satires, the strange fauna of heraldry and the origins of some of the Bestiary legends, must all be ignored. What I hope to have shown is that even the most crudely hacked out creature, if its identifying attributes were clearly shown, could suggest to a medieval beholder a strange tale, a moral simile or the starting point for an exalted meditation, according to the bent of his own mind. In the words of Honorius of Autun, 'Every created thing is but the shadow of the truth of life',[21] and if our picture of what the churches meant to medieval people is to be true it must embrace not only the simple credulity which accepted griffins, basilisks and human monstrosities without question, but also the mysticism of Adam of St. Victor to whom a nut in the palm of his hand could present an image of Christ. Its outer covering betokening His humanity, the shell, the wood of the Cross, and the sweet kernel that hidden Godhead which is the food of man's salvation.[22]

Perhaps the most fitting conclusion, not only to this chapter but to my whole book, may be found in the words of St. Augustine: 'For God made all, and when, or how, He would form this, or that, He knows best, having the perfect skill to beautify this Universe by opposition and diversity of parts. But he that cannot contemplate the beauty of the whole, stumbles at the deformity of the part, not knowing the harmony that it has with the whole.'[23] That lesson might well be pondered by those who see only confusion in the strange mingling of lofty symbolism and grotesque baberies to be found in medieval imagery. Many of the beliefs therein expressed now seem naïve, or even crude; compared with the majesty of the Christian faith they are as the candle in the hands of St. Joseph to the glory of light surrounding the new-born Child, or the shepherds' scrannel pipes to the song of the angelic host. Yet, underlying them all, there is a direct personal experience of religion, a homely reverence before the dimly apprehended splendour of the Divinity, which is often missed amid the tortured uncertainties of our scientific age. We shall almost certainly smile sometimes as we seek to unravel the mysteries of medieval iconography, but it is to be hoped that we shall also learn.

Appendices, Bibliography and Notes,
and General Index

ARRANGEMENT OF SUBJECTS IN THE *BIBLIA PAUPERUM*

(From Block-book printed in Netherlands)

Eve tempted	Annunciation	Gideon and the fleece
The Burning Bush	Nativity	Aaron's rod burgeons
Abner visits David at Hebron	Adoration of Magi	Queen of Sheba visits Solomon
Presentation of first-born in the Temple	Purification	Presentation of Samuel in the Temple
Rebecca sending Jacob to Laban	Flight into Egypt	Mychal assisting David's escape
Adoration of the Golden Calf	Destruction of the idols in Egypt	Dagon falling
Saul causing Ahimelech and the priests to be slain	Massacre of Innocents	Athalia's massacre of the sons of Ahaziah
David consulting God about his return after death of Saul	Return out of Egypt	Return of Jacob to his country
Passage of the Red Sea	Baptism of Christ	Spies bearing grapes
Esau sells his birth-right	Temptation of Christ	Fall of Man
Elijah and the widow's son	Raising of Lazarus	Widow's son restored to life by Elisha
Abraham and the angels	Transfiguration	Children of Israel in the fiery furnace
Nathan reproving David	Mary Magdalene at the the feet of Christ	Miriam punished with leprosy
David with head of Goliath	Entry into Jerusalem	Children of the prophets meet Elisha
Esdras asked by Darius to purify the Temple	Christ driving out the money-changers	Judas Maccabeus orders the purification of the Temple
Jacob told of death of Joseph	Judas betrays Christ	Absolom incites the people to rebellion
Joseph sold to the Ishmaelites	Judas paid 30 pieces of silver	Joseph sold to Potiphar
Melchizedek meets Abraham	Last Supper	Manna from Heaven
Micaiah prophesies the death of Ahab	Christ leaves the disciples at Gethsemane	Elisha prophesies plenty in Samaria

Foolish virgins	Christ in the Garden of Olives	Fall of the Angels
Abner treacherously killed by Joab	Kiss of Judas	Tryphon treacherously takes Jonathan captive
Jezebel seeks to kill Elijah	Pilate washes his hands	Daniel accused by the Babylonians
Shem covers nakedness of Noah	Crowning with thorns	Children mock Elisha and are eaten by bears
Isaac carrying faggots	Christ bearing the Cross	Widow of Zarephath holding two pieces of wood crosswise
Sacrifice of Isaac	Christ on the Cross	Moses and the brazen serpent
Creation of Eve	The soldier pierces the side of Christ	Moses striking the rock
Joseph put into the well	The Entombment	Jonah swallowed by the whale
David cuts off the head of Goliath	Descent into Limbo	Samson and the lion
Samson and the gates of Gaza	The Resurrection	Jonah cast up
Reuben seeking Joseph at the well	Three Maries at the Sepulchre	Daughter of Sion seeking her spouse
Daniel released from the lions' den	Christ appears to the Magdalene	Daughter of Sion finds her spouse
Joseph discovers himself to his brothers	Christ appears to the disciples	Return of the prodigal son
Angel appears to Gideon	Incredulity of St. Thomas	Jacob wrestles with the angel
Enoch taken up to Heaven	Ascension	Elijah in the chariot of fire
Moses receives the Tables of stone	Pentecost	Sacrifice of Elijah consumed by fire from Heaven
Solomon seats his mother by his side	Coronation of Blessed Virgin	Esther and Ahasuerus
Judgment of Solomon	Last Judgment	The Amalekite who slew Saul is slain
Destruction of Korah, Dathan and Abiram	Hell	Sodom and Gomorrah
Feast of the children of Job	Christ holding His saints in His mantle	Jacob's ladder
Daughter of Sion crowned by her spouse	Reward of the righteous	St. John and the Angel

THE LABOURS OF THE MONTHS

Month and Sign of Zodiac	Brookland Font	Ripple Misericords	Worcester Cathedral Misericords
January (*Aquarius*)	Two-faced Janus drinking at table	Man emptying two jugs (Aquarius)	Woman with distaff. Man with spade
February (*Pisces*)	Man sitting by the fire	Man and woman sitting by the fire	Man by the fire
March (*Aries*)	Man pruning a vine	Man sowing and leading horse and cart	Sowing seed
April (*Taurus*)	Figure in long robe holding foliate branch	Bird-scaring	Man holding branches
May (*Gemini*)	A mounted knight hawking	Woman holding nosegays between sheaves of flowers	Man with hawk, horse and page
June (*Cancer*)	A man mowing hay	Full Sun	Mowing with scythe
July (*Leo*)	Man raking hay	Building ?	Weeding with crotch and hook
August (*Virgo*)	Man reaping with sickle	Man and woman cutting corn	Reaping with sickles
September (*Libra*)	Man threshing with flail	Hunting with hawk (broken) and hound	Huntsman with horn
October (*Scorpio*)	Man treading out grapes	Pruning	Swineherd knocking down acorns for his pigs
November (*Sagittarius*)	Swineherd getting acorns for his pigs	Pig killing	. . .
December (*Capricornus*)	Pig-killing	Splitting logs	Killing an ox

Note.—On the Brookland font the names of the months are given in Norman French, also the of the signs of the Zodiac, although the latter are sometimes incorrectly allocated and spelt. In me other cases there is some measure of uncertainty as to which Labour is supposed to represent whi month. The agricultural programme varies according to local climatic conditions and the gener weather conditions and the craftsmen's work reflected their own experience or that of the scribes who illuminated psalters they copied. That the latter influence was the stronger is shown clearly by t fact that sheep-shearing, the most important event to an English medieval farmer, is not include while the tending of vines often appears. Many of the illuminated calendars were probably of Co tinental origin, or based their conception of the agricultural year upon foreign prototypes.

THE APOSTLES AND PROPHETS OF THE CREED SEQUENCE

St. Peter (keys) : 'I believe in God the Father Almighty, Maker of Heaven and earth' :

Jeremiah : 'Thou shalt call me, My father' (iii. 19). 'Ah, Lord God behold, thou has made the heaven and the earth by thy great power.' (xxxii. 17).

St. Andrew (saltire cross) : 'and in Jesus Christ, His only Son, Our Lord',

David : ' The Lord hath said unto me, "Thou art my son ; this day have I begotten thee" ' (Psalm ii. 7).

St. James Major (pilgrim's habit) : 'who was conceived by the Holy Ghost, born of the Virgin Mary',

Isaiah : 'Behold, a virgin shall conceive, and bear a son' (vii. 14).

St. John (dragon emerging from chalice) : 'Suffered under Pontius Pilate, was crucified, dead and buried',

Zechariah : 'They shall look upon me whom they have pierced' (xii. 10).

St. Thomas (spear) : 'He descended into Hell ; the third day He rose again from the dead',

Hosea : 'O death, I will be thy plagues ; O grave, I will be thy destruction' (xiii. 14).

St. James Minor (a club) : 'He ascended into Heaven and sitteth on the right hand of God the Father Almighty' ;

Amos : 'It is he that buildeth his stories in the heaven' (ix. 6).

St. Philip (loaves or tall cross) : 'From thence He shall come to judge the quick and the dead'.

Zephaniah : 'And I will come near to you to judgment ; and I will be a swift witness'. (This mistaken attribution of Malachi iii. 5 is often seen.)

St. Bartholomew (flaying knife) : 'I believe in the Holy Ghost' ;

Joel : 'I will pour out my spirit upon all flesh' (ii. 28).

St. Matthew (money-box, bag, or sometimes a sword) : 'The Holy Catholic Church ; the Communion of Saints' ;

Micah : 'They may all call upon the name of the Lord, to serve him'. (Mistaken attribution of Zephaniah iii. 9.)

St. Simon (fish, oar or sword) : 'The forgiveness of sins' ;

St. Jude (a boat) : 'The resurrection of the body',

St. Mathias (halberd) : 'and the life everlasting'.

Malachi : 'The God of Israel saith that he hateth putting away' (ii. 16).

Daniel : 'Many of them that sleep in the dust of the earth shall awake' (xii. 2). By confusion the text given to Daniel is often 'I will open your graves' (Ezekiel xxxvii. 12).

Obadiah : 'The Kingdom shall be the Lord's' (21).

Note.—The order of the Apostles is generally the same but that of the Prophets may vary, or different texts be allotted to them.

APPENDIX 4

LIST OF ANIMALS IDENTIFIABLE IN CHURCHES

REAL ANIMALS

Antelope.—Has long serrated horns which become entangled in bushes as man is trapped by his sins. (Walpole St. Peter, bench-end), or misericord in Manchester Cathedral.

Ape.—Much used in satires on human frauds such as the 'ape doctor' holding up a urine flask.

Bat.—General appearance naturalistic but details of anatomy never correct. Misericords: Chichester, Christchurch, Lincoln, Wells, Edlesborough (Bucks).

Bear.—Shown in scenes of bear-baiting, etc., or heraldically as Warwick badge of the bear and ragged staff. Also in the Reynard the Fox beast epic.

Boar.—Boar hunts. Wild boar on tympanum of St. Nicholas' Ipswich.

Camel.—Except for its hump, or humps, its anatomy is imaginary.

Cat.—Usually shown holding a mouse. As a character in the Reynard the Fox epic, on the misericords in Bristol Cathedral.

Crane.—Only distinguishable from other long-necked birds when it holds a stone in one claw (Denston misericord (Suffolk), poppy-head Lincoln Cathedral). One crane said to stand sentinel, while the others slept, with a stone in upraised foot which it would let fall should it sleep.

Crocodile.—Real form unknown so it can only be identified when shown swallowing the small serpent (*Hydrus*, q.v.), as on the corbels of Kilpeck (Herefs).

Deer.—Frequent in hunting scenes and in legends of St. Hubert and St. Giles.

Dog.—A starving dog gnawing bone is finely carved on a misericord at Christchurch (Hants) and on a bench-end at Lakenheath (Suffolk) a dog is licking itself, because the Bestiary says that thus dogs heal their wounds.

Doves.—When drinking from a chalice they symbolise the Holy Communion.

Duck.—Rare, but correctly represented on a misericord at Stratford-on-Avon.

Eagle.—(See page 179.) Only distinguishable from other birds of prey when used as emblem of St. John the Evangelist. Legend of the Lathom baby in the eagle's nest carved on stall-end in Manchester Cathedral.

Elephant.—(See page 178.) Common, but generally grossly inaccurate : any beast with a long nose probably meant to be an elephant.

Fox.—Sometimes shown shamming dead to trap birds (misericord Whalley, Lancs) ; more often making off with a goose over its shoulder. Symbol of fraud, as when it preaches to the geese, in monk's robe. Beast epic on misericord in Bristol Cathedral.

Frog.—Symbol of heretics, and is shown issuing from a dragon's mouth in one of the Apocalypse bosses in Norwich cloister. On misericord at Edlesborough (Bucks) all four feet are webbed.

Goat.—Generally shown browsing upon bushes (Winchester College misericord).

Hawk.—In hawking scenes or alone, grasping some small animal in its talons.

Hedgehog.—Said to roll on fallen fruit and carry this back to its young on its spines. Shown with fruit thus impaled on a misericord in New College, Oxford.

Hippopotamus.—A possible example, which might equally be a rhinoceros, on a misericord in St. George's Chapel, Windsor.

Hoopoe.—The young are said to tend their aged parents by plucking out their old feathers. Only shown on a misericord in St. George's Chapel, Windsor, where the birds' crests are clearly marked.

Horse.—Only shown incidentally in hunting scenes, etc.

Hyena.—(See page 179.)

Ibex.—Was said to throw itself over precipices and land safely upon its horns. A possible, and very beautiful, example on a bench-end in St. Nicholas', Kings Lynn.

Ibis.—Said to live by the side of water and to feed upon carrion (misericord at Lavenham (Suffolk) shows two of them pecking a human head), or upon serpents (misericord St. George's Chapel, Windsor).

Lion.—Very common and generally naturalistic.

Lizard.—Hard to distinguish from the many forms of dragon. Carving on a corbel in Wells Cathedral of a lizard among vine leaves and fruit.

Ostrich.—(See page 181.) I know of no representation earlier than a misericord in Henry VII's Chapel, Westminster Abbey, which indicates that the craftsman knew at all what the bird looked like.

Owl.—(See page 183.) Different species sometimes indicated : short-eared owl on misericord at Hemington (Northants) and long-eared owl on misericord at Edlesborough (Bucks).

Panther.—(See page 179.)

Pard.—Said to be born of a panther and a lioness, and to be very bloodthirsty. Generally shown in profile with branching tail but with its head turned full face and its tongue extended from gaping jaws.

Parrot.—Rare. Misericord in Wells Cathedral.

Peacock.—Eyes in its tail symbolised foresight, which a man often loses, as the bird moults. The bird was associated with the Roman empresses who were deified at death and so came to represent immortality. Carved on the font at Hodnet (Salop).

Pelican.—Never naturalistic earlier than the 19th-century monument in Gloucester Cathedral. Always shown plucking its own breast with the young birds below. (See page 176.)

Phoenix.—Birds with curiously branching tails may represent the phoenix but the characteristic design of the bird rising from the flames only occurs on a misericord in Henry VII's Chapel, Westminster.

Pig.—Sow and farrow a symbol of a divinely appointed spot, for the site of a church.

Rabbit.—Sometimes shown as the prey of a hawk, but not common.

Raven.—Only identifiable in scenes of Noah in the Ark, when it feeds upon carrion.

Serpent.—Except in representations of the Fall of Man a naturalistic snake is rare. Font at Ashover (Derbs) has serpent with knotted tail apparently wriggling through the bowl. This may allude to the belief that snakes slough off their old skin (here symbolising sin) by wriggling through a crack in a wall.

Sheep.—Rare except in genre subjects. Rams used as a rebus on the chantry of Abbot Ramÿnge in St. Albans Cathedral.

Squirrel.—Generally shown naturalistically, sitting up to eat a nut.

Swan.—Mostly heraldic, often with a coronet round its neck (*ducally gorged*).

Tiger.—(See page 177.)

Whale.—(See page 180.)

Wolf.—(See page 179.) When holding a crowned head it refers to the legend of St. Edmund.

Fabulous Creatures

Amphisbaena.—Winged serpent with a second head at the end of its tail, which the Greeks knew as a symbol of deceit. Medieval craftsmen apt to bestow the second head on any monster they wished to make horrific.

Asp.—Two-legged beast with a long tail, which was supposed to lay one ear to the ground and block the other with its tail, typifying the sinner making himself deaf to the divine message. Misericord in Exeter Cathedral.

Basilisk.—(See page 181.) Should have the head, wings and feet of a cock and the body and tail of a serpent, but is not always correctly shown. Weasel can attack it because it first protects itself by eating rue. This is shown on misericord in Worcester Cathedral.

Blemya.—Human abnormality with its face in its stomach. Misericord in Norwich Cathedral.

Caladrius.—(See page 180.)

Centaur or *Sagittarius.*—Its human half typifies Christ upon earth, and the horse His vengeance upon those who betrayed Him. Frequent representations of centaur aiming its arrows at the throat of a monster perhaps associated with the Harrowing of Hell.

Cynocephali.—Dog-headed race of men shown on the World Map in Hereford Cathedral but elsewhere impossible to distinguish from mere grotesques.

Dragon.—The commonest symbol of evil. Distinguished from Wyvern by having four legs.

Griffin.—(See page 181.)

Hydrus.—Small snake said to cover itself in mud, slip down the throat of a crocodile and then burst out of its side, thus typifying Christ descending into Hell in human form. Kilpeck (Herefs).

Mantichora.—Has head of man with three rows of teeth, the body of a lion and the tail of a scorpion. Perhaps incised on exterior of North Cerney (Glos).

Salamander.—Two-legged winged dragon with a long tail which is always branched, or knotted. Supposed to live in fire, it symbolised the man who could pass through temptation unscathed. Sometimes shown on fonts, as at Salehurst (Sussex) and Youlgreave (Derbs).

Sciapod.—(See page 182.)

Siren.—There are two types, the bird-siren and the fish-siren or mermaid. In medieval art the latter predominated but transitional types having feathers and claws as well as fish tails occur on misericords at Carlisle and Hereford, All Saints. The mermaid approaches her prey, two sailors in a boat, on a misericord at Boston (Lincs). The fish which the mermaid sometimes holds in one hand (Exeter Cathedral misericord) typifies a soul in the grasp of the Evil One, but she is generally shown with mirror and comb. Mermen are rare but both sexes appear together on a misericord at Stratford-on-Avon.

Terrobuli.—(See page 180.)

Unicorn.—Shown as a goat, or a deer with one spiral horn. (See page 176.)

BIBLIOGRAPHY AND NOTES

A COMPLETE bibliography of this book would take up far more space than can be spared, so I have either quoted from accepted authorities in support of my statements or indicated sources from which the ordinary reader can learn more about some particular point. I have deliberately referred to books and periodicals likely to be available through any good reference library rather than to the less accessible original source-books and foreign journals.

ABBREVIATIONS

Apocryphal New Testament. Translated by M. R. James. (Oxford, 1926.)

Biblia Pauperum. Most references are to the facsimile edition edited by J. Ph. Berjeau (1859).

Cave, Bosses. C. J. P. Cave, *Roof Bosses in Medieval Churches* (1948).

Didron—Stokes. A. N. Didron, *Christian Iconography* (1907), English translation completed and added to by Margaret Stokes.

Dives and Pauper. Edition printed by Wynkyn de Worde (1496). British Museum copy.

E.E.T.S. Early English Text Society publications.

Festial. *John Mirk's Festial: a Collection of Homilies*, E.E.T.S. (Extra Series) XCVI, ed. Theodore Erbe.

The Golden Legend, or Lives of the Saints as englished by William Caxton, 1483, ed. F. S. Ellis, Temple Classics, 7 vols. (1927).

Gougaud. Dom Louis Gougaud, *Devotional and Ascetic Practices in the Middle Ages* (1927).

Keyser, Murals. C. E. Keyser, *A List of Buildings having Mural Decorations* (1883).

Keyser, Tympana. C. E. Keyser, *Norman Tympana and Lintels* (1904).

Künstle. K. Künstle, *Ikonographie der christlichen Kunst*, 2 vols. (1928).

Mâle, XIIe. Émile Mâle, *L'Art religieux du XIIe siècle en France* (1928).

Mâle, XIIIe. Émile Mâle, *L'Art religieux du XIIIe siècle en France* (1910).

Mâle, fin M.A. Émile Mâle, *L'Art religieux de la fin du moyen-âge en France* (1931).

Millet. Gabriel Millet, *Recherches sur l'iconographie de l'Évangile au XIVe, XVe et XVIe siècles d'après les monuments de la Macédoine et du Mont Athos* (1916).

Nelson. P. Nelson, *Ancient Painted Glass in England* (1913).

Owst, Lit. G. R. Owst, *Literature and the Pulpit in Medieval England* (1933).

Rackham. B. Rackham, *The Ancient Glass in Canterbury Cathedral* (1949).

Rushforth. G. McN. Rushforth, *Medieval Christian Imagery as illustrated by the Painted Windows of Malvern Priory Church* (1936).

Woodforde, Norwich. Christopher Woodforde, *Norwich School of Glass Painting in the 15th Century* (1950).

Woodforde, Somerset. Christopher Woodforde, *Stained Glass in Somerset, 1250–1830* (1946).

INTRODUCTION

1. *The Journal of William Dowsing*, ed. C. H. Evelyn White (1885). He charged each parish 6s. 8d. for his services in destroying imagery, although this was not always collected. Sometimes only a few windows were broken and 'popish inscriptions' on brasses erased, but at Clare 'a thousand pictures' were destroyed together with other imagery.

2. *A Pocket Guide to the Church of St. Mary at Kersey*.

3. E. Milner White, *The Ancient Glass of St. Michael, Spurriergate, York*, p. 5.

4. Canon Wickenden, 'The Choir Stalls of Lincoln Cathedral', *Archaeological Journal* (1881), XXXVIII, 42–61.

PART I

1. THE PARSON'S APPROACH

1. A. F. Leach, *Educational Charters* (1911), p. 122.

2. A. F. Leach, *The Schools of Medieval England* (1916), *passim*.

3. L. F. Salzman, *English Life in the Middle Ages* (1926), pp. 136 ff.

4. C. G. Crump and E. F. Jacob, *The Legacy of the Middle Ages* (1926), pp. 254.

5. Owst, *Lit. passim*, and G. R. Owst, *Preaching in Medieval England* (1927).

6. Vincent of Beauvais did not himself complete his great encyclopaedia, and the *Speculum Morale* was added by another writer.

7. M. R. James and E. W. Tristram, *The Wall-paintings in Eton College Chapel and in the Lady Chapel of Winchester Cathedral*, Walpole Soc., XVII (1929).

8. G. G. Coulton, *Europe's Apprenticeship* (1940), p. 79.

9. A. Hamilton Thompson, 'Pluralism in the Medieval Church, with Notes on the Pluralists in the Diocese of Lincoln in 1366', *Associated Archit. and Arch. Soc. Reports*, XXXIII, 35 ff. The author quotes two extreme cases. John Mansel (d. 1265), the trusted Minister of Henry III, who was accounted as the richest man in the world by Matthew Paris, and was commonly said to have held 300 benefices, and Bogo de Clare, younger son of the Earl of Gloucester, who held 2 canonries and prebends, which were sinecures, 3 dignities in cathedrals or collegiate churches (including the Treasurership of York) and 24 parish livings, or portions of such, involving the cure of souls.

10. J. H. Harvey, 'The Medieval Office of Works', *British Archaeological Ass. Journal* (3rd Series), VI (1941).

11. T. D. Atkinson, *Local Style in English Architecture* (1947), pp. 159–61, gives a list of buildings known to have been built in imitation of others.

12. A. Hamilton Thompson, *The English Clergy* (1947), p. 115.

13. F. H. Crossley, 'Monastic Influence on the Construction of Parish Churches', *Chester and North Wales Archaeol. Soc. Journal*, XXXIII (1939), 138–49. Gives a list of Cheshire churches which were appropriated to various monasteries.

14. T. R. Boase, *English Art, 1100–1216* (1953), *passim*.

15. Audrey Baker, *Lewes Priory and the Early Group of Wall-paintings at Hardham and Clayton*, Walpole Soc. XXXI (1946).

16. G. C. Druce, 'Queen Camel, Bosses on the Chancel Roof', *Somerset Arch. and Nat. Hist. Soc. LXXXIII* (1937), 89–106.

17. William Durandus, *Rationale divinorum officiorum*, ed. J. M. Neale and B. Webb, 1893.

18. M. R. James, 'Pictor in Carmine', *Archaeologia*, XCIV, 141-66.

19. St. Antoninus, *Summa*, pars. iii, tit. viii, c. 4. The translation is quoted from G. G. Coulton, *Art and the Reformation* (1928), pp. 382-3.

20. 'Myrc's Duties of a Parish Priest' (*c.* 1420) (Original Series), No. 31.

21. Giraldus Cambrensis, *Opera*, R.S. II, 341.

22. See also G. G. Coulton, *Europe's Apprenticeship* (1940), pp. 64 ff.

23. For Archbishop Peckham's 'Constitutions' see *The Lay Folks Catechism*, E.E.T.S. (Original Series), No. 118.

24. A. K. Wickham, *St. Michael's Church, Brent Knoll* (1949), p. 2.

25. *Owst, Lit.* p. 249.

2. THE CRAFTSMAN'S APPROACH

1. D. Knoop and G. P. Jones, *The Medieval Mason* (1935), p. 75.

2. G. G. Coulton, *Art and the Reformation* (1928), p. 199.

3. R. H. C. Davis, 'Masons' Marks in Oxfordshire and the Cotswolds', *Oxfordshire Arch. Soc. Report 84* (1938), pp. 69 ff. See also Coulton, *op. cit.* pp. 143-64, on masons' marks.

4. Knoop and Jones, *op. cit.* p. 166.

5. P. B. Chatwin, 'The Decoration of the Beauchamp Chapel, Warwick, with Special Reference to the Sculptures', *Archaeologia*, LXXVII (1937), 313 ff. The will of Sir Richard Beauchamp, Earl of Warwick, made in 1437, orders the building of the Beauchamp Chapel to contain his tomb. The work was carried out under the direction of Thomas Huggeford, one of the Earl's Council, Nicholas Rody, Steward, and William Berkeswell, priest-dean of the collegiate church of St. Mary at Warwick. The various contracts have survived and among those concerned was Roger Webbe, barber, who is known to have been the Warden of the Worshipful Company of Barber Surgeons of London in 1449.

6. R. Willis, *The Architectural History of Canterbury Cathedral* (1845), p. 36.

7. George Zarnecki, *Later English Romanesque Sculpture, 1140-1210* (1953), pp. 1-8.

8. *Keyser, Tympana*, repr. plates 73, 79, 80.

9. T. S. R. Boase, *English Art, 1100-1216* (1953), p. 240.

10. *The Trinity Apocalypse*, ed. M. R. James (Roxburghe Club, 1909).

11. M. D. Whinney, *The Interrelation of the Fine Arts in England in the Early Middle Ages* (1930), *passim*.

12. A. Saxl and R. Wittkower, *British Art and the Mediterranean* (1948), p. 14.

13. C. Mowbray, 'Eastern Influence on Carvings at St. Andrews and Nigg', *Antiquity* (Dec. 1926), pp. 428 ff.

14. E. W. Tristram and W. G. Constable, *English Medieval Wall Paintings, 12th Century* (1944), p. 64.

15. Geoffrey Webb, 'The Decorative Character of Westminster Abbey', *Warburg Journal*, XII, pp. 16-20.

16. J. van den Gheyn, *Le Psaultier de Peterborough*, 1911; M. R. James, 'On Paintings formerly in the Choir at Peterborough', *Cambridge Antiq. Soc. Proc.* No. 38, IX, 178 ff.

17. M. R. James, 'On Two Series of Paintings formerly at Worcester Priory', *Cambridge Antiq. Soc. Proc.* No. 42, X, 99 ff.; Mary Chamot, *English Medieval Enamels* (1930), pp. 26-31.

18. George Zarnecki, *English Romanesque Sculpture, 1066–1140* (1951), plates 39–40. The manuscript referred to is in the British Museum, Cotton MS., Claudius, E. V.

19. Bertram Colgrave, 'The St. Cuthbert Paintings on the Carlisle Cathedral Stalls', *Burlington Magazine*, LXXIII, 17 ff.

20. J. A. Knowles, 'Medieval Methods of Employing Cartoons for Stained Glass', *Master Glass Painters' Journal*, I, No. 3, pp. 35 ff.

21. *Rushforth, passim.*

3. THE PARISHIONER'S APPROACH

1. Francis Bond, *Fonts and Font Covers* (1908), includes a chapter on inscribed fonts, pp. 107-17.

2. G. G. Coulton, *Medieval Panorama* (1938), pp. 164-5.

3. *Gougaud*, pp. 131-45.

4. A. G. Little, 'Sculpture Miscellaneous' in *Franciscan History and Legend in English Medieval Art* (1937). The Conington effigy is here quoted as the only example of a Franciscan habit on the effigy of a layman.

5. G. H. Cook, *Medieval Chantries and Chantry Chapels* (1947), *passim.*

6. D. Rock, *The Church of Our Fathers* (1905), III, 109 n. and 266 n.

7. A. R. Dufty, 'The Stathum Book of Hours', *Archaeological Journal*, CVI, Memorial Volume to Sir Alfred Clapham (1952), pp. 83-90, quotes some other examples of brasses and tablets commemorating obits : two examples in the parish church of Corfe Castle and brasses at Finchley, St. Mary's and Shipton-under-Wychwood (Oxon). The prayers specified on the second brass are as follows : *De Profundis*, etc. ; *Pater Noster*, etc. ; *Ave Maria* ; *et ne nos* (indicating the penultimate clause of the Lord's Prayer and the prayers following in the Office of the Dead) *requiem eternam*, etc. (the beginning of the refrain used after every psalm and canticle in that Office) ; *Domini exaudi orationem, with this orison Inclina domine*, etc. (the collect for the departed in the Use of Sarum), *John Stathum ordained this to be said and more written in other divers books.* Mr. Dufty has recently identified one of these 'other books', and the rings on its binding suggested that it may have been originally chained near the brass which it supplements.

8. The Ashwell Graffito reads :

> MCter X Penta miseranda ferox violanta
> . . . ? (pestis) superest plebs pessima testis
> In fine IIe ventus validus
> . . . oc anno Maurus in orbe tonat XCCCLXI

See letters in *East Herts. Archaeological Soc. Trans.* IX, 67.

9. H. F. Westlake, *The Parish Gilds of Medieval England* (1917), *passim.*

10. *Regist. Test. Ebor.* V, 108, quoted from J. A. Knowles, 'Gild Windows', *British Master Glass Painters' Soc. Journal*, VII.

11. J. A. Knowles, 'The East Window of Holy Trinity, Goodramgate', *Yorkshire Archaeol. Journal*, XXVIII, pt. i (1924).

12. E. K. Chambers, *The Medieval Stage* (1903), II, 116-48, on 'Guild Plays and Parish Plays', also gives a bibliography of the subject.

13. M. D. Anderson, *Looking for History in British Churches* (1951).

14. G. G. Coulton, *Art and the Reformation* (1928), pp. 281-5.

15. Arnold Foster, *Studies in Church Dedications* (1899), II, 114.

PART II

1. THE SIGNIFICANCE OF PLAN

1. A. Hamilton Thompson, *The Ground Plan of the English Parish Church* (1911), *passim*, and G. H. Cook, *The English Medieval Parish Church* (1954), pp. 76-123.
2. A. W. Clapham, *English Romanesque Architecture before the Conquest* (1930), pp. 26-8.
3. William Durandus, *Rationale Divinorum Officiorum*, ed. J. M. Neale and Benjamin Webb (1893), pp. 21-34 *passim*.
4. C. J. P. Cave, 'The Orientation of Churches', *Antiquaries' Journal* (1949), pp. 47-51.
5. H. Munro Cautley, *Norfolk Churches* (1949), pp. 14-17.
6. F. C. Eeles, 'The Orientation of Scottish Churches', *Publ. Soc. Antiquaries of Scotland*, XLVIII (1914), 169 ff. Analyses examples in Aberdeenshire and Banffshire. Out of 62 churches surveyed only 8 were orientated due east. 38 inclined to the north and 16 to the south. 15 inclined more than 20° north, the extreme case being 35°. Only 3 inclined as much as 20° south.

2. THE STRUCTURAL SETTING OF IMAGERY

SHORT BIBLIOGRAPHY

General Works
   G. W. O. Addleshaw and Francis Etchells, *The Architectural Setting of Anglican Worship* (1948).
   G. H. Cook, *The English Medieval Parish Church* (1954).
   C. J. Cox and H. Harvey, *English Church Furniture* (1907).
   C. J. Cox, *Church Fittings, Furniture and Accessories* (1923).
   C. J. Cox and C. B. Ford, *The Parish Churches of England* (1935).
   F. H. Crossley, *English Church Craftsmanship* (1941).
   F. E. Howard and F. H. Crossley, *English Church Woodwork* (1927).
   A. Needham, *How to Study an Old Church* (1944).
   D. Rock, *The Church of our Fathers* (1905).
   A. Hamilton Thompson, *The Historical Growth of the English Parish Church* (1911).

Churchyard Crosses
   A. Vallance, *Old Crosses and Lychgates* (1935).
   W. G. Collingwood, *Northumbrian Crosses* (1927).

Consecration Crosses
   F. C. Eeles, 'Consecration Crosses in Somerset and Dorset Churches', *Somerset Arch. and Nat. Hist. Soc. Proc.* LXXVI, 22.

   J. H. Middleton, 'Consecration Crosses', *Archaeologia*, XLVIII, 436.

Mass Dials
   Dom Ethelbert Horne, *Scratch Dials, Their Description and History* (1929).
   A. R. Green and P. Green, *Saxon Architecture and Sculpture in Hampshire* (1951), has a section on scratch dials.

The Porch
   Ulric Daubeny, *Ancient Cotswold Churches* (1921), gives a list of the Gloucestershire churches which have niches in their porches.

The Font
   Francis Bond, *Fonts and Font-covers* (1908).

Seating
> Francis Bond, *Wood Carvings in English Churches*: I, 'Misericords' (1910) ; II, 'Stalls and Tabernacle Work' (1910).
> C. J. Cox '*Bench-ends in English Churches* (1916).

Pulpits and Lecterns
> C. J. Cox, *Pulpits, Lecterns and Organs* (1915).

Chantry Chapels
> G. H. Cook, *Medieval Chantries and Chantry Chapels* (1947).

Tombs
> F. H. Crossley, *English Church Monuments* (1921).
> K. A. Esdaile, *English Church Monuments 1510–1840* (1946).
> A. Gardner, *Alabaster Tombs of the Pre-Reformation Period in England* (1940).

Rood-screens
> Francis Bond, *Screens and Galleries in English Churches* (1909).
> Francis Bond and B. Camm, *English Church Screens and Roodlofts* (1909).
> A. Vallance, *English Church Screens* (1936).
> A. Vallance, *Screens of Greater English Churches* (1947).
> H. Munro Cautley, *Royal Arms and Commandments in Our Churches* (1934).

The Chancel Fittings
> Francis Bond, *The Chancel of English Churches* (1916).
> Archibald Macpherson, 'Scottish Sacrament Houses', *Soc. Antiquaries of Scotland Proc.* XXV, 89-116.
> Rotha M. Clay, *Hermits and Anchorites of England.*

PART III

1. THE SEVEN SACRAMENTS AND DEVOTIONAL IMAGES

1. *Gougaud*, pp. 3-47.
2. *Gougaud*, pp. 26-7.
3. A. C. Fryer, 'Seven Sacrament Fonts', *Archaeological Journal*, LIX, 17 ff. ; LXII, 102 ff. ; LXX, 171 ; LXXVII, 1 ff. Examples may be seen at the following places :
   > *Norfolk* : Alderford, Brooke, Burgh-next-to-Aylsham ; Cley, Earsham, East Dereham, Gt. Witchingham, Gorleston, Gresham, Little Walsingham, Loddon, Marsham, Martham, Norwich Cathedral, Salle, Sloley, Walsoken, West Lynn, Gayton Thorpe, Seething, Wendling and South Creake.
   > *Suffolk* : Badingham, Blythburgh, Cratfield, Denston, Great Glemham, Laxfield, Melton, Monk Soham, Westhall, Weston and Woodbridge.
4. D. Rock, *The Church of Our Fathers* (1905), IV, 178-9.
5. *Myrc's Duties of a Parish Priest*, E.E.T.S. (Original Series), No. 31.
6. D. Rock, *op. cit.* IV, 201.
7. G. McN. Rushforth, 'Seven Sacrament Compositions in English Medieval Art', *Antiquaries' Journal*, IX, 83 ff.
8. Other incomplete examples of Seven Sacrament windows are recorded at : Tattershall (Lincs), Cartmel Fell (Lancs), St. Anthony's Chapel, Burrington and Bishop's Lydeard (Somerset), Frampton (Glos), Malvern Priory, Nostell Priory (Yorks), Llandyrnog (Denbighs). A wall-painting of the subject was found at Kirton (Lincs) in 1860 but has perished.
9. *Mâle, fin M.A.* p. 100 repr.
10. Campbell Dodgson, *English Devotional Woodcuts of the Late 15th Century*, Walpole Soc. XVII.

11. E. S. Prior and A. Gardner, *Medieval Figure Sculpture in England* (1912), p. 464 repr.

12. G. McN. Rushforth, 'The Kirkham Monument in Paignton Church', *Exeter Diocesan Archit. and Arch. Soc. Trans.* XV (1927), 192.

13. Campbell Dodgson, *loc. cit.* repr.
    Other examples of the Mass of St. Gregory occur in windows at Alston (Glos), Blakeney (Norfolk), Tattershall (Lincs) and All Saints, North Street, York. The carving on the west door of St. Mary Magdalene's, Taunton (Somerset), is a copy of the original now in the Castle Museum, Taunton.

14. H. Macklin, *The Brasses of England* (1907), p. 233. G. Marshall, 'The Church of Edwin Ralph and Some Notes on Pardon Monuments', *Woolhope Naturalists Field Club* (1924–6), pp. 40 ff., discusses the incised tomb slab of Matilda Eddefen, *c.* 1320, at Edwin Ralph, which has a Latin inscription round it recording that the Bishop of Worcester has granted 30 days' pardon, and the Bishop of Hereford, 60 days, to those who should pray for her soul. Such inscriptions are fairly common, dating from the late 13th and early 14th centuries, but thereafter become rare until the late 15th century. These later examples show the important difference that the bishops no longer observed the ruling of the Lateran Council of 1216 which limited such grants of pardon to 40 days, except at the dedication of a church when 100 days might be granted to those present. The later tombs mention periods of pardon ranging from 100 days to 26,000 years. Mr. Marshall gives the following list of tombs bearing pardon inscriptions:

    English Bicknor, Glos. Two tombs, one of them commemorating Urian de St. Pierre, d. 1294.
    Great Coates, Lincs. Brass of Sir Thomas Barnardiston. 100 days.
    Hatfield Broad Oak, Essex. The Earl of Oxford, d. 1221. 40 days.
    St. Buryan, Cornwall. Clarice Bolleit. 10 days.
    Semington, Wilts. A fragment. 40 days.
    Stambourne, Essex. Edward Mackwilliams. 300 days.
    Winchester Cathedral. Prior William de Basingstoke, d. 1295. 350 days.
    The unusual length of pardon granted at this early date may have been accounted for by a direct grant from the Pope.

    In Hungerford church (Berks) there is a marble slab bearing an Anglo-Norman inscription, within, and around, an incised quatrefoil design. This may be translated: 'Whoso shall pray for Sir Robert Hungerford whilst he shall live, and for his soul after death, shall have 550 days of pardon, granted by 14 Bishops, whilst he was alive. Wherefore in the name of charity [say] a Pater and Ave.' The slab has been temporarily detached from the wall owing to alterations.
    Sometimes the indulgence is associated with the whole church. By the door of St. Catherine's Chapel, overlooking Milton Abbey (Dorset), there is a 13th-century inscription which promises 110 days' indulgence to those who come to this holy place. In the little church of Clapton (Glos) an inscription on the chancel arch, thought to date from the 13th century, seems to promise 1000 days' pardon to those who say a Pater and an Ave, devoutly kneeling, but why so long a period of indulgence should have been granted to such an unimportant church is not known. See G. McN. Rushforth, 'An Indulgence Inscription in Clapton Church, Glos.', *Antiquaries' Journal*, III (1923), 338.

15. *The Lay Folks Mass Book*, E.E.T.S. (Original Series), No. 71, ed. Canon Simmons from the manuscript in the British Museum, Royal MS. 17B, xvii.

16. *Legends of Holy Rood, Symbols of the Passion and Cross Poems*, E.E.T.S.

(Original Series), No. 46, ed. R. Morris. The poems quoted are from British Museum, Royal MS. 17A, xxvii.

17. C. J. P. Cave, 'The Bosses on the Vault of the Quire of Winchester Cathedral', *Archaeologia*, LXXVI, 161, gives a full description of these bosses, with many illustrations.

18. *Gougaud*, p. 83.

19. James Fowler, 'Note on Bowness Church', *Proc. Soc. Antiquaries* (2nd Series), IV, 420

20. *Gougaud*, p. 79.

21. *Woodforde, Somerset*, p. 262 repr. For the theological and historical development of this iconographical theme see Evelyn Underhill, 'The Fountain of Life', *Burlington Magazine*, XVII, 99-109.

22. Edmund Kite, 'Note on Desk at Bishop's Cannings', *Proc. Soc. Antiquaries* (1st Series), IV, 277.

2. THE SIGNIFICANCE OF POSITION

1. *Didron—Stokes*, II, 189 ff. The text of 'The Byzantine Guide to Painting' is translated in Appendix II of this work.

2. O. M. Dalton, *Byzantine Art and Archaeology* (1911), p. 649.

3. *Keyser, Tympana*, p. xxviii.

4. A. R. Green, *Saxon Architecture and Sculpture in Hampshire* (1951), p. 36 repr., plate XI.

5. W. H. St. John Hope and W. R. Lethaby, 'The Imagery and Sculptures on the West Front of Wells Cathedral', *Archaeologia*, LIX (1904).

6. E. W. Tristram and W. G. Constable, *English Medieval Wall Paintings, 12th Century* (1944), pp. 113-15.

7. *Mâle, XIIIe*, p. 18.

8. Clive Bell, *Twelfth-century Paintings at Hardham and Clayton* (1947), p. 15.

9. *Rackham, passim.*

10. *Rushforth*, p. 328.

11. F. T. S. Houghton, 'Astley Church and its Stall Paintings', *Birmingham Arch. Soc. Trans.* LI, 19 ff.

12. O. G. Farmer, *Fairford Church and its Stained-glass Windows* (1931).

3. THE CHOICE OF SUBJECTS

1. G. Wilpert, *La fede della Chiesa nascente secondo i monumenti dell' arte funeraria antica* (1938), *passim*.

2. Françoise Henry, *Irish Art in the Early Christian Period* (1940), pp. 169-70. An Irish version of the *Ordo Commendationis Animae*, which is embodied in the 9th-century Calendar of Aengus, differs from the original adaptation of a Jewish invocation, made by St. Cyprian of Antioch in the 2nd century, by being addressed throughout to Jesus. Whitley Stokes, 'The Martyrology of Oengus the Culdee', *Henry Bradshaw Soc.* (1905), pp. 283-4.

3. Origen, *De Principiis*, Bk. IV, chap. ii.

4. St. Augustine, *Confessions*, Bk. V, chap. 6.

5. Bede, *Historia Abbatum*, 9, *Opera Historica*, ed. C. P. Plummer (1896), I. 373.

6. *Rackham*, pp. 51-65.

7. J. Lafond, 'The Stained-glass Decoration of Lincoln Cathedral in the 13th Century', *Archaeological Journal*, CIII, 119-56.
8. M. R. James, 'On the Paintings formerly in the Choir of Peterborough', *Cambridge Antiq. Soc.* IX, 178-94.
9. J. H. Cornell, *Biblia Pauperum* (Stockholm), 1926. J. Ph. Bergeau, *Biblia Pauperum* (1859), a facsimile reproduction of a 15th-century Netherlandish block-book.
10. J. Lutz and P. Perdrizet, *Speculum Humanae Salvationis* (1907). *Speculum Humanae Salvationis*, facsimile of a 14th-century Italian MS. with preface by M. R. James (Roxburghe Club, 1926).
11. J. S. Purvis, 'Use of Continental Woodcuts and Prints by Ripon School of Woodcarvers in the Early 16th Century', *Archaeologia*, LXXXV.
12. *Mâle, XIII*, p. 184.
13. M. R. James, *Abbeys* (1925), pp. 28-30.
14. M. R. James, 'The Verses formerly inscribed in the Twelve Windows in the Choir of Canterbury Cathedral', *Cambridge Antiquarian Soc. Publ.* No. 38 (1901).
15. M. R. James, 'Pictor in Carmine', *Archaeologia*, XCIV, 141-66.

4. GENERAL CONVENTIONS OF RELIGIOUS IMAGERY

1. *Mirrour of the Blessed Lyf of Jesu Christ*, translated by Nicholas Love from the *Meditationes Vitae Christi* of St. Bonaventura. Facsimile of the edition printed by William Caxton (Roxburghe Club, 1908).
2. M. D. Anderson, *Lincoln Choir Stalls* (1951), repr. fig. 51.
3. *Didron—Stokes*, I, 201-34, describes the forms adopted for the portrayal of God the Father, and 234-417 the forms in which Christ is either portrayed or symbolised.
4. *Apocryphal New Testament*, pp. 477-8, gives the description of Christ which was supposed to have been written by Lentulus, a Roman official in Judea at the time of Tiberius Caesar, to the Roman Senate. Dr. M. R. James considers that this was more probably in Italy in the 13th century. See also E. von Dobschütz, *Christus Bilder* (1899).
5. R. Pettazoni, 'Pagan Origins of the Three-headed Representations of the Christian Trinity', *Warburg Journal*, IX, 135 ff.
6. *Didron—Stokes*, I, 1 ff., deals at length with the various forms and applications of the nimbus. See also Künstle, I, 25 ff. J. Tavernor Perry, 'The Nimbus in Eastern Art', *Burlington Magazine*, XII (1907), 20 ff.
7. Otto Brendel, 'Origin and Meaning of the Mandorla', *Gazette des Beaux-Arts* (6th Series), XXV (1944), 5-24.
8. *Cave, Bosses*, fig. 114.
9. A. G. Langdon, 'The Chi Rho Monogram upon Early Christian Monuments in Cornwall', *Archaeologia Cambrensis* (5th Series), X (1893).
10. *Rushforth*, p. 26.

5. OLD TESTAMENT SUBJECTS

1. *E.g.* the Ashburnham Pentateuch in the Bibl. Nationale, Paris.
2. Anthony Blunt, 'Blake's Ancient of Days', *Warburg Journal*, II (July 1938).
3. *Künstle*, I, 277, repr. fig. 110.

4. Goblet d' Alviella, *The Migration of Symbols* (1894), reproduces a cameo (fig. 69) on which this pagan subject has been deliberately changed into that of the Fall and the relevant text from Genesis engraved on it. Dom F. Cabrol and H. Leclerq, *Dictionnaire de l'archéologie chrétienne et de liturgie* (1907–35), in the article on 'Arbres' reproduce a gem of the late Imperial period showing Medea feeding the serpent while Jason seizes the Golden Fleece as another possible pagan prototype, and also suggest association with Hercules and the apples of the Hesperides. Perhaps this is the source of the apple-of-the-Fall tradition.

5. J. Romilly Allen, *Christian Symbolism in Great Britain and Ireland before the 13th Century* (1887), pp. 185 ff.

6. J. K. Bonnell, 'The Serpent with the Human Head in Art and Mystery Play', *American Journal of Archaeology* (New Series), XXI (1917), 255 ff.

7. *Didron—Stokes*, II, 257. The Byzantine Manual directs that the form of the forbidden tree shall be 'a great tree, like a fig-tree, covered with fruit'.

8. *Dialogue of Salomon and Saturnus*, ed. J. M. Kemble, Aelfric Soc. (1848). The quotation comes from a fragment of a prose version in the British Museum, Cotton MS. Vitel. A, xv.

9. J. Fowler, 'On Medieval Representations of the Months and Seasons', *Archaeologia*, XLIV, 137 ff. J. C. Webster, *The Labours of the Monks* (1938).

10. William Jordan, 'The Creation of the World and Noah's Flood', edited and translated from the Cornish by Whitley Stokes, *Philological Soc. Trans.* (1864).

11. Meyer Schapiro, 'Cain's Jaw-bone that did the First Murder', *Art Bulletin*, XXIV (Sept. 1942). A. K. Coomaraswamy, in a letter printed in *Art Bulletin*, XXIV, 383-4, commenting on the article quoted above, describes how the ass or the camel are used in Islamic art as symbols of carnal individuality, as opposed to spirituality. In Indian mythology wicked persons are said to use 'ass-magic' against their enemies. Cain may thus have been said to use a jaw-bone of an ass as a symbol of his brutality.

12. Walter Hilton, *The Goad of Love*, ed. Clara Kirchberger (1952), p. 80. A 14th-century translation of the *Stimulus Amoris* of St. Bonaventura.

13. O. F. Emerson, 'The Legends of Cain', *Publ. Modern Language Assoc. of America*, XXI (1906), 831-929.

14. *Rushforth*, p. 161, quoting St. Gregory, *Homil.* IV, 16 (Migne, *Patrol. Latina*, LXXVI, col. 983), *Hom. in Evangelia*, *ii Hom.* XXXVIII, 8 (Migne, LXXVI, col. 1287).

15. *Cursor Mundi*, ed. R. Morris, E.E.T.S., vols. 57, 59, 62, 66, 68, 101. This quotation is from lines 1881-92.

16. *Künstle*, I, 283.

17. Alison Moore Smith, 'The Iconography of the Sacrifice of Isaac', *American Journal of Archaeology*, XXVI (1923), 159 ff.

18. M. R. James, *Cathedrals* (1926), p. 35.

19. *Queen Mary's Psalter*. Facsimile reproduction with introduction by Sir George Warner (1912).

20. *Cursor Mundi* (see note 15), lines 4784 ff.

21. *Historia Scholastica*, chap. lxxiii.

22. *Cursor Mundi* (see note 15), lines 6615-26.

23. *Rushforth*, p. 186.

24. *Woodforde, Norwich*, p. 61 repr.

25. J. Lutz and P. Perdrizet, *Speculum Humanae Salvationis* (1907), reproduces this page of the block book, and the carving is reproduced in C. J. Cox, *Bench-ends in English Churches* (1916), p. 39.

26. Wolfgang Born, 'Samson and the Lion', *Gazette des Beaux-Arts* (Series 6), XXV (May 1944), 257.

27. A. K. Coomaraswamy in letter quoted under note 11 notes a parallel between the legend of Indra wielding the bones of the horse's head once used by the Indian deity Dadhyañc, in order to rout the Titans, and Samson's use of the jaw-bone to vanquish the Philistines. See also *Journal of American Oriental Soc.* XVIII, 17.

28. A. Watson, *The Early Iconography of the Tree of Jesse* (1934), and A. K. Coomaraswamy, 'The Tree of Jesse and Indian Parallels or Sources', *Art Bulletin*, XI, 217-20.

29. C. Mowbray, 'Eastern Influence on Carvings at St. Andrews and Nigg', *Antiquity* (Dec. 1926), pp. 428 ff.

30. M. R. James, Introduction to *A Book of Old Testament Illustrations in the Pierpont Morgan Library* (Roxburghe Club, 1927), p. 49 n.

31. André Chastel, 'La Rencontre de Salomon et de la reine de Saba dans l'iconographie médiévale', *Gazette des Beaux-Arts* (1949), pp. 99 ff.

32. J. Romilly Allen, *op. cit.* p. 218.

6. THE INFANCY OF CHRIST

1. *The Mirrour of the Blessed Lyf of Jesu Christ*, by Nicholas Love. Facsimile of William Caxton's edition (Roxburghe Club, 1908).

2. *Apocryphal New Testament*, 'Protevangelium', chap. x, p. 43.

3. *Millet*, p. 91, associates it with the words of St. Bernard, '*o inviolabile castitatis lilium*'.

4. *Mâle*, XIIIᵉ, pp. 288-90.

5. *Dialogue of Salomon and Saturnus*, ed. J. M. Kemble, Aelfric Soc. (1848).

6. *Festial*, pp. 108-9.

7. L. Duchesne, *Christian Worship*, 3rd English ed. (1910), pp. 261-5, discusses the origin of this tradition and the dates assigned at various times and places to the Birth and Death of Our Lord. From at least the 4th century onwards there was a deeply rooted tradition that the Crucifixion took place on March 25th, although Mgr. Duchesne shows that this was historically impossible since in the years 29 and 35, when March 25th fell on a Friday, the age of the moon was not right for the Jewish Passover. The other dates were calculated from the Death of Christ, on the following basis. He must have lived a perfect number of years, for the imperfection of fractions was not tolerated in symbolical numbers, and since the Incarnation was reckoned from the first moment of the conception of the Virgin Mary the Annunciation must have taken place on March 25th and the Nativity on December 25th.

8. *The Mirroure of Man's Salvacionne*, ed. A. H. Huth (Roxburghe Club, 1888), chap. iv.

9. D. M. Robb, 'Iconography of the Annunciation in the 14th and 15th Centuries', *Art Bulletin*, XVIII, 480 ff.

10. *Mâle, fin M.A.* p. 47, quoting *Meditationes Vitae Christi*, chap. vii.

11. *Apocryphal New Testament*, p. 74.

12. G. Wilpert, *La fede della Chiesa nascente secondo i monumenti dell' arte funeraria antica* (1938), pp. 24-7 repr.

13. *Festial*, pp. 22-3.

14. Translation quoted from J. H. Cornell, 'The Iconography of the Nativity of Christ', *Upsala Universitets Arsskrift* (1942). This passage does not

figure in the 15th-century English translation of 'The Revelations of St. Birgitta', ed. W. P. Cumming, E.E.T.S. (Original Series), No. 178.

15. *Apocryphal New Testament*, pp. 46-7.

16. *The Book of Margery Kempe*, E.E.T.S., No. 212, ed. Sanford Brown and Hope Emily Allen, p. 214. The notes quote a 12th-century English nun's book of devotion, known as the Shaftesbury Hours (B.M. Lansdowne MS. 383), as containing a prayer of gratitude to the Virgin for giving the Christ Child His bath. Margery Kempe is here referring to her capacity as handmaid to the Virgin in her meditations on the Infancy.

17. *Two Coventry Corpus Christi Plays*, ed. Harden Craig, E.E.T.S. (Extra Series), No. 87, p. 11. The other two shepherds offer one his hat and the other his mittens.

18. *Millet*, pp. 114-35.

19. *Mâle, XIII*, p. 254, states that it is in a Greek chronicle, early 6th century, translated into Latin by a Merovingian monk, that the names of the Magi first appear in the forms Bithisarea, Melichior and Gathaspa. (*Excerpta Latina Barbari.*)

20. This association appears in Bede's 'Commentary on St. Matthew', *lib.* I, chap. ii.

21. *Mirrour of the Blessed Lyf of Jesu Christ* (Roxburghe Club, 1908), pp. 51-3.

22. *Chester Plays*, ed. Herman Deimling, E.E.T.S. (Extra Series), vols. 62 and 115, p. 210, xi, line 141.

23. *Festial*, p. 59.

24. *Apocryphal New Testament*, 'Gospel of Pseudo-Matthew', chap. xxi, p. 75.

25. M. R. James, 'The Sculptures in the Lady Chapel at Ely' (1895).

26. M. R. James, 'Rare Medieval Tiles and their Story', *Burlington Magazine*, XLII, 32.

27. P. M. Johnston, 'Shorthampton Chapel and its Wall-paintings', *Archaeological Journal*, LXII, 157 ff. The legend is told in *Apocryphal New Testament*, Gospel of Thomas, chap. ii, p. 49.

7. THE MINISTRY OF CHRIST

1. *Mâle, XII*, p. 71.

2. G. McN. Rushforth, 'The Baptism of St. Christopher', *Antiquaries' Journal* (1926), p. 152, discusses the pouring of water from a vessel in Baptism, giving examples in glass at Birtsmorton near Malvern and on a font at Gresham (Norfolk).

3. J. Strzygowski, *Ikonographie der Taufe Christi* (1885), p. 16. *Millet*, p. 178, quotes from Greek liturgies references to the presence of angels at the Baptism of Christ.

4. *Mâle, XII*, p. 110, points out that in the art of the Eastern Church the attendant angels sometimes have their hands covered by part of their own robes and quotes the instruction of the Mount Athos 'Manual for Painters' that the reverent angels should cover their hands beneath their robes. This misunderstanding was not confined to ignorant carvers, such as the maker of the West Haddon font, for the first appearance of the angel holding out the tunic in French ecclesiastical art occurs in the windows of Chartres Cathedral, *c.* 1150. See *Mâle, XII*, fig. 98.

5. In *Queen Mary's Psalter*, see facsimile edition 1912, ed. G. Warner, plate 198, the *architriclinus* is shown with a nimbus and the editor refers to this as being 'under his medieval guise as St. Architriclin'. Christopher Woodforde, 'The Medieval Stained Glass of the East Harling and North Tudden-

ham Churches, Norfolk', *British Archaeological Ass. Journ.* (1940) (3rd Series), V, 5, quotes the late Dr. M. R. James as saying that he only knew of further medieval references to the Architriclinus as a person, not as a saint.

6. A. V. Peatling, *Ancient Stained and Painted Glass in the Churches of Surrey* (1930), p. 50 repr.

7. Meyer Schapiro, 'The Religious Meaning of the Ruthwell Cross', *Art Bulletin*, 258 ff., suggests that the subject of Mary Magdalene at the feet of Christ appearing in conjunction with other subjects having an association with deserts, indicates that the legend of her living and dying in the desert, which was widely propagated by the monks of Provence and Vézelay in the Middle Ages (her bones were claimed by Vézelay) was known in England by the 7th century. It occurs in *An Old English Martyrology* (E.E.T.S. (Original Series), No. 116) which dates from the mid-9th century but is based on a Latin original *c.* 750. Mr. Schapiro suggests that this priority in England may be connected with the English custom of having double monasteries, often under the rule of an abbess.

8. E. W. Tristram and W. G. Constable, *English Medieval Wall Paintings, 12th Century* (1944), p. 117, repr. plate 78.

9. The parable is represented in the Roman Catacombs on two 4th-century tombs of women, where it apparently expresses the prayer that the dead woman shall be numbered among the Wise Virgins. See G. Wilpert, *Pitture delle catacombe romane*, pp. 833 ff.

10. *Nelson*, p. 82.

11. M. R. James, 'The Verses formerly inscribed in the Windows of the Choir at Canterbury', *Cambridge Antiquarian Soc. Publ.* (1901), No. 38.

8. THE PASSION AND RESURRECTION

1. *Apocryphal New Testament*, p. 97.

2. E. K. Chambers, *The Medieval Stage* (1905), II, 5.

3. O. G. Farmer, *Fairford Church and its Stained-glass Windows* (1931). For description of the Palm Sunday processional procedure see Adrian Fortescue, *The Ceremonies of the Roman Rite described* (1943), p. 262.

4. Clark D. Lamberton, *Themes from St. John's Gospel in the Early Catacomb Paintings* (1905).

5. Migne, *Patrol. Latina*, XXXV, col. 1966.

6. *The Northern Passion*, ed. F. F. Foster, E.E.T.S., Nos. 145 and 147.

7. E. Dobbert, 'Das Abendmahl Christi in der bildenden Kunst bis gegen den Schluss des 14. Jahrhunderts', *Repertorium für Kunstwissenschaft*, XIV (1891), 175-203.

8. Otto Demus, *Byzantine Mosaic Decoration* (1948), p. 8.

9. *Künstle*, I, 412.

10. *Mirrour of the Blessed Lyf of Jesu Christ* (Roxburghe Club, 1908).

11. P. M. Johnston, 'Shorthampton Chapel and its Wall-paintings', *Archaeological Journal*, LXII, 157 ff.

12. Quoted from G. G. Coulton, *Medieval Panorama* (1938), p. 420.

13. S. A. Callison, 'The Iconography of the Cock on the Column', *Art Bulletin*, XXI, 160 ff.

14. *Rushforth*, p. 70.

15. *The Book of Margery Kempe*, E.E.T.S., No. 212, ed. Sanford Brown Meech and Hope Emily Allen. In a note to this passage (p. 334) the editors

attribute this multiplication of torturers to a desire to relate the text of Isaiah i. 6, 'From the sole of the foot even unto the head there is no soundness in it ; but wounds and bruises and putrefying sores ; they have not been closed, neither bound up, neither mollified with ointment', to the Flagellation, but without contravening the Mosaic limitation expressed in Deut. xxv. 3, 'Forty strokes may he give him, and not exceed'.

16. Dom Ethelbert Horne, 'The Crown of Thorns in Art', *Downside Review* (Jan. 1935), pp. 48 ff. In an article on the Crown of Thorns in the *Catholic Encyclopaedia*, Herbert Thurston suggests that the band of rushes preserved in Notre-Dame de Paris was used to hold a helmet of thorns upon the head of Our Lord, these being probably the twigs of the jujube tree (*Zizyphus spina Christi*). The Crown of Thorns was not mentioned as extant by Christian writers before the late 6th century, but it was venerated for several centuries at Jerusalem before its journey to France. Separate thorns were presented as holy relics to European sovereigns, including King Athelstan who gave it to Malmesbury Abbey.

17. Arthur Gardner, 'Lincoln Angels', *Minster Pamphlets*, No. 6 repr.

18. *Festial*, p. 121.

19. *Owst, Lit.* p. 308.

20. C. R. Morey, 'Christus Crucifer', *Art Bulletin*, IV, 117 ff., states that the earliest examples of Christ bearing His own Cross occur on 4th-century sarcophagi of a type always associated with figure subjects suggestive of Eastern origin. The subject is treated symbolically rather than realistically. In the art of the early Egyptian Church Christ often carries a small cross, like a sceptre, in the scenes of His miracles and in the Entry into Jerusalem.

21. *Mâle, fin M.A.* p. 64.

22. Mrs. Jameson and Lady Eastlake, *The History of Our Lord* (1888), pp. 41 ff.

23. C. J. Cox, *Bench-ends in English Churches* (1916), p. 64 repr.

24. *The Northern Passion*, ed. F. A. Foster, E.E.T.S., No. 145, pp. 188-91.

25. L. H. Gondijs, *L'Iconographie byzantine du Crucifié mort sur la Croix* (1947).

26. D. Talbot Rice, *English Art, 871–1100* (1951), pp. 101-6, discusses the probable relation of the Langford Rood with the robed figures of Christ crucified in Syria or Palestine, dating from the 6th century onwards, and also with the crosses in Ireland and the Isle of Man in the 8th and 9th centuries.

27. A. R. and P. Green, *Saxon Architecture and Sculpture in Hampshire* (1951), p. 36 repr., consider that the Breamore Rood also has had the arms reset in the reversed position although the wall shows no definite evidence of this. A drawing of how the carving would appear were the arms to be again reversed is certainly more naturalistic.

28. St. Anselm, Migne, *Patrol. Latina*, CLVIII, col. 761.

29. Quoted from G. G. Coulton, *Medieval Panorama* (1938), p. 567.

30. Aron Andersson, *English Influence on Norwegian and Swedish Figure Sculpture, 1220–70* (1941), pp. 285 ff., gives an interesting discussion of the position of the feet on a 13th-century crucifix.

31. *Legends of Holy Rood, Symbols of the Passion and Cross Poems*, ed. R. Morris, E.E.T.S. (Original Series), No. 46.

32. Where the shoots protruding from the stem of the Cross are foliate and apparently living we may perhaps assume that the allusion is to the Tree of Life, but when they are dead stumps the artist has perhaps known the legend that, while Christ hung upon the Cross, its wood burst into flower and bloomed from midday till compline, after which it died once more. See W. L. Hildburgh, 'A Medieval Bronze Pectoral Cross', *Art Bulletin*, XIV, 79-102.

33. Dorothy Shorr, 'The Mourning Virgin and St. John', *Art Bulletin*, XXII, 61 ff., illustrates parallels from Hellenistic and early Roman grave reliefs of the poses in which the Virgin and St. John are sometimes shown, she with her left hand touching her cheek, the left elbow supported by her right hand, and he with his wrists crossed in front of his body. An ivory book-cover of the Echternach School, 11th century, in the British Museum (repr. *loc. cit.*) shows both figures in these classical poses.

34. St. Ambrose, *Comm. in Luc.* I, 27 ; Isidore of Seville, *Allegories*, 138, 139.

35. *Mâle, XIIIᵉ*, pp. 227-30, says that on the Saturday after Easter the reading of this passage from St. John was followed by that of a homily of St. Gregory the Great in which this symbolical interpretation was explained. (*Homil. XXII in Evang. Joan.*)

36. Betty Kurth, 'Ecclesia and an Angel on the St. Andrew Auckland Cross', *Warburg Journal*, VI, 213, suggests that the female figure holding a sceptre, and accompanied by an angel, carved above the Crucifixion on this fragmentary cross, represents *Ecclesia*, as the Bride of Christ, being led to the Cross. This figure, based on Ephes. v. 32, which speaks of the marriage between Christ and the Church, occurs in Byzantine and Syrian manuscripts. O. M. Dalton, *Byzantine Art and Archaeology* (1911), p. 660, stresses that the introduction of *Ecclesia* and the rejection of Synagogue, by angels, is an Eastern feature. The companion subject of the Synagogue being driven away may have been carved upon the lost panel of the St. Andrew Auckland Cross (Durham).

37. Mrs. Jameson, *op. cit.* pp. 11-160 ff.

38. F. J. Dölger, *Antike und Christentum*, IV (1934), 81-94, analyses the Longinus legend and quotes a Passion Play of *Christus Patiens* attributed to an 11th-12th-century Byzantine writer which describes the soldier with the spear as overwhelmed by the sight of the Blood and Water issuing from the wounded side of Christ and touching his head with his blood-stained hands as if cleansing it.

39. W. L. Hildburgh, 'Iconographical Peculiarities in English Medieval Alabasters', *Folk Lore* (March and June 1933).

40. The names of the thieves, Dysmas and Gestas, are taken from later versions of the apocryphal *Acts of Pilate* (*Apocryphal New Testament*, pp. 116 and 161 ff.), where we also read of their past lives and their relative positions on each side of Christ.

41. *The Southern Passion*, ed. E. D. Brown, E.E.T.S. (Original Series), No. 169.

42. L. H. Gondijs, 'Le Soleil et la lune dans les scènes de Crucifixion', *Inst. Arch. Bulgare Bulletin* (1936), p. 250. In Babylonian imagery the sun represented the perfect ideal world and the moon the pale reflection of this cast upon imperfect matter. The writer suggests that the introduction of this motive into the iconography of the Crucifixion may be connected with the Manichean heresy which was widespread when it first appears, in the 5th century. See also Louis de Hautecœur, 'Le Soleil et la lune dans les scènes de Crucifixion', *Revue Archéologique* (5th Series), XIV, 13. Martigny, *Dictionnaire des antiquités chrétiens*, pp. 230 and 739, interprets the sun and moon as symbols of the divinity and humanity of Christ.

43. *Künstle*, I, 484.

44. *Apocryphal New Testament*, pp. 117-44.

45. T. E. R. Boase, *English Art, 1100-1216* (1953), p. 218 repr.

46. For the evolution of the liturgical drama see K. Young, *The Drama of the Medieval Church* (1933), or E. K. Chambers, *The Medieval Stage* (1903). See also A. Heales, 'Easter Sepulchres', *Archaeologia*, XLII, 263-308. The action of Christ stepping on to a soldier's back is generally peculiar to England. To compare a Flemish rendering of this subject, in which Christ

seems to soar out of the tomb without His feet touching the ground, see a carved panel in the church of Knowsley (Lancs). See also W. L. Hildburgh, 'Medieval English Representations of the Resurrection', *Folk Lore* (March 1937), pp. 95-8.

47. *The Book of Margery Kempe*, E.E.T.S., No. 212, p. 75. Notes by Hope Emily Allen, p. 336.

48. E. T. Dewald, 'The Iconography of the Ascension', *American Journal of Archaeology* (2nd Series), XIX, 277 ff.

49. K. Young, *op. cit.* quotes a 14th-century *Ordinarium* from Moosberg which describes the hoisting of an Ascension image through a ring of silk cloths under the roof. Such an image is preserved in the Museum für Völkerkunde, Basle. Meyer Schapiro, 'The Image of the Disappearing Christ ; the Ascension in English Art around the Year 1000', *Gazette des Beaux-Arts* (6ᵉ Série), XXIII (1943), 135-58, ascribes this convention rather to Anglo-Saxon literary sources.

50. *Apocryphal New Testament*, p. 488.

51. Abel Fabre, 'L'Iconographie de la Pentecôte', *Gazette des Beaux-Arts* (1923), p. 33.

9. HEAVEN AND HELL

1. *Nelson*, pp. 234-5.

2. M. R. James, *The Apocalypse in Art* (1931), *passim.*

3. E. W. Tristram, 'The Cloister Bosses, Norwich Cathedral', *Reports of the Friends of Norwich Cathedral* (reprinted 1938).

4. *Keyser, Tympana*, p. lvi.

5. L. B. Ellis, 'The Animal Symbols of the Evangelists', *Ancient Egypt* (1930), p. 109.

6. L. Delisle and P. Meyer, *L'Apocalypse français au XIIIᵉ siècle* (1890), has an appendix dealing with glossed manuscripts, p. 19.

7. Zofia Ameisenowa, 'Animal-headed Gods, Evangelists, Saints and Righteous Men', *Warburg Journal*, XII, 21 ff., quotes instances of animal-headed figures representing the planets in the Zodiacs of Dendera, and as participating in the Mithraic initiation ceremonies. There may also have been a connection with Jewish angels. In Hebrew illustrated Bibles heavenly beings, or righteous men and women, are shown with animal heads, associating them with the stars, *e.g.* the 13th-century 'Milan Bible' (Ambrosiana MS. B30-32), f. 136, shows a Banquet of the Just with such figures, and a 14th-century Hebrew Bible in the British Museum (MS. Or. 22413) shows Boaz, Naomi and Ruth with the heads of various animals while the servants in the same miniature have human heads.

8. *The Mirroure of Man's Salvacionne*, English text ed., H. A. Huth (Roxburghe Club, 1908), chap. 37.

9. *Owst, Lit.* p. 19.

10. *Mâle, XIIᵉ*, 3-17.

11. E. W. Tristram and W. G. Constable, *English Medieval Wall Paintings, 12th Century* (1944), pp. 102-5 repr.

12. M. R. James, *The Sculptured Bosses in the Cloisters of Norwich Cathedral* (1911), p. 5.

13. *The Trinity Apocalypse* (Roxburghe Club, 1909), ed. M. R. James.

14. *Friends of York Minster Annual Report* (1949).

15. *Summa Predicantium : Furtum.* Translation quoted from *Owst, Lit.*

16. A. Hollaender, 'The Doom Painting of St. Thomas of Canterbury, Salisbury', *Wiltshire Magazine*, L, 351 ff.

17. *Gesta Romanorum*, E.E.T.S. (Extra Series), No. 33, ed. S. H. Heritage, pp. 384-5. The sinners were a pair of adulterous lovers and the tale is of the vision shown to the husband of a woman who brought them together but who escaped like punishment by repentance.

18. O. G. Farmer, *Fairford Church and its Stained-glass Windows* (1938), pp. 72-3.

19. M. P. Perry, 'The Psychostasis in Christian Art', *Burlington Magazine*, XXII, 94 ff. The Weighing of the Souls before Osiris is reproduced in E. A. Wallis Budge, *The Book of the Dead* (1898).

20. Françoise Henry, *Irish Art in the Early Christian Period* (1940), p. 159.

21. W. L. Hildburgh, 'An English Carving of St. Michael weighing a Soul', *Burlington Magazine* (May 1947). In his article on the Rosary, in the *Catholic Encyclopaedia*, Herbert Thurston dismisses the legend that the Rosary was originally instituted by St. Dominic. The use of beads, or counters, in connexion with repetitive devotions goes back to ancient Nineveh, and in *c.* 1075 the Countess Godiva of Coventry left a certain statue of the Blessed Virgin a circlet of precious stones, threaded on cord, which she used to reckon her prayers. Such strings of beads were known as 'Paternosters' throughout the Middle Ages and the craftsmen who made them constituted a special gild having its London centre in what is still called Paternoster Row.

22. F. Lugt, 'Man and Angel', *Gazette des Beaux-Arts* (6ᵉ Série), XXV (1944), 265.

23. P. B. Chatwin, 'The Decoration of the Beauchamp Chapel, Warwick', *Archaeologia*, LXXVII (1927), 313 ff.

24. M. D. Anderson, *Design for a Journey* (1940), 58-68, gives a brief account of the various instruments included in these angelic orchestras. For information about the instruments see F. W. Galpin, *Old English Instruments of Music* (1910).

25. *Woodforde, Norwich*, pp. 124-48, describes the dress and accoutrements of many angels and quotes the inscribed scrolls held by them in many East Anglian church windows.

26. *Jacob's Well*, E.E.T.S. (Original Series), No. 115, ed. A. Brandels.

10. THE LIFE OF THE VIRGIN MARY

1. Charles P. Parkhurst, 'The Madonna of the Writing Child', *Art Bulletin*, XXIII (1941), 292-306.

2. Victor Lazareff, 'Studies in the Iconography of the Virgin', *Art Bulletin*, XX, 26, discusses, amongst other points, the evolution of the type of '*Virgo Lactans*' from the representations of Isis nursing Horus which was a favourite mythological subject in Egypt.

3. Mrs. Jameson, *Legends of the Madonna* (1879), *passim*.

4. F. Bond, *Dedications and Patron Saints of English Churches* (1914), p. 31.

5. *Mâle, XIIᵉ*, pp. 426 ff.

6. *Apocryphal New Testament*, pp. 38 ff.

7. M. R. James, *The Sculptures in the Lady Chapel at Ely* (1895).

8. *Apocryphal New Testament*, p. 40, 'Protevangelium', chap. iii.

9. *Rushforth*, pp. 272-5, describes the panels of glass at Malvern showing the childhood and betrothal of Mary the Virgin.

10. *Ludus Coventriae*, ed. J. O. Halliwell, Shakespeare Soc. (1841), pp. 82-5. Authorised version. Psalms cxx-cxxxiv.
11. M. R. James and E. W. Tristram, 'Wall Paintings in Croughton Church', *Archaeologia*, LXXVI.
12. *Ludus Coventriae* (as note 10), pp. 79-80.
13. Pseudo-Matthew xiii, *Apocryphal New Testament*, p. 74.
14. Narratives of the Assumption of the Virgin, *Apocryphal New Testament*, pp. 194-227.
15. *Woodforde, Norwich*, p. 30 repr., plate iv. Life of the Virgin. The 'Burial of the Virgin' at Stoke d'Abernon is of 16th-century Flemish glass, recently inserted. It was formerly in Lord Rochdale's collection and other panels from the same series are at Prittlewell (Essex). See *Country Life* (Nov. 3rd, 1950).
16. Betty Kurth, 'The Iconography of the Wirksworth Slab', *Burlington Magazine*, LXXXVI (April 1945), pp. 114 ff.
17. E. T. Long, 'Recently discovered Wall-paintings', *Burlington Magazine*, LXXVI, 156-62.
18. Cave, *Bosses*, p 43 repr., fig. 181. See also Mr. Cave's article, 'The Roof Bosses of Peterborough Cathedral', *Archaeologia*, LXXXVIII, 271 ff.
19. The incident of the girdle occurs only in the narrative of the Assumption attributed to Joseph of Arimathaea (*Apocryphal New Testament*, pp. 217-18) and Dr. James considered that the prominence there given to the story of the relic honoured at Prato indicated that this text, which is certainly late, was written in Italy in the 13th century.
20. *Festial*, p. 224.
21. C. S. Bland, *Miracles of the Blessed Virgin Mary* (1928), translated from Johannes Herolt, called Discipulos (1435-40). *Miracles of Notre-Dame*, ed. G. F. Warner (Roxburghe Club, 1885).
22. A. C. Fryer, *Theophilus the Penitent in Art* (1936).
23. Jean Lafond, 'The Stained-glass Decoration of Lincoln Cathedral in the 13th Century', *Archaeological Journal*, CIII, 119-56.
24. *Mâle, XIIᵉ*, p. 434.
25. E. W. Tristram, *The Cloister Bosses, Norwich Cathedral*, reprinted from *Reports of the Friends of Norwich Cathedral* (1938).
26. E. W. Tristram and M. R. James, *Wall Paintings in Eton College Chapel and in the Lady Chapel of Winchester Cathedral*, Walpole Soc., XVII (1929).
27. M. R. James, *The Sculptured Bosses in the Roof of the Bauchun Chapel, Norwich Cathedral* (1908).
28. E. Horne, 'Wings, Heart and Sword Badge', *Antiquaries Journal*, XI, 286 ff.
29. D. Rock, *Church of Our Fathers* (1905), III, 162-7.
30. *Woodforde, Somerset*, pp. 204-5.
31. *Festial*, pp. 228 ff.

11. THE SAINTS

1. Suggested books of reference :
   S. Baring Gould, *Lives of the Saints*, 16 vols. (1914–   ).
   F. Arnold Foster, *Studies in Church Dedications*, 3 vols. (1899).
   F. C. Husenbeth, *Emblems of the Saints* (1882).
   R. L. P. Milburn, *Saints and their Emblems in English Churches* (1949).
2. G. G. Coulton, *Art and the Reformation* (1928), p. 281, quotes P. Saintyves,

Les Saints successeurs des dieux (1907), chap. ii, as reckoning about eighty saints who are reputed to have carried their own heads.

3. F. Wormald, 'Some Illustrated Manuscripts of the Lives of the Saints', *Bulletin of the John Rylands Library*, XXXV (Sept. 1952).

4. *The Golden Legend*, William Caxton's translation, ed. F. S. Ellis, in The Temple Classics (1900), 7 vols.

5. *Rushforth*, p. 141.

6. Migne, *Patrol. Latina*, XXXIX, col. 2189. See also Herbert Thurston, the *Catholic Encyclopaedia*, I, 629.

7. F. T. S. Houghton, 'Astley Church and its Stall Paintings', *Birmingham Archaeological Soc. Trans.*, LI, 19 ff., quotes the following examples of Creed figures :
   Painted Screens. Kenton and Chudleigh, Devon. The apostles only on screens in Norfolk churches of Gooderstone, Mattishall and Weston Longueville. The damaged paintings at Thornham (Norf) may have represented the prophets alone.
   Painted roof of St. Helen's Church, Abingdon, has prophets and kings.
   Windows. Norbury (Staffs) and Lanwade (Cambs), Drayton Beauchamp (Bucks) and Hayles (Glos). In the clerestory of the Lady Chapel of York Minster there are 7 prophets and 6 apostles. (This list could easily be prolonged, for many churches show the remains of Creed windows.)

8. Christopher Woodforde, *The Stained Glass of New College, Oxford* (1951), p. 69.

9. *Mâle, fin M.A.* pp. 253-79. For complete list of the Sibyls' prophecies and attributes see F. C. Husenbeth, *Emblems of Saints* (1882).

10. *Rushforth*, p. 95, discusses the possible origin of this feature and quotes examples in windows at Coombe (Oxon), East Brent (Somerset), Ludlow (Salop), Norwich, St. Peter Hungate, and York, All Saints, North Street.

11. W. L. Hildburgh, 'Folk Lore Recorded in English Medieval Alabaster Carvings', *Folk Lore*, LX (1949). The feasts are : St. Peter, June 29th ; Decollation of St. John Baptist, Aug. 29th ; St. Thomas, Dec. 29th ; traditional date of Crucifixion, March 25th.

12. W. H. St. John Hope, 'On Sculptured Alabaster Tables called St. John's Heads', *Archaeologia*, LII, pt. 2, pp. 669 ff.

13. *Acta Sanctorum*, XXV.

14. Louis du Broc de Segange, *Les Saints protecteurs des corporations et protecteurs spéciaux* (1887).

15. *Ibid.* II. 49-52, quotes several of these hymns and invocations.

16. *Festial*, pp. 199-202.

17. *Woodforde, Somerset, passim.*

18. P. Perdrizet, *La Vierge de miséricorde* (1908), repr.

19. *Keyser, Murals, passim.*

20. F. Kendon, *Mural Paintings in English Churches during the Middle Ages* (1923), discusses the probable influence of such woodcuts.

21. See also John Salmon, 'St. Christopher in Medieval Life and Art', *British Archaeological Ass. Journal*, LXI (1936), 76 ff. H. H. Brindley, *St. Christopher*, in supplement to Blomefield's *Norfolk* (1929). G. McN. Rushforth, 'The Baptism of St. Christopher', *Antiquaries Journal* (1926), pp. 152 ff., is concerned with a fragment of glass formerly in Birtsmorton Church (Worcs) which showed the Christ Child pouring water on to the saint's head from a jug.

22. Castle Acre Pulpit inscriptions :
    St. Gregory. *Gloria predicantium est profectus audientium.*
    St. Jerome. *Ne te decipiat sermonis pulcritudo.*
    St. Ambrose. *Evangelium mentes omnium rigat.*
    St. Augustine. *Impletus spiritu sancto predicavit.*

23. Christopher Woodforde, *The Stained Glass of New College, Oxford* (1951), pp. 4-5.

24. *Woodforde, Somerset,* pp. 260-62. For Shrewsbury windows see H. E. Forrest, *The Old Churches of Shrewsbury* (1920), pp. 75-9.

25. E. W. Tristram, 'Franciscan Influence in English Medieval Wall-painting', in *Franciscan History and Legend in English Medieval Art,* ed. A. G. Little (1937).

26. E. G. Bowen, 'Travels of the Celtic Saints', *Antiquity* (March 1944), and 'The Settlements of the Celtic Saints', *Antiquity* (Dec. 1945).

27. Hobart Bird, *Old Warwickshire Churches* (1935), p. 125, quotes Dugdale as authority for the tradition that Wroxall Priory Church was built by Hugh de Hatton as a thank-offering for his deliverance after seven years of chained captivity in Palestine.

12. THE MIRROR OF MORALS

1. Dan Michael, *The Ayenbite of Inwit,* E.E.T.S., No. 23, ed. R. Morris (1866). This is a translation of *La Somme des vices et des vertues* composed in *c.* 1279 by Frère Lorens of the Order of Friars Preachers for the use of Philip II of France, but Dan Michael does not refer to the original author.

2. *The Prykke of Conscience,* ed. R. Morris, Philological Soc. (1863).

3. A. Katzenellenbogen, *Allegories of the Virtues and Vices in Medieval Art* (1939), deals with the early development of this theme.

4. Details of the Malmesbury and Stanton Fitzwarren carvings are reproduced in G. Zarnecki, *Later English Romanesque Sculpture* (1953), figs. 96-7. A very fine late 10th-century English manuscript of the Psychomachia which belonged to Malmesbury during the Middle Ages is now in the Library of Corpus Christi College, Cambridge (MS. 23).

5. *Woodforde, Norwich,* p. 196.

6. Archbishop Thoresby, *The Lay Folks Catechism,* E.E.T.S. (Original Series), No. 118, ed. Canon Simmons and H. E. Nolloth (1901).

7. See A. Katzenellenbogen, *op. cit.* pp. 63 ff.

8. A. Watson, 'The *Speculum Virginum* with Special Reference to the Tree of Jesse', *Speculum,* III (1928), and also 'A Manuscript of the *Speculum Virginum*', *Journal Walters Art Gallery, Baltimore* (1947), pp. 61 ff.

9. C. E. Keyser, 'Mural Paintings in the Churches of Little Horwood and Padbury, Bucks.', *Buckinghamshire Records,* VII. *Keyser, Murals,* quotes examples of Seven Deadly Sins or Works of Mercy at Arundel (Sussex).

10. J. G. Waller, 'Wall Paintings at Raunds and Slapton, Northants', *Archaeological Journal,* XXXIV, 219 ff.

11. See article in *The Times* (June 19th, 1937) reporting the discovery of the paintings and letter from G. R. Owst, June 29th, 1937. Other examples of such moralities are at Hook Norton (Oxon), Hoxne (Suffolk).

12. John Piggot, 'Notes on a Wall Painting discovered in Ingatestone Church', *Essex Archaeological Soc. Trans.* IV, 137 ff.

13. G. McN. Rushforth, 'The Wheel of the Ten Ages of Life in Leominster Church', *Proc. Soc. Antiquaries* (1914), pp. 47-60.

14. P. B. Chatwin, 'A Tile Pavement of "the Wheel of Fortune" at St. Mary's Priory Church, Nuneaton', *Birmingham Archaeological Soc. Trans.* LXV, 126-7.

15. E. Carleton Williams, 'Mural Paintings of the Three Living and the Three Dead in England', *British Archaeological Ass. Journal* (3rd Series), VII (1942), 31 ff.

16. K. Künstle, *Die Legende der Drei Lebenden und Drei Toten* (1908), quoted by E. Carleton Williams, *loc. cit.* p. 36.

17. See also W. F. Storck, 'Aspects of Death in English Art and Poetry', *Burlington Magazine*, XXI, 249 and 314. This article includes a list of paintings of the Three Living and the Three Dead, still extant or recorded.

18. F. Douce, *The Dance of Death* (1833), and E. C. Williams, 'The Dance of Death in Painting and Sculpture in the Middle Ages', *British Archaeological Ass. Journal* (Jan. 1937), pp. 229-57.

19. M. R. James, *St. George's Chapel, Windsor : the Woodwork of the Choir* (1933).

20. M. R. James, *Suffolk and Norfolk* (1930), p. 183.

21. *Owst, Lit.*, 420-21.

22. E. C. Rouse, 'Wall Paintings in the Church of St. John the Evangelist, Corby, Lincolnshire', *Archaeological Journal*, C, 151-2.

23. *Woodforde, Norwich*, pp. 183-92, gives a very interesting study of the Heydon window and the various wall-paintings which are related to its theme.

24. E. W. Tristram, 'Piers Plowman in English Wall Painting', *Burlington Magazine*, XXXI, 135-6.

13. THE MIRROR OF NATURE

1. A. C. Seward, 'The Foliage, Flowers and Fruit of Southwell Chapter House', *Cambridge Antiquarian Soc. Com.* XXXV. Nikolaus Pevsner, *The Leaves of Southwell*, King Penguin Books (1945), reproduces many of these exquisite carvings and illustrates the medieval approach to natural history at various periods, by quotations from contemporary writers. For the stylistic development of foliage-sculpture in British churches see S. Gardner, *English Gothic Foliage Sculpture* (1927).

2. G. C. Druce, 'The Lion and the Cubs in the Cloister', *Canterbury Cathedral Chronicle* (1936).

3. M. R. James, Introduction to *A Bestiary of the Twelfth Century* (Roxburghe Club, 1928).

4. *Batman upon Bartholome, his book De Proprietatibus Rerum* (1598), or Robert Steele, *Medieval Lore from Bartholomew Anglicus* (1924).

5. *Queen Mary's Psalter*, facsimile edition (1912), ed. G. Warner.

6. H. H. Humphreys, 'The Horn of the Unicorn', *Annals of the Royal College of Surgeons of England*, VIII (May 1951), traces the origin of the unicorn legend. The Hebrew word *re'em* which was rendered as *monoceros* in the Septuagint, meant a wild ox and it is possible that the convention of Assyrian and Persian art, by which horned animals were shown in profile as having only a single horn, gave rise to the legend of the indomitable, single-horned creature. See also Odell Shepard, *Lore of the Unicorn* (1930).

7. Robert Steele, *op. cit.* pp. 149-50.

8. *Ibid.* p. 166.

9. *The Bestiary of Guillaume le Clerc* written *c.* 1210 and translated by G. C. Druce (1936). See also G. C. Druce, 'The Caladrius and its Legend', *Archaeological Journal* (1923), LXIX.

10. G. C. Druce, 'Queen Camel Church : Bosses on the Chancel Roof', *Somerset Archaeological and Nat. History Soc. Proc.* LXXII, 89-106 repr.

11. Fritz Lügt, 'Man and Angel', *Gazette des Beaux-Arts* (6e Série), XXV, 265-82, suggests that the Hebrew word *K'rub* may have had links with the Sanscrit *gribh* and the Persian *griftan*. The Jewish cherub was sometimes shown as a winged quadruped.

12. P. Ansell Robin, *Animal Lore in English Literature* (1936), p. 164, illustrates by quotations the varying attitude of writers towards this belief at different periods.

13. St. Augustine, *De Civitate Dei*, Bk. xvi, chap. ix.

14. G. R. Crone, *The Hereford World Map* (1948).

15. G. C. Druce, 'Some Abnormal and Composite Human Forms in English Architecture', *Archaeological Journal*, LXXII, 1915, describes most of the human abnormalities to be found in churches, other than grotesque creations of the craftsmen's fancy.

16. Paris, Bibliothèque de l'Arsenal, MS. 3516.

17. C. A. Williams, 'Oriental Affinities of the Legend of the Hairy Anchorite', *University of Illinois Studies in Language and Literature*, X, No. 2, and XI, No. 4 ; also 'German Legends of the Hairy Anchorite', *op. cit.* XVIII, Nos. 1-2.

18. Francis Wormald, 'A Wall-painting at Idsworth, Hants, and a Liturgical Graffito', *The Antiquaries Journal*, XXV (1945), 43-7 repr.

19. Allardyce Nicoll, *World Drama* (1949), p. 162.

20. See also R. Bernheimer, *Wild Men in the Middle Ages*, Harvard (1952), and H. D. Ellis, 'The Wodewose in East Anglian Church Decoration', *Suffolk Institute of Archaeology and Nat. History Trans.* XIV, 287.

21. *Mâle, XIIIe*, pp. 41-82.

22. Adam of St. Victor, *Sequentiae, Patrol.* CXCVI, col. 1433.

23. St. Augustine, *De Civitate Dei*, Bk. xvi, chap. 8.

For further information about animal subjects in British churches consult the following :

G. C. Druce, *Animals in English Woodcarvings*, Walpole Soc., III.
G. C. Druce, 'Medieval Bestiaries and their Influence on Ecclesiastical Decorative Art', *British Archaeological Ass. Journal*, XXV and XXVI.
G. C. Druce, 'Notes on Birds in Medieval Church Architecture', *The Antiquary* (1914).
A. H. Collins, *Symbolism of Animals and Birds in English Church Architecture* (1913).
M. D. Anderson, *Animal Carvings in British Churches* (1938).

GENERAL INDEX

PRINTED BY R. & R. CLARK, LTD., EDINBURGH